WHERE DOLPHINS WALK:

A Memoir of Bridging National Lifestyles, Positive Change and the Powers of Silence

By

DOUGLAS ANDREW KEEHN

WHERE DOLPHINS WALK:

A Memoir of Bridging National Lifestyles, Positive Change and the Powers of Silence

By

DOUGLAS ANDREW KEEHN

Café con Leche

Where Dolphins Walk: A Memoir of Bridging National Lifestyles, Positive Change and the Powers of Silence

Published by

Café con Leche

3 Griffin Hill Court
The Woodlands, TX. 77382
281-465-0119
www.cafeconlechebooks.com

ACKNOWLEDGMENTS

To Elaine and Jack:
Mom, you skillfully cleared numerous paths to see that all of my dreams came true; and because of you they indeed have.

Dad, as you are resting in Arlington surrounded by America's elite, know that I think of you each and every day. You never had a bad word to say about anyone—even your captors. You were and always will be my hero.

Mom and Dad, thanks for all your unconditional love and support. Without your incalculable selfless sacrifices my life could never have been so complete.

Captain Davie Dryer:
Calm and collected, you always placed the concerns of others before your own. A gentleman in every sense of the word, I could not have been blessed with a better mentor. Like my dad, you have a heart larger than life.

Monica (Moni):
Your uniquely patient and careful guidance successfully steered me through a complex maze of cultural differences. The genuine compassion you possess for those less fortunate is a model for all to follow. Your combination of an innate kindness and gentle spirit kept a bright candle burning during some of the darkest of hours. I'll always be indebted for having you by my side.

Leticia:

I'm truly humbled. Without your support, conviction, dedication, and countless hours of work on my behalf, none of this would have been possible. Words just can't express how grateful I am for all of your trust.

To the Dolphins:

Always captivated by your auras, you honored me time and again with your remarkably opportune presence.

P.S. - I'm going to place some copies in a bottle. When you find it floating somewhere offshore please break it open, and feel free to read at your leisure. I look forward to hearing from all of you soon.

Special Note from the Author To My American and Latino Neighbors

After years of sporadically jotting down private notes, and mentally storing a variety of experiences, something began to dawn on me. It would take an extended period of time for the significance of this "something" to finally unravel and come into focus. In fact, whether it was intentional or not, I didn't recognize what was constantly weighing on my mind. All I knew with some semblance of certainty was that I had developed a powerful inner feeling–a sensation that was growing stronger with each and every day. Eventually I would awaken to acknowledge there were many realities that ran quite contrary to what I had always believed.

Living together in the Western Hemisphere, Americans and Latinos often have perceptions of what each other's lives are truly like; perceptions that are influenced more than ever before via the expansion of the modern media and internet. Frequently overlooked is another crucial component that affects our beliefs; it's the power these influences not only have on how we view one another, but also how we tend to view ourselves. So let me offer some examples of what I am trying to convey. Many Americans see their southern neighbors as poor, and struggling to escape to the U.S. for a better life. Then in turn, my American friends look inward and see themselves as fortunate, convinced that they are generally "better off." After all, if this were not the case, then why would so many want to enter the "land of opportunity?" And this belief becomes even more solidified from the Latino perspective as the U.S. is frequently defined in broad terms as a "modern" nation; a nation offering security, and superior chances for economic advancement. Consequentially many then see themselves as less fortunate, disadvantaged, and frustrated that they aren't living the "American dream."

Without a doubt, there are undeniable truths that have skewed each culture's thoughts concerning one's quality of life. It's factual that the average American's standard of living is higher compared to those who reside in Latin America. And in some Latin American nations economic conditions remain excessively punishing. Therefore, logically it would seem the previously mentioned rationalizations are fairly straightforward, understandable, and simple enough to accept?

At least on the surface, the grass seems to be much greener on one side of the fence? . . . At least on the surface . . .

TABLE OF CONTENTS

Acknowledgments v
Special Note from the Author to My American
and Latino Neighbors... vii
Introduction 1
Chapter 1: Spark and Ignition 11
Chapter 2: Foundation 18
Chapter 3: In the Shadow of a Glider 31
Chapter 4: The Seeds of Change 37
Chapter 5: The Strength of Straw 49
Chapter 6: Mystic Lima...60
Chapter 7: Switching Gears 73
Chapter 8: Nossa 82
Chapter 9: Sampa: Many Bright Shining Moments 104
Chapter 10: Beyond the Andes................................125
Chapter 11: Midnight in Recoleta 145
Chapter 12: A Hidden Gem 162
Chapter 13: The Magic of Floripa 172
Chapter 14: Fica Tranquilo 201
Chapter 15: Compass Reversal................................211
Chapter 16: Carefully Packed Parachute? 222
Chapter 17: External Darkness – Internal Light 236
Chapter 18: Final Approach and Landing 242

INTRODUCTION

. . . With my eyes shut I frequently envision so much of life's beauty void of its many harsh realities. And with my eyes wide open, with my unrestricted visibility, I can readily see so much pain and injustice. Yet, hidden within so much suffering is a certain type of magnificence that is unmatched—unparalleled even in my most vivid and uplifting dreams.

—*Douglas Andrew Keehn*

I can still picture Dad standing by my side near a fence at Kennedy Airport. Watching those jumbo jets scream overhead as they came in for a landing always filled him with awe. His eyes lit up and he beamed with excitement every time he heard the roar of their powerful engines. My dad was a simple salesman but those days at the airport, he became someone else. He was in command of one of those "dream machines." My father didn't have an easy life but that never stopped him from living life to its fullest. At the airport, I knew where he really wanted to be, where his heart was at. I so regret that fate never granted him his wish.

At times I confess to overthinking and reflecting excessively on my life, considering my past and comparing it to where I am today. We tend to believe we have a fair amount of control over our destinies, and that we can sense what our

1

future will entail. And the closer our present draws to that span of time, the more confident we feel about our forecast. But from the moment we are born, what really lies ahead is one mysterious and unscripted journey. Who and what will our partners and friends be like? What interests will drive our attention? Which places will we explore? What will we ultimately achieve? The possibilities and questions seem boundless.

It's also fascinating that we often experience our time and act in ways we never anticipated. Although our dreams and aspirations can sometimes become a reality, they often are only partially achieved or are unrealized. Our lives are fluent, filled with peaks and troughs, triumphs and disappointments. At any moment, lightning can strike; an event causes us to pause, to rethink, and possibly alter our direction. If that happens, the signal can be confusing, complicated, challenging, and even a bit frightening.

For me, it would take almost forty years for the right storm to gather, for the claps of thunder to finally waken me from within. After the storm passed I realized a great deal more about myself. It was as if the rains had soaked through, with each drop containing a different mixture of delicate hints. The drenching taught me that the only guarantee is there are no guarantees. How dramatically we overestimate the expected, and how greatly we underestimate the significance and power of the unexpected.

If I were a betting man I would have lost big. I never would have anticipated the many instrumental influences that found their way into my life. Even when I was in my thirties, I had no forewarning of how much my outlook would change.

Thus, I have a journey I want to share, a journey that has been life-altering. The changes were subtle, strong, and arrived not through any intentional plan or design. A certain sequence of events and experiences eventually created a deep and lasting impression—an awareness that I was often observing and seldom seeing.

To put some of the building blocks of this journey into place, I first have some explaining to do. Often, when we meet new people we are curious about their profession or occupation. What they do for a living, on a superficial level, helps us define the person. In addition to providing conversational footing, the question points us toward possible common interests.

The trap that we often build is to make too tight a connection between a person's profession and their overall character. It is a dangerous trap and one that I urge you to approach with caution. A person's values, intelligence, beliefs, morality, manners, honesty, determination, sense of fairness, reliability—the list can go on and on—are individual attributes that should be recognized as such. In other words, don't paint a picture of someone based on what he or does for a living. You might find yourself getting on the wrong train and getting off at the wrong station, far away from where you intended to travel.

With that in mind, I will now reveal that I am an airline pilot with more than thirty years of experience and an excess of 25,000 flight hours. Currently, I fly a Boeing 777 for a major US international airline. I really do fly a "dream machine."

My profession is relevant to this story. Not so much because of what is involved in becoming an airline pilot or what it takes to maintain the various skills required by my employer and the Federal Aviation Administration (FAA). The real relevance concerns the foreign places I visited. Every trip allowed me to experience people from different cultures; people who rank the hierarchies of life in ways quite different than most Americans.

When you board a commercial jet, you are placing yourself in an aluminum tube that will travel around 600 mph. The cruising altitude is often near 35,000 feet, the equivalent of stacking twenty new World Trade Centers on top of one another. The outside air temperature can easily reach -65 degrees

F, and the winds are frequently in excess of 100 mph. It's safe to say that the external environment isn't very hospitable.

I ask that you embrace my leadership and the high level of confidence I have been afforded by thousands of passengers; a level that I never take for granted. Together we will weave in and out of multiple cultural views in both direct and subtle ways. By sharing some of my experiences, I hope you might be prompted to look at yourself, at others, and innumerable surroundings from a new perspective. There is no right or wrong here, at least not in the literal sense.

Please stay close by my side, and possibly see as I finally did, that too many of us strive for and admire things out of proportion to what should truly matter. A great deal of living this way is no fault of our own. We are raised in a culture that has certain values, many of which are unique and admirable. But because many Americans don't have the opportunity to live or frequently travel abroad, it's extraordinarily difficult for them make objective judgments about what might be missing within our own cultural boundaries, to see for themselves how others live and truly feel. We are often forced to accept at face value what is portrayed to us via the media— an often quick and abstract snapshot of what is out there. The photos often come in frequent bursts, sometimes lasting for weeks. Whether true or not, partial or impartial, we develop a subliminal picture of various people and places. So how can we know if we're really missing things of value?

Again, I ask that you allow yourself to be completely open. Imagine that I am your seeing eye dog. Take the time to permit your senses to receive all that is around; allow everything, even if you might not understand or even agree with the message, to penetrate your soul. Accept everything that you feel and visualize while whiting out preconceived notions. When reading through our journey, never be afraid to periodically close your eyes and absorb the places, their undertones, and the relevance they might offer for your life.

People who are blind are often razor sharp in imagining and sensing their environment. And many of us with our perfect eyes walk around with a limited vision conditioned and influenced by a complexity of factors. All too often we look at things through too narrow a prism. It's the way we were raised and taught, which leads to each of us having certain expectations. Our behaviors are perfectly understandable.

Let's be honest . . . we are conditioned to act and think within the confines of certain socially approved and accepted norms. Yet, why should each and every one of us not be open to seeing things in different ways? Why can't we allow ourselves to hone the skills of a person who has developed a unique and diverse way of seeing without sight? The short answer is that we can and we should.

Our minds should always remain open but that does not mean we should be complacent and just thoughtlessly follow any path. That course would be unproductive and irresponsible. However, if we keep our thoughts untainted, we have an advantage because we do not have to follow the same road. The roads untraveled might be quite useful in getting us to a better place.

Throughout this journey I will act as your guide and do my utmost not to sugarcoat anything. Like anyone I am fallible but I am committed to bringing you my story as clearly and as truthfully as possible. You will discover many different paths, and it is completely up to you as to which ones, if any, you ultimately follow.

This book then is not about airline pilots. To a certain extent this story is about me and how I now view my life's priorities; yet that just scratches the surface of our journey. Ultimately this concerns not only me but your own personal processes. The trip will shed light on the philosophies and routines of many people within our culture and some cultures abroad.

It's my intention to objectively guide your attention to a wide range of hints and messages I experienced. I will at times mention how I felt and was influenced; other times I will purposely remain silent. Ultimately, I want to stand clear and allow you to decide the relevance of each experience. There will be moments that feel as if you're touching a hot stove. Some experiences might be uncomfortable and yes, at times even hurt. There will be concepts, ideas, realities and visions you might find strange to your ways of thinking.

The bottom line is that I might strike personal cords that you find painful. So be it. It's my hope to share my experiences in such a way that they strike not just one but several private cords; and that they strike in positive ways that encourage you to continue the journey.

Some realities that I had never seen nor felt before I wanted to flush out and voice for all to hear. It takes a great deal of courage to cross an angry river, a river void of any bridge, a river that contains impediments and a powerful current. Complex, new and controversial ideas are never easy, and are often consciously and subconsciously avoided. On our journey we are not going to avoid anything. I take full responsibility for dragging you along with me across several angry rivers.

One of the most important things that I discovered during my journey was how to be patient. Patience is another of those words that is so loosely tossed around. But the most significant thing about being patient is that it's much easier said than done. Patience is not a quality many people possess even though many people truly believe they are patient. I am calling this to your attention because you might consider parts of my journey as just "a story" without much meaning. However, to recount my journey in full I had to devote some time to descriptions and backgrounds.

You will frequently follow me in and out of various countries, airports, cafes, restaurants and neighborhoods. Some of these stops might seem mundane but within each visit lay quiet messages, messages from commonplace people from wide-ranging backgrounds. Their messages might have been soft but they were nonetheless powerful. Ultimately what I absorbed would have a lasting impact on the ways I viewed my surroundings. And over time, I was also forced to take an objective scan of my own values.

In some of my travels I built acquaintances that lasted a fair amount of time. In other spheres my interactions were short, passing and often not sustained. Regardless of the period, no matter how brief, I allowed myself to be open to messages and hints of change. At times I found crucial and interesting clues in the briefest of exchanges. So, I ask that you not brush aside what might appear to be small talk; when many conversations are combined, essential lessons are contained within their innocence. Without building upon these unassuming yet captivating interactions, it would be unreasonable to expect anyone to understand why and how my life changed.

I used to be overly punctual and consumed with work. Earning as much money as possible took priority over time with family and friends. I enjoyed owning brand-name clothing and expensive items. Frequenting malls, I often indulged myself with too much stuff. I ate "on the run" and didn't have much tolerance for waiting in line. When people think of change in their lives they often refer to obvious things: eating a healthier meal, spending less money on electricity, etc. But as I was to learn, this is only a microcosm of what true change really entails.

A genuine alteration first involves an unbiased recognition of one's flaws. To actually see this can be uncomfortable, painful, and is therefore often masked by false or misleading justifications. Before one can see his or her surroundings in a different light, one first has to build a fire from within. In other words, one first has to have a burning sensation that something is truly not working.

In my case, I just couldn't quite get my hands around what could possibly be wrong. My life seemed to be good but it just didn't feel right. Things, whatever they might have been, were missing. I didn't know if these things were big, small, or even critical. All I knew was what I felt: that something very necessary had not been incorporated into my life. It would take an unusual chain of events to finally awaken a fire that had been building in me. A crescendo that felt like it had been eternally boiling.

I am confident that I am likely not alone in admitting feeling trapped in a bubble bloated with unhappiness. It took the craziest of accidental events to finally piece together a road that would lead to my escape, a way for me to burst free of the stagnant bubble. Once and for all I wanted to exhale all the stale air out of my system and inhale a life-lasting breath filled with a fresh, positive transformation. In order to accomplish that, in order to connect to others in a dramatically different way, I first had to find a path that would allow me to be at peace with myself.

As so often happens, people change due to a life-threatening illness, a near-death experience, or a major life-altering event. None of these had anything whatsoever to do with my personal reversal. It shouldn't take something so dramatic or horrific to set any of us on a different path. If you feel a fire building, even if the flame is small, then let yourself go and stay with me to the very end. I wasn't changed by any major event, religious experience or teachings. Nor was I at all influenced by any medical, educational or scholastic journals. Ordinary people moved me away from a tainted path, people whose thinking and approaches to life I found more than magical.

I came to one major conclusion when I decided to write this book. My journey had to capture your interest, and the ideas along with my discoveries really had to matter. You know the old saying, "Does it really matter?" Well, my answer is a firm yes. It really does matter. It matters that I might open your mind to a different way of viewing so much of what surrounds us.

I also want to point out that the same or similar discoveries will appear throughout the book. This process is intentional, as I wanted to reinforce important ideas, ideas that I attempted to view from different angles. Some of the opinions, and hopefully revelations, you arrive at over time can be drawn out because of the ways the ideas were packaged. Since we are all unique, it's not uncommon to attempt to convey an idea in more ways than one. That's why, for example, when someone tries to express a point using only a single dimension, one person understands and someone else just doesn't get it . . . at least at that moment. But later, through an experience, picture, or different explanation, the light bulb is finally lit.

It's extraordinarily rewarding to develop a high level of clarity on something that's of personal interest and importance. While stepping incrementally thru our journey, I'm hoping you ultimately experience this same degree of clarity. Finally, I will try to tie together any loose ends to clarify misconceptions or expectations of what has been stated or implied.

Envision yourself by my side as I take you to places scattered throughout Latin America. Beautiful hills, valleys, forests, and unique shorelines await. Places that will capture most anyone's awe year-round in daylight or in darkness. Ride with me along roads while crossing though upscale and impoverished neighborhoods. Allow yourself to travel with me on lanes that twist around astonishing mountains, paths that can lead to tiny unspoiled and unknown communities. Come along and hear the ocean and smell the salt air. While appreciating the treasures of silence, take note of the brilliant stars and the echoes of the still evenings.

Expect to walk through many spaces that might seem conventional and even outdated: apartments, homes, stores and hallways with dilapidated interiors and no heating or air conditioning, comforts Americans often take for granted. Within these walls you will meet people from a very different history. People who generally have substantially less than most Americans' certain "standard of living."

You will hear their messages and undertones while witnessing their actions, inactions and behaviors. There is a good deal of poverty, suffering, and masking of pain coupled with tranquility, determination, kindness, cohesiveness and laughter. Sometimes clearly and often inconspicuously, you will view beautiful and unpleasant circumstances. Allow yourself to see past the obvious while trying to absorb the invisible. Often what we don't immediately see can later come into focus. Occasionally the picture becomes clear in minutes; sometimes the process takes years. Relax and fine-tune the constant whispers, permitting many messages to be captured in a fair and positive way.

This journey unlocked paths that provoked new ways for me to think, understand, and even imagine. I hope that sharing my experiences will be at least as beneficial to you, and that they will take you to new and exciting places. I hope they will elevate you to view things in different dimensions and to incorporate a diverse approach to your life.

CHAPTER 1
Spark and Ignition

It is the small things in life which count. It is the inconsequential leak which empties the biggest reservoir.
— Charles Comiskey

There are no such things as accidents. Only fate redesigned. —Soroosh Shahrivar

A rather ordinary incident triggered me to write this book. I never really realized a spark lay dormant inside me, a spark in need of an igniter. When the spark finally occurred, it was almost invisible. It would take some time for this spark to ultimately flare, to ultimately lead me in a new direction, a direction that would have a lasting impact on how I would live my life.

One evening in Fort Lauderdale, Florida, I was driving with my girlfriend Lindsey. We had been living together for a while in a townhouse in front of a busy canal. Our destination that evening was a restaurant called Houston's, one of Lindsey's favorite places. The evening sky was clear, the temperature rather refreshing. We were both looking forward to a relaxing dinner, and to some of our usual joking and good conversation.

Lindsey and I connected well on many levels, and this special connection made almost any occasion with her that much more enjoyable. I always looked forward to spending my free time with her. She had long, beautiful black hair and, like myself, looked forward to daily exercise. She also loved the ocean, the beach, windsurfing and fishing. We spent a lot of time relaxing on my boat while drifting off the coast of Fort Lauderdale. Never one to complain, Lindsey was smart, honest and very caring.

After living together for several years, Lindsay and I decided to go our separate ways. We were traveling different paths and agreed it was in both our interests to be apart. I still talk to her from time to time and will remain her friend forever. Lindsey brought only good energy into my life and was a strong force in my eventually capturing so much that took years for me to realize. She will always remain a special person in my heart. Her direction and chemistry were certainly instrumental in pulling together so many crucial pieces of the puzzle.

This particular sundown, Lindsey chose US1, also known as Federal Highway, as our route to Houston's. Both dressed casually in jeans and sneakers, we were sitting low in my two-seat black Mazda RX7. It was a great car that I had recently purchased as used. The interior was small and the design was enticingly sporty. As I slowly came to a stop a few miles from home, a car struck us from behind.

At first the impact didn't seem significant but both Lindsey and I were shaken. After gathering my thoughts, I stepped out of the car and just stood still. I wasn't hurt and fortunately neither was Lindsey. Two people, a lady and a man, were still seated in the other car, an upscale European import. After some time, the man got out. He was tall and slender, well-dressed, wearing grey slacks and some brown-laced business shoes.

Lindsey had some medical training and was concerned about everyone's condition. She walked over to see if the lady was hurt. Almost simultaneously, the tall man walked over to the passenger side of my car. Then he worked his way back to the rear and stopped beside me. His companion stayed in her seat toying with her bleached blonde hair. Clutching a brown Louis Vuitton bag, she was fashionably dressed in a pair of brand-name black jeans complimented by a white striped vest. Both appeared to be in their mid-fifties.

Finally, the man approached me and said, "There doesn't seem to be any real damage but if you find any here is my card."

I took his card and saw that he was an attorney. I thanked him for the card and was at a loss for other words. The damage was so minor it didn't require immediate repair—just a few scratches around the rear bumper and a cracked brake light. His car didn't have so much as a nick. After placing his information in my wallet, I pondered for a moment.

I joined Lindsey to see how the lady was doing. She reluctantly rolled down her window and reassured me that she was okay. I nervously laughed to myself as I saw her pull some lipstick out of her bag. She managed to carefully place some red gloss on her lips. I then asked the attorney if he really was all right. Rather curtly, he also claimed to be fine, and they hastily drove away.

I was a bit bewildered but did my best to calm Lindsey and salvage our night out together. We continued on our way to Houston's and managed to turn a bad start into a decent time. Seated in a large booth, we enjoyed a nice dinner of mixed salads and roasted chicken. But there was no denying that each of us still had the accident on our minds. Our normal free-flowing conversation was somewhat subdued. After paying the check, we drove home and watched a late-night movie. I never needed, nor did I frankly want to reach out to the attorney. The damage just wasn't worth the effort. Eventually, I paid for the repairs myself. Nonetheless, the accident troubled me; there was something about it that just didn't seem right.

Early the next morning I awoke from a deep sleep in a way that I had never experienced before. I was alert but not really conscious. My eyes were half open, and my thoughts were really racing. I was an audience to a movie my mind had constructed. The movie ran backwards, taking me from the previous night's car accident to a time several years earlier. The visions were vivid, tying all my travel experiences into a package that seemed to contain an abundance of messages. It was as if the movie was trying to rearrange and then organize a deck of cards with specific photographs from my past. My mind placed the cards in a way that allowed me to decipher a newly established collection of hidden messages. Moving at the speed of light, I was remembering every detail of the movie.

Upon waking, something inside of me was different. It's impossible to define or to even describe—I just felt very distinctive, filled with something I strongly wanted to share. The previous evening also struck a chord. Not the accident but what had occurred after the collision. Neither the man nor the lady had thought it necessary to ask if Lindsey or I were hurt. There didn't appear to be a shred of concern for anything other than a possible monetary penalty. For whatever reason, neither one asked anything remotely human.

At the time of the accident, this detachment did not register with me as being anything significant. The movie highlighted this coolness. During the playback, I felt myself being physically pulled by someone trying desperately to show me something. And then the picture came more into focus. Finally, that deck of cards became clearer. I don't know exactly how I got to the end of the movie; all I knew is that I arrived.

With the photos now stored in my mind, I asked what my next steps should entail. What should I do with this stuff? Was this some sort of wakeup call? Had there been a message in front of my eyes all along? Why hadn't I seen it? Upset that I never saw this movie before, I asked myself why it had taken so long for my mind to produce a sequel. Why hadn't I had this experience long ago? I then realized that the dream, the movie, had been ignited by the car accident.

The next evening another dimension began to take shape. I went to sleep extra late having spent much of the day over thinking. At around 3 AM, I felt mentally drained and retreated into another deep sleep. Soon I began to have visions of when I was a boy and thought about how less complicated life had seemed: a small black and white television with only a few channels, a life without cell phones and computers. All I needed was some Tootsie Roll candies and a baseball.

Then, as if I were slowly cooling down on a treadmill, I entered a state of tranquility. I could literally see and almost feel the ocean while its waves crashed down on large multi-colored rocks. Surrounding me was the pure aroma of the ocean's salt air. The scenery then expanded to mountain lush with greenery surrounding the sea. The echoes of the waves were interrupted by the cries of seagulls flying over the beach. The pristine shoreline was polished with white sand and scattered shells. Finally, I felt as if I were swimming beneath the surface. Dunes made of clean-shaven sand lined the bottom. Brilliantly colored blue and yellow striped fish were swimming in and out of an untouched coral reef.

That dream was one I wanted to capture in a bottle and hold for the rest of my life. On this morning, again something was different, but exactly what required more thought. What was this dream trying to teach me? Did it follow the previous night's movie for a reason? Had I been missing out on some important themes germane to my life? If so, how could I interpret them? How could I regain that exceptional tranquility? Was it only possible to experience that in a dream? All along, have I been going in the wrong direction?

The visions were shortly cemented by the oddest of voices. Lindsey and I frequently shared time on a twenty-four-foot Ocean Master fishing boat. The center console was perfectly designed for fishing; it allowed anyone to walk around the entire deck free from obstruction. Located at the stern was a well that kept bait alive through a constant exchange of seawater. The boat docked directly behind my condominium in southeast Fort Lauderdale. The craft was white and had a T-top outfitted with aluminum outriggers (spreaders.) Since I didn't have a cabin, the T-top offered shelter from the sun and the occasional rain. Used by anglers for trolling, the outriggers acted as makeshift flagpoles with lines hoisted along their entire length; this allowed for the separation of several fishing rigs to prevent tangling. A single outboard engine provided sufficient power to maneuver the boat and enough energy to escape any threatening storms.

In summer Lindsey and I often ventured far offshore in search of cooler waters. Every once in a while, we had the great luck to be surrounded by a school of dolphins. It always amazed me how they would somehow appear out of nowhere. At times they would sneak up from behind, and before I knew it we were the floating center of attention.

To describe what one feels when surrounded by dolphins is not all too difficult. But to actually feel the sensation(s), to really seize the moment . . . to accomplish this you will one day have to place yourself in their midst. I am keenly aware that isn't easy to realize. However, I can guarantee that if you are ever lucky enough to place yourself in their care, even if for just a few minutes, you will carry that experience for the rest of your life.

The encounter is so positive, so amazing that it's virtually impossible to explain the actual sensations. When a school of dolphins engulfed our small boat I immediately felt an aura, a special sense of security. It was almost as if I were a king on a floating chariot being escorted by a group of special gods. They toyed with the boat as if it was a giant rubber ball floating for their entertainment. I didn't understand how they so easily transferred their all-embracing happiness and sense of security.

Looking alongside the boat and watching their true grace is really something to behold. One can't help but be reassured by their defining, bigger than life smile. While watching their leader jump directly in front of the bow, I was overcome with a complete sense of safety and serenity. Dominating the entire surface of the ocean was the shine of their sleek white and grey coloration. The others followed their leader, performing Olympic ballets over this small part of the ocean. It's a dance anyone would repeatedly want to watch, the audience would never grow tired of the mystical show.

The dolphins are bound only to life's great freedoms—the freedom to eat, communicate, play, laugh, and enjoy each other's company. With my adrenalin pumping, the dolphin's magic always made me feel as if I were the center of attention. But of course, they were the true stars, the gods, the magicians; how so alive and fundamentally happy I always felt under their supreme presence. And just as suddenly as their ballet began, surrounding our boat with their kindness and grace, the gods escorting us vanished into their secret world of the sea. Before I left my dock I always hoped the dolphins would again select me. Honor me with their presence. Shine their powerfully positive energy in my direction.

A funny thing happened soon after the fender bender. I was on the boat alone but was escorted by an enormous school of dolphins. It was the most extensive group I had ever encountered. Coincidence? Maybe. But somehow their presence acted as a type of bond or reinforcement of what was subliminally going through my mind. It was if they were desperately trying to hint, "Where else have I seen such a consistency of happiness, tranquility, and playfulness?"

With their images and grace now firmly embedded, I found myself repeatedly asking, "Where else have I seen this behavior? Where else?"

CHAPTER 2

Foundation

We make a living by what we get, but we make a life by what we give.

— Winston Churchill

W hen I think of my parents, I have a confession to share that was prompted by the changes wrought by my travels. Before I reveal a very personal admission, it's necessary to quickly touch on a bit of my parent's history. My mom, Elaine, is ninety-two years old and resides in New York City where she has lived all of her life. She simply adores that town. My mom grew up with little money or possessions; even to this day, she doesn't crave luxurious items or a fancy lifestyle. She lives in a modest apartment under rent control, one of the few remaining under the city's regulations. Fortunately, her health is excellent, and weather permitting, she does quite a bit of walking.

One great benefit of residing in the city is the ease of travel. Buses, trains and taxies can provide transportation within the city and extend to the outer boroughs. However, in terms of what my mom needs, everything is within walking distance. As did my father, she grew up during the Great Depression.

After finishing high school, she went to work for a company in the garment industry. In my heart I know that she always did her best. Even to this day she is constantly supportive and checks that I am doing well.

One special memory I carry of her was my desire for a toy seaplane. I was a student of the New York City public school system all the way through high school. From kindergarten up to fifth grade, I attended my designated local public elementary school. P.S. 11 was a typical New York City public school. The students and teachers came from diverse socio-economic and cultural backgrounds. Standing just a few stories high, its exterior was composed of dark bricks; a thick iron mesh protected the heavy large windows that opened from the bottom. The first floor had a big open cafeteria, and steel stairs led up to different levels. A few disorderly pupils frequently pulled fire alarms to create daily mischief. The classrooms had wooden floors, wooden desks, and tall stained wooden closets.

One of my schoolrooms, the music history class, faced a building that had a heliport on its roof. I could even see the orange windsock blowing in the distance. I always looked forward to attending that particular class because the teacher made it a point to open the large squeaky windows. This allowed the noise of the churning blades to echo into the room. While most of my peers were paying attention to the lesson, my mind was focused on the constant helicopter traffic outside. I regularly daydreamed that I would one day fly in a helicopter; that I would hear up close the whipping blades whisking me into the sky. Every so often I would be embarrassed as the music teacher awakened me from my personal imaginative jaunt over the New York City skyline.

While walking me home from school, Mom and I often passed a tiny toy store located on Eighth Avenue. Sitting in the crowded window was a plastic seaplane accompanied by a key used to spin its propeller. The yellow and white plane remained in that window for a long time. Each time we passed, I was fixated on that golden toy. Its possibilities drew my imagination to my school day focus on that heliport.

There was just one problem. The seaplane cost five dollars. At the time, that was a large amount of money. Twenty-five cents could buy all the candy in the world. Although I wanted that toy, I never expected to receive such a super gift. Nevertheless, when the holidays arrived, I woke up to find that seaplane on the living room table. I was in heaven, and I wound that propeller celebrating my first piloting job! It might not have been a helicopter but it certainly did the trick! How much fun that moment was. More importantly, it signified the countless sacrifices my parents made for me over the years.

My mom was a strong believer in education and kept me focused on school. I was lucky that she was always there to guide me. She reinforced the importance of obtaining a college degree. On this point there wasn't any room for negotiation, as she understood the value of that piece of paper. Clearly, she dreamt of a better life for me, one with fewer struggles than she'd endured.

My dad, Jack, recently passed away at the age of eighty-eight, and I think of him often. He was a tall and handsome man up until the last moments. I had only fond memories of his extraordinary sacrifices. Serving in the 101st Airborne Division, he was a recipient of the Purple Heart and the Bronze Star. He was from the Greatest Generation and was laid to rest in Arlington National Cemetery. I was very touched by the gun salute, honor, professionalism, and dignity the military afforded my father's funeral.

Although it was uncomfortable for him, my dad shared some memories from when he was younger. One such story centered on good old-fashioned luck. In World War II, he was a staff sergeant and paratrooper in the 502 Infantry Parachute Regiment, Company E, of the 101st Airborne Division. His first entrance into the war came on D-Day during the Normandy invasion.

At one o'clock in the morning on Omaha Beach, the weather was lousy. Heavy winds forced him and his fellow paratroopers to be dropped from three hundred feet or less. Few landed where they were supposed to, and the altitude didn't permit enough time for many of the parachutes to open. As a result, many broke their legs and several others drowned in the water. Some landed in church steeples and were cut down by German machineguns. Unharmed, my dad spent the rest of the night searching for fellow paratroopers and gathering up the wounded. He was so far unharmed. This was lucky number one.

On the seventeenth day in Normandy, my dad delivered a trailer of heavy mortar ammunition. When he returned from the delivery, a captain sat on his right and two corporals were in the back of the jeep. They hit a land mine. The jeep went up in the air and spun several times. My dad hit his head and was knocked unconscious. When he woke, the captain's leg hung by some skin. The arms of both corporals had been badly mangled. My dad got some sodium packets, dressed their wounds and applied tourniquets. The ambulance that transported the wounded men also blew up. My dad only remembered that he passed out and woke up three days later in a field hospital on a beach. He was later shipped to a British hospital for three weeks to recuperate. He only had a bruise and a bump on his head. Call this luck number two.

The next battle my dad faced was the invasion of Holland. This time he managed to talk his way into flying a glider. It was a day invasion and the Germans were well prepared; they shot down many gliders like sitting ducks. But my dad and a few others landed safely. This was luck number three.

My dad along with his chief warrant officer commandeered a German truck and placed a machinegun on the back. Their mission was to destroy three bridges. On September 26, 1944, in Eindhoven Holland, my dad was taking ammunition to a company that had arrived the previous evening. He and another soldier drove by the ditches along the road; lying in them were German paratroopers dressed in camouflage who opened fire.

They captured my dad and his buddy. They were both taken to a nearby hut where the Germans agreed to take them outside and shoot them. Normally, German paratroopers took no prisoners. They started marching them down a road; my father was dying with every step. After about two hundred yards they reached a farmhouse and were taken to a stone wall behind a house. They stood shaking in front of the wall and were allowed to urinate. By chance, they were joined by a German major who graduated from Columbia University in New York. The major instructed the soldiers to take them to a POW camp. Indeed, luck number four.

The next day my dad was packed into a boxcar like a sardine. The car had one hole to use as the toilet but it was impossible to maneuver toward it. Basically, the guys went in their pants. They rode for two days and two nights and were taken to Limberg Prison where the Germans separated the officers and the enlisted men.

For the next forty-eight hours, he sat in another boxcar on its way to a camp near the Polish border. He was imprisoned at Stalag XIIA for seven months. In the morning they were given one slice of ersatz bread and one cup of ersatz coffee . . . no lunch. At night some ersatz soup with beet tops; if he was lucky he would get horsemeat. Many of the men combated dysentery; my dad went from 155 to 105 pounds.

Then at 4 AM. on a cold winter morning the Germans, brandishing their bayonets, rousted all the prisoners. They were taken outside, lined up, and marched out of the camp. They were presented as fresh German troops to fool the Russian army closing in on the area. Russian tanks mistook them for the enemy and killed hundreds of the prisoners. Soon the Russians liberated the camp and killed many of the guards in gruesome ways. My dad and five other soldiers spent two weeks walking two hundred miles to Warsaw, Poland. They stayed alive by eating canned foods they found in abandoned cellars and hunting wild pigs. They arrived in Warsaw hungry but free. This was certainly lucky number five!

Two days later they were rounded up by the US Navy and were taken to Odessa via Stalingrad. They were examined, deloused, fed, and placed on a ship to Constantinople, Turkey, then to Port Said, Egypt, and then to Naples, Italy, where he was hospitalized for three weeks with double pneumonia. One day an Air Force colonel came and said, "Keehn, we're sending you home." He arrived in Miami via Casablanca and then the Azores. When he finally stepped on American soil, he was assigned as an instructor at parachute school. He was later discharged at Camp Shelby, Mississippi, on October 7, 1945, exactly four years to the day after he enlisted.

On the day of my dad's burial at Arlington National Cemetery, I was reminded of the many who weren't so lucky; so many were killed at such young ages. The neatly spaced rows of tombstones went on as far as the eye could see. When the gun salute to my father ended, the views of the many graves and the stillness of the trees were sobering. I never realized silence could be so gripping. If not for that German major who had been educated in the States, I would not be here to write my story. So much in life is indeed luck. Don't let anyone tell you otherwise.

When my dad returned from the war he looked like a toothpick. He managed to get some work selling dresses in the midtown garment district. At the outset, his salary was between five and ten dollars per week. He became close friends with an Italian couple, Mary and Patsy. They were both great chefs who owned an Italian restaurant called Mary's on Bedford Street in the lower part of Manhattan. The décor was rather bland; the two levels were connected by a steep flight of dark wooden stairs. The small dining area on the ground floor contained only a few ordinary tables covered with white cloth. The walls could have used a fresh coat of white paint, and the uneven wooden flooring was warped.

On the first level was the open kitchen in plain view. At times the steam and enticing smells from the giant pots traveled directly into the tight quarters. Both chefs were short with a mix of silver and grey hair. They were madly in love. Mary often wore a hairnet, and while cooking, Patsy touted a tall white hat. My dad partook in their fantastic food for years. Whenever an opportunity arose, he would take me to their restaurant.

We were always seated on the first floor, which was considered an honor. If I didn't finish everything on my plate, Mary gave me quite the scolding; she didn't hesitate to do so in front of other customers. Patsy, a quiet and gentle man, referred to the gas stoves as his secretaries. He played those stoves like a maestro. Judges and politicians frequented the unpretentious restaurant. My dad always made certain that I maintained proper manners. Unfortunately, Mary and Patsy passed away many years ago; they were unforgettable gems.

When I was a boy, my dad would take me to the Seaman's Institute in the lower part of Manhattan. He knew I loved to look at the old ships that had been skillfully sealed inside tanks or glass bottles. After visiting we normally walked to the South Street Seaport. The pier had antique shops that sold boating, sailing, fishing and whaling knickknacks. On display in one store was a white whale's tooth; and just like the seaplane, it sat there for months. My dad bargained with the shopkeeper to afford me this white prize.

For the longest time I wanted to go on a helicopter ride offered off a nearby pier on the Hudson River. I wanted my classroom dream to finally become a reality. The heliport was located in Chelsea, and I was beyond excited by the chance to climb into that noisy chopper. The fee was fifteen dollars per person for a five-minute jaunt; a great deal of money at the time. But my dad, never thinking of himself, always found a way to make me smile.

Accompanied by friends who also wanted to go for a ride. To satisfy everyone was just too expensive; dad simply didn't have anywhere near that amount of disposable income. My dad instructed us to wait outside while he went into the heliport's trailer. The next thing I knew, a helicopter appeared, blades roaring, ready to take us for a ride. The single pilot wore a thick headset, and a boom microphone was placed directly in front of his mouth.

As my hair and shirt was blown wildly about, he waved me to join him. For about thirty seconds I just stood frozen in wonder. I couldn't imagine what in the heck my dad had said to persuade them to take us all for a ride. Apparently, he convinced the manager that he simply didn't have the money (which was true), and that to let us down would be too disappointing. It was another of the countless magical moments my father managed to pull off. Even now, I can still recall my uncontained excitement. The tour might have been only five minutes but for me it felt like a lifetime. I pretended I was lifting off from the building I had watched from the P.S. 11 classroom. This time, like so many others, my dad turned my dream into reality.

* * *

When I wanted a bicycle, dad made a connection with an older Italian gentleman, Tony, who owned a neighborhood bicycle store. After a few trips to the shop, Dad offered to pay for a bicycle in installments. Upon receiving the bike, my dad gave Tony a box filled with dresses for his niece. Tony was so elated he insisted we take the bike at no cost. The gesture was completely unexpected, and my dad tried everything to convince him to accept the payments. My dad had a special way with people as he really had the gift of gab.

When Dad gave a present, it was never with intention of receiving anything in return. He taught me at an early age to "give from the heart and only from the heart," and to never give with the expectation of receiving something back. He said, "When you give from the heart, you are rewarded in more ways than you can ever imagine."

* * *

Because he'd barely finished high school, my dad was not an educated man. Both his brothers had received more schooling and were well read. But my father possessed a rare and powerful combination of a tremendous heart and a unique way with people. He worked like a dog to ensure that I had a better life.

With some luck, he found employment as a salesman for an established clothing company. He worked first for an outfit named JLH, and later for a firm in midtown with a plant in Lancaster, Pennsylvania. Both companies manufactured children's dresses. One day I was introduced to dad's boss, Mr. Martin K. I was nervous; it was the first time I had met someone of his caliber. He stood tall with perfect posture and was impeccably dressed. Mr. K was educated, polished, and spoke with a confident and soft elegance.

Because I was somewhat shy, my dad prodded me to initiate a presentation. Before I could get a word out, Mr. K reached for my hand and gave it a firm shake. He had a way of quickly making one feel at ease. A gracious man, Mr. K owned a nice condominium in Pompano Beach, Florida; he offered it to my dad for family vacations. A remarkably gifted gentleman, Martin K died far too young from cancer. He was another one of those diamonds my dad managed to have by his side.

* * *

An avid fisherman, Dad frequented the Palace II and III party boats docked in Hoboken, New Jersey. The boats, converted WWII submarine chasers, picked up customers on the New York side. Accompanying dad, I fished for years on these boats and later worked on them as a deck hand. During the voyage, my dad managed to squeeze his way into some poker games.

Poker was a game my dad truly found relaxing. Afterwards, if he won, he would hand me a portion of his monies.

In his eyes, my needs always came first. When possible, we would travel to the Great South Bay of Eastern Long Island. There we rented a small motorboat and fished for the much sought-after sea trout. He loved the escape offered by the open water; the tranquility always relaxed him.

One sunny afternoon, my dad drove me to Farmingdale, Long Island's airport. When I asked where he was taking me, he said it was a surprise. On that day I climbed into a small Piper airplane for an introduction flight. I was uneasy yet excited. The brief flight was with an elderly instructor confident enough to allow me to handle the controls. My dad waited patiently on the ground hoping I was enjoying my time. The hook was set. I couldn't wait to fly in one of those small planes again. My parents would sacrifice a ton to see that my dreams would one day be realized.

* * *

Our family had some close friends in Bethesda, Maryland, so we occasionally flew the Eastern Airlines shuttle into the small Washington, D.C. airport. Dad always snuck me into the cockpit so I could meet the pilots. But he escorted me there for another reason, too. He always imagined himself sitting behind those dials and fancy controls. As a boy, I was fascinated by those instruments, switches and buttons. To me, the pilots were the Gods of the sky. I looked forward to the long walk out to the Lockheed Electra, soaking in the sounds of the airplanes roaring down the nearby runway. Once aboard the stumpy four-engine plane, I purposely took a seat near the wing. I wanted to watch and hear the winding vibrations of the noisy turboprops.

Then came the day I walked out expecting to board another Lockheed Electra. Parked in the distance was a shiny new McDonald Douglas DC-9 they named the whisper jet because it was a comparatively quiet machine. My dad knew of the change but he hadn't wanted to spoil the surprise. When I realized I would ride in a jet for the first time, my heart began to pound. I was overwhelmed and thrilled by this sleek, state-of-the-art machine. I ran up the stairs and couldn't wait to sit by any window! As trivial as it might seem now, that day was truly a monumental dream come true.

* * *

In my late teens, I began taking regular flying lessons out of New Jersey's Teterboro Airport. When I finally received my private pilot's license, the elderly Mary and Patsy were my first passengers. Imagine how thrilled I was to take them for a plane ride up the Hudson River; these two people were so special to my father.

My dad really cherished everything about airplanes. From his hidden spot at Kennedy Airport, he watched in amazement and repeatedly asked, "How can such a large thing get off the ground?" A sky covered by a low ceiling formed his favorite day; the huge planes appeared out of nowhere and somehow found their way to the runway. He watched in awe as the jumbo jets took off and vanished into the low clouds that looked like clusters of cotton. My dad never grew tired of watching, and I think his greatest dream was that he could have commanded one. At times he might have been reminiscing about his time in the glider, and how that feeling of happiness and freedom had been stolen by so much horror. His life did not allow the space for his dream to come to fruition. His youth was, like those of many others, just too difficult.

* * *

My dad was a very relaxed man and never got stressed about much of anything. He once told me that life is like a train. You will always see many people in front who appear to be doing so much better but your mind doesn't capture the many people behind you who are truly suffering and struggling. Be happy and make the best of what you have at the moment. And if for some reason you aren't able to do that, then take a moment, pause, and adjust your rearview mirror.

Both my parents taught me about certain stages of life. They said if I placed life's experiences on a graph, the line would be like a wave vacillating between ups and downs. Our lives are filled with triumphs and tragedies, successes and failures. They taught me to understand that we are only human, and we fail not once or twice but time after time throughout our lives. They believed it was important to learn from failure and to build from mistakes. My parents stressed the importance of managing with failure. Anyone can shine when everything is going well. The real test lies in how an individual copes when so much goes wrong. The degree of power to rebound from the abyss and rise even higher demonstrated inner strength and ultimately revealed true character.

As I grew older, I noticed how easy it is to believe we are surrounded by so-called friends, people who embrace us when everything is on track. I saw what happened when things started to go wrong . . . the herd of friends quickly thins out, leaving one with the real deal. True friends will stand by a person who is struggling through their lowest point. My parents were spot on when they taught me the accuracy of this litmus test of human nature.

* * *

Once my dad was gone, his absence forced me to do a lot of thinking. As painful as it is for me to admit, I often took him for granted. I squandered a great treasure placed right into the palms of my hands. As my dad got older, instead of focusing on and spending time with him, my attention shifted to other dynamics—my career, money, and the stock market all took precedence over sharing priceless moments with my parents. I was too involved with my own life and my selfishness was an enormous mistake.

My dad was a beautiful person, a very gentle and giving man. What I had was an almost perfect diamond, and instead of wearing it around my heart, I left it in a drawer to gather dust. My mistake brought home the importance of family that is rooted in many of the Latin cultures. Regrettably, it would take me all too long to recognize that I had let go of a real treasure. How much time, energy and effort I spent thinking of finance . . . what was I really investing in? How much was I investing in my relationship with my parents, or for that matter, with my own friends?

My dad had this secret: he once told me that if you are good to people, make them happy and laugh, then the personal reward will be something that no amount of money can buy. How fitting it is that my dad is at rest surrounded by America's heroes, those who made the ultimate sacrifice. My dad will always be my hero. If one day I can grow to be half the man he was then I will feel truly blessed. He, and so many like him, gave us the ability to get into any airplane and fly with wings built on freedom.

My dad was never able to fulfill his dream but he will always be my captain.

CHAPTER 3

In the Shadow of a Glider

It's the possibility of having a dream come true that makes life interesting.

— *Paulo Coelho*

Because I started flying lessons very young, I had a good start on that boyhood dream to make flying my profession. My first year attending college in upstate New York, the local airport was just outside town. When I had time, I would rent a small plane for an hour or two to maintain my skills. The main airline that serviced the community was Allegheny, which utilized the British Aircraft Corporation One-Eleven. Commonly referred to as the BAC-111, the echoes of the short-range jetliner's takeoffs and landings could be heard quite far from the airport.

In my accounting and philosophy classes I purposely sat by the windows. They offered a view of the arrival and departure paths of the Allegheny jets. I cracked the windows open when the professors weren't looking so I could hear the booms of the noisy BAC-111 Rolls-Royce engines. Just like the sights and sounds of the helicopter blades during elementary school, my focus was again elsewhere. Only this time I was captured by a bigger and sleeker flying machine. I might have been in college but my imagination never wandered too far from those PS11 days.

Throughout my college years, I gained enough flying experience to become an instructor. The Teterboro flight school where I trained was gracious enough to give me my first real break. There, I instructed in both single and multi-engine Piper planes. I had a solid following of students, and within a short period of time landed a copilot job with a small commuter airline. After building enough multi-engine turboprop experience, I was hired by a small regional airline. From there, I was interviewed by several major US airlines; eventually my current company hired me. My dream was now realized. I was part of a large international airline with a route structure to many parts of the world. I would fly in and out of those clusters of cotton.

I was only in my mid-twenties, still quite young, when I began my career with this new company. Suitcase in hand, I was given a one-way ticket to the flight training center in the Midwest. My initial position was as a flight engineer on a Mc-Donnell Douglas DC-10, a large three-engine, wide body jetliner. The position entailed monitoring aircraft instruments, handling system emergencies, and calculating a variety of performance data on an older generation of planes. Most of these planes are not in service anymore, and computers have replaced the need for the three-man cockpit.

Upon arriving near the training center, I had to pay for my own hotel room. I was on probation for the first year. Training and testing lasted almost two months, and the entire event was grueling. My partner, Susan, was really friendly and we worked well together as a team. Her father was an airline pilot, so the profession ran in her family. She was of medium build with long blonde hair, and always positive and supportive.

Finally, we were told who would give us our final practical test in the simulator. The Japanese gentleman named Joe had a reputation for being difficult. We were warned that he was precise and extra particular. Fortunately for Susan and I, our European instructor Hans was also quite demanding. He made sure we were 110 percent ready before he released us to the wolves. Still, we were both nervous about our final check rides. Joe lived up to his reputation but he was also fair. Susan and I survived.

To celebrate, we were taken to dinner by two other classmates who had been with the company for a long time. Each had been flight engineers for more than ten years and were upgrading to become DC-10 co-pilots. Both were in their fifties. They drove us to a large restaurant famous for its prime quality steaks. Cut-off ties hung on all the walls and sawdust had been sprinkled on the wooden floors. I took a menu and confidently ordered some Rocky Mountain oysters. Being from the northeast, I thought I was getting oysters.

The two older guys smirked but didn't utter a peep. I figured they were both meat and potato eaters. Susan ordered a salad but she also displayed a certain grin. My Rocky Mountain's arrived and they tasted just like oysters. I finished my entire portion and washed it down with a cold beer. Then all three of my guests began laughing. The older guys pounded their fists on the table as they laughed uncontrollably.

"What in the hell is so damn funny?" I asked.

Susan gently broke the news . . . those Rocky Mountain oysters were actually the testicles of bulls! Of course, no one mentioned that until I had finished every last one. Rocky Mountain oysters = bull balls. Plainly, the joke was on me. So that's how my initial training concluded—very rocky indeed!

* * *

Soon after I completed training, I had a rather short layover at a hotel near the Detroit metro airport. It was an extremely cold Monday evening and snowing quite heavily. The snow was so intense I had difficulty seeing a few feet in front of me. Nothing much was located near the hotel, so I agreed to meet the captain downstairs an hour after we checked in. He liked to be called Dens, which was slang for something; I just can't recall what.

We were both a bit tired and thought it best to find a place to eat that was close to the hotel. A few blocks away, we stumbled upon a run-down bar/restaurant. Between the snow and the freezing wind, our walk seemed like an eternity. On a normal night, I wouldn't have entered this particular place but the chill was punishing and the proximity made this place feel welcoming. I didn't have a warm jacket, a hat, or even a pair of gloves. And my shoes were wet from the snow and slush.

I walked briskly in front of the captain and firmly pulled the metal door handle. It took a few tugs to finally pry it free from a small coat of ice. I stomped my feet to shake off the melted water. I was shivering and rubbed my hands together. We walked over to some high chairs at the bar, which encompassed the main area of the restaurant. I could smell the remnants of spilled beer on the stained mantle.

The tavern was poorly lit, and an assortment of wooden chairs and tables had been spread throughout. Most of the furniture looked worn, and the tables were covered with dark red, torn cloths. Because of the weather, there weren't many patrons. Only two or three people were at the bar, and a sparse few sat at the uneven tables. Our bartender was an older gentleman, seemingly in his early sixties. He had a grey beard and a large tattoo of a horseshoe on his right arm. We were quickly handed some sticky menus with not much of a food selection. The soup of the day didn't seem appealing, so we ordered club sandwiches; they seemed the lesser of two evils. We also selected some draft beer. I just wanted to wind down for a few minutes.

No more than five minutes after we sat down a large man entered. He was tall and built like a football player. He wore some black decorated leather boots and a black wool mask that covered his entire face. Draping his body was a long blue overcoat that looked like it had never been washed. He slowly walked past us around to the other side of the bar. At first, I didn't think his scouting was of any significance. But after about two minutes, I realized he had never taken off the hat.

The interior became still. I could hear the piercing wind coming through the cracks of a nearby exit. I got an eerie feeling that something was just not right. Then the man reached inside his coat and withdrew a rifle. In a very deep voice, he commanded that nobody move. He was going to collect our money. Dens and I sat motionless. I thought that this was going to be a memorable layover.

The large man went to the tables and quickly gathered wallets and watches. He was fast, calm, and methodical, he had done this sort of thing before. He carried a small green duffle bag into which he stuffed everything he thought to be of value. His large forearm supported that rather large gun quite comfortably. After the longest few minutes of my life, he approached us. The captain, being much older and wiser, quietly handed over his money. He stared at the floor and he was shaking.

Then it was my turn. I placed a ten-dollar bill on the bar. The robber stopped and demanded, "Is this all you have?"

I thought about what my dad would say. Having been through so much in his life, he was always so calm and collected. With my heart pounding, I nervously replied, "If I knew you were coming I would have made it a point to have brought more."

Dens gave me a look that to this day I can easily recall. His stare held such disbelief and horror. He must have thought my answer was going to get us both killed. Fortunately, despite my wisecrack and stupidity, the thief just pounded the bar, took the money, and proceeded to the exit.

By then my chill was long gone and I needed a scotch to replace my beer. The police never did catch the Monday night gunman but it certainly was an evening to remember. As for the captain and I . . . well, we both lost our appetite. After the police arrived and questioned us along with the other patrons, we bolted back to the hotel. When I entered into my room, I took off my shirt and rested on the bed. Staring at the ceiling, my adrenalin was still in high gear. It was beginning to dawn on me just how risky my antics had been. I didn't sleep a wink.

But as dangerous as that event had been, it paled in comparison to what my dad had gone through. With that realization, the fear began to subside; I was then overtaken by a tremendous sense of relief. I was shaken but happy to be able to put on my uniform the next morning! My dad would have shrugged off the entire event. In my heart I knew he would have given anything to be in my place, to fly one of those big jets. That evening in Detroit was certainly an unusual introduction to a glamorous career but I never lost sight of the bigger picture. I was so lucky to be where I was, living a great dream in the shadow of my dad's glider.

CHAPTER 4

The Seeds of Change

Where the horse reaches, the jackass does reach and pass.
The race is not for the swift, slow and steady wins.

My first five years of flying for my present airline consisted mostly of domestic trips—cities within the boundaries of the United States. At times, however, I was assigned
flights to Canada, a truly magnificent country. I stayed in
cities such as Vancouver, Ottawa and Toronto. I especially
remember frigid winter nights in Ottawa. The snow covered
the streets, grass, rivers and buildings and gave the entire city
a beautiful appearance. It was as if a perfectly smooth white
blanket draped the area. And at night, the lights of the homes
and buildings reflected off of the frozen layers to create an
almost tranquilizing glow. One thing was certain though: I
could really feel the cold. To reside there in the winter was
not for the weak. Thank goodness for the kindness of the Ca-
nadian people as their warmth more than made up for the
punishing winters.

Later on, my career began a major change. Some pilot positions became available at our crew base in Miami, Florida. I put in a request to be transferred from New York and

was quickly awarded the move. I was a bit nervous because I was changing offices from one location to another. This meant I would be working with a completely new group, people I likely had never seen before. But in my profession, one can be called on to quickly adapt. Anxious but excited, I packed my bags and boarded our next flight to south Florida.

Our Miami office specialized in flights to the Caribbean, and Central and South America. It did offer limited domestic service to transfer passengers to some major US cities like Chicago, Denver, San Francisco, New York and Los Angeles. These cities, including Miami, are called hubs, an airline term for connecting flights/passengers to other destinations. The jargon "hub and spoke" is often used to describe most of today's complex airline networks.

Soon after my arrival in Miami, I began flying to the Caribbean and South America. My first assignment was to the Islands of Trinidad and Tobago. These twin islands are located off the cost of northeastern Venezuela. The country has a solid amount of oil and natural gas reserves, and on a clear night, you can sometimes see flames emanating from the offshore rigs. There are beautiful sandy beaches, especially on the island of Tobago. The water is crystal clear, warm and soothing. Throughout the chains you encounter low hills and mountains, and plenty of natural vegetation. More than 90 percent of the population resides on the Trinidad side. The combination of heat and humidity, palm trees, and dense rain are all reminders that you are indeed situated in the tropics of the Caribbean.

I arrived in my little Mazda at the employee parking lot at Miami International Airport. It was evening, and I waited for the crew bus that would transport me to the airport's main terminals. Miami airport has grown over the years into a rather larger international destination. It's a busy place bustling with passengers, skycaps, and airport and airline employees. At times I partook of the Latin cuisine offered by the airport restaurants.

Our pilot operations were located up some short escalators leading to the F concourse; there we would meet and discuss the flight plan, weather, and anything relevant to our work. The room was compact and partitioned with cubicles, tables, and older desktop computers. I punched in the security code and waited for the assigned captain. Before he showed, I logged into one of the computers and printed off the information pertinent to our route.

After about twenty or so minutes Russ appeared. He firmly shook my hand and introduced himself. Rather short and thin, he was a quiet and polite older gentleman. Not noticing anything out of the ordinary in the flight plan, aircraft papers, and fuel, we agreed that everything was proper. He signed the papers accepting the flight release and then we strolled down to the fingers of the F concourse. At the gate, we introduced ourselves to the flight attendants and coordinated the estimated time, weather, and in-route flight conditions.

Once the passengers had boarded, we commenced our push back and completed the required checklists. It wasn't long before we were off in the darkness headed to Trinidad. I was secretly excited because I had never visited that part of the world before. Fortunately, the time zones we would cross closely coincided with the ones where I resided. Those who haven't experienced time zone changes shouldn't underestimate their effect. Your body keeps its internal clock set on the accustomed region; if you deviate from your normal sleep cycle you will quickly be alerted. To put it in laymen's terms, you will be dragging it.

Sometimes at night, without the glow of a bright moon, you just can't see much out a cockpit window. At times I felt as if I was locked inside a closet. The flight to Trinidad was only a few hours from Miami. Russ and I talked to pass the time. The hours quickly ticked by, and we fast approached the point to begin our descent into Piarco International Airport.

Controllers often cleared pilots to fly to the "shark" intersection. The point served as an identifier/location so pilots could commence on the correct final path to the airport runway. I always thought the name was a great motivator to fly with extra precision. The air traffic control procedures were quite safe but noticeably much less regimented compared to other parts of the world.

Some showers around the islands appeared on our radar. We were prepared in case the landing became challenging. The plane was bouncing, tossed around by some low-level windshear. At the correct fix, Piarco issued a landing clearance. At approximately a few hundred feet, we broke out of a thick layer of clouds; the runway was barely visible. The captain turned on the wipers and landing lights as a driving rain blew directly across the airstrip. He lowered the left wing slightly into the crosswind and did a nice job touching down.

The ground controller instructed us to an area for parking. Wearing a yellow poncho and holding two dimly lit red wands, a man signaled where to turn and stop; the poor guy was literally bombarded by buckets of heavy rain. The plane was now set to remain overnight. The area didn't have a jet bridge, so portable stairs were wheeled to the airplane's front door. Everyone had to walk a fair distance to the terminal. By the time I finally got to the field's shelter, I was soaked.

Having never been to Piarco International, I wanted to do some quick exploring. The first thing that struck me was the age of the terminal; it seemed a bit antiquated. The architecture and infrastructure of the building were rather ordinary. No marble or tiled flooring was in evidence as the structure consisted of either concrete or wood. For a moment I thought I had entered a large hangar. Despite its age and appearance, the terminal served its purpose. Like many things in life, it would just take some getting used to.

Past the customs area were stores selling liquor, sauces and seasonings. I went into a small spice store and purchased a jar of hot sauce. The choices were overwhelming. Soon I would discover that the people of Trinidad have a unique understanding of the meaning of hot. The sauce could have burned a hole through an armored truck. After you ingest some of Trinidad's spices, you will find the experience unforgettable. Be prepared for a very spicy and new eating experience.

The lady who sold me the hot sauce wore a light dress and was calm and polite. The temperature was exceedingly hot. The store was void of air conditioning, yet she didn't seem disturbed. Her demeanor remained upbeat and positive; her face carried a large and genuine smile. How she wasn't bothered was a mystery. The tiny space was almost suffocating. I wondered if those conditions would have been considered legal in my own country. Saying goodbye, I thanked her for her kindness and promised to return.

Russ caught up with me. Accompanied by the flight attendants, we crawled into an old greenish-grey Volkswagen Kombi. Our uniforms were waterlogged as we began the forty-five minute trip to the hotel. During the drive I didn't see much lighting and was thinking about what I had seen at the airport. The culture of simplicity was new to me.

The Trinidad Hilton is located within the confines of the capitol, Port of Spain. The hotel has the distinguished honor of being referred to as the upside-down Hilton. Because the building is situated at the top of a hill, its levels descend; when pressing the elevator's button from the lobby to a higher floor, you are actually going down. I was tired and the experience caught me a bit off guard. I couldn't quite understand why I was going down when I was supposed to being going up. It made for a good laugh but my more immediate concern was to get out of my wet uniform and towel myself dry! I wished Russ a good rest.

The assigned room was modest with a decent bed and an adequate bathroom. Just like my home in Florida, some tiny ants patrolled the windowsill. In the morning, the sounds of birds filled the air. They were up at the crack of dawn softly singing and chirping. The symphony was so calming it lulled me back to sleep. Finally waking late in the morning, I was in need of something to eat. I put on a pair of shorts and went down to the hotel's tremendous pool. There, sitting by a table and canapé, I selected a fish snack called a shark and bait sandwich. Russ and others from the crew were already lounging by the pool.

A middle-aged lady wearing a yellow dress, protective hat, and brown sandals strolled over to take my order. She had quite the Trinidadian accent. The pace of the workers was justifiably slow as they had to cope with the oppressive heat. As a visitor, you quickly learn to slow your activity. If you don't, the sun will zap every ounce of your energy. It's also imperative to stay hydrated or you can literally pass out from heat exhaustion.

It took almost an hour for my food to arrive but it was worth the wait. I wanted to discover other dining possibilities outside the hotel. I waited for the sun to wane before I walked carefully down some shabby steps to the bottom of the hill. In a large park, a game of soccer was taking place. The locals were scattered about, some jogging, others resting on the grass. Even though I resided in Florida, I was not used to this degree of heat and humidity.

Still hungry and now thirsty, I scanned the area. I found a little store that sold vegetable and meat patties. The clerk informed me that each cost only a dollar. It seemed a lot of food for little money. At the first bite of the vegetable patty, the quality was obvious. Hard to believe: a super meal for one dollar? Where in the States could I equal that level of trade? The store also offered natural fruit juices that quenched my thirst.

The entire experience of inexpensive, freshly prepared food was new. I thought of my Jamaican nanny Inez who'd helped raise me. Inez was one great calypso cook! She could prepare codfish a hundred different ways and give each dish its own unique flavor. From time to time, I still crave her masterfully prepared meals. Inez was a special lady who passed away in her nineties. I will always miss her dearly. I felt her presence all the while I was in that tiny store. Before I left, I promised the elderly owner I would soon return for more of his home-cooked food.

I followed some locals to a bus stop on the other side of the park where I could catch a ride downtown. After a lengthy wait, an old Kombi arrived with barely enough room for two. I paid the driver and squeezed in between two elderly ladies. There wasn't any air conditioning. The seats were torn and the shocks almost nonexistent. I wasn't comfortable and sweated profusely; the breeze would have to sustain me. Candidly, I was anxious to exit the van as soon as possible! Not one of the other passengers showed any signs of dissatisfaction. Closing my eyes, I imagined how my American friends would cope with the experience. Maybe I was exaggerating the circumstances and was simply overreacting? At the time, I couldn't see how.

The van stopped in the middle of a crowded market. Relieved, I stepped out and randomly chose a direction. Several outdoor shops sold clothing, hats, shoes and furniture. The merchandise appeared to be conventional and correctly priced to conform to people's budgets. Some stores had windows filled with a hodgepodge of piled-up stuff. Sometimes it was difficult to decipher exactly what some of these places sold. The merchants could tell I was a foreigner, and I was often stopped in an attempt to convince me to make a purchase. I just didn't find anything of interest; although I admired their persistence, I respectfully declined. Dressed in very thin clothing and wearing sandals or flip-flops, all the locals seemed nice yet they didn't have much in a material sense.

The sun's powerful rays were vanishing and I was tired. Having taken in enough for one day, I returned to the hotel via taxi. My thoughts were going in all directions. There was much for me to continue to discover about the culture of this calypso land.

* * *

Having walked for hours, I was again hungry. I changed into clean clothes and entered the hotel's upscale restaurant. A young man placed me at a square table draped in a bright white cloth. The dishes and glasses were sparkling clean; soothing music played in the background. The room was relatively empty, and the waiters were mostly of Indian descent; a fairly large percentage of people in Trinidad apparently migrated from India.

The waiters were polite and eager to help. At their suggestion, I ordered a spicy dish of rice. It was flavorful and filling. When I was finished, some of the waiters wanted to talk; they were curious about where I was from and what I thought about Trinidad. After explaining my neighborhood in Florida, I then responded with kind words about their country. The workers were low key, soft-spoken and relaxed. They seemed genuinely happy. Their calm demeanor had an immediate impact. Their composure was something I didn't often encounter back home. That evening, I felt completely at ease.

With my hotel room dimly lit, I lay in bed with the ceiling fan sending a breeze across my sheets. I could see the shadows of the blades on the ceiling and walls as the motor chattered throughout the night. When I thought of my stay, I was somewhat perplexed. All I'd had to eat was a simple sandwich, a vegetable patty, and some rice. Other than food, I hadn't bought anything. The transportation was lousy, and at times I had been exhausted. Then why was I so happy? It just didn't make sense.

The following day I again enjoyed the birds. I slowly consumed coffee and a plate of fresh fruit. Time to leave. I went upstairs to the lobby and dropped off my key. The van was waiting curbside, and I was the last crewmember to arrive. It was another one of those Volkswagens from the 1960's. The interior was in poor condition but at least we had air conditioning.

This time I could clearly see what surrounded our route to the hotel. Older and quaint homes were fenced in by tall iron gates; most buildings appeared to be in fair condition. In many cases the structures needed exterior repair. The van passed by hills and a large bird sanctuary. We cruised by the town's marine port, and the age of the many ships made them look like a photo out of a pirate movie. The cargo and fishing vessels were old compared to those at my hometown harbor. Despite their age, I was informed that they functioned quite well. We drove through cobblestone streets and dirt roads but most of the lanes were in fine condition.

Back at the airport, I couldn't resist returning to the spice store. The same saleslady sat behind the counter. She stood up and immediately greeted me with a warm smile. I couldn't resist and purchased another bottle of liquid fire. When I convinced Russ to buy some items, the lady's smile grew even larger. We both waved goodbye and passed several parked trucks to reach our company's minuscule operations room. Dragging our luggage and heavy flight bags made the walk difficult. The rundown space had a single computer along with a rudimentary printer.

After reviewing the flight plan, we walked toward the airplane. The weather remained stubbornly hot and humid without the slightest hint of a breeze. As required, I inspected the outside of the airplane to make sure everything appeared mechanically correct: no fuel or oil leaks, normal brake and tire pressures, and no damage to any section of the aircraft's exterior. We in the pilot profession call this the walk around.

When I returned to the cockpit, I noticed that the BWIA (British West Indies Airways) planes had been parked on the opposite side of the field. I wondered what it would be like to live in Trinidad and fly for BWIA. It's only natural for the mind to wander now and then, so no harm in a quick daydream. Peering out of my window, I saw passengers heading our way. Now it was time to get the departure instructions from the Piarco controllers. I called on the radio and asked for our flight clearance to Caracas, Venezuela. We would stop there before continuing on to Miami.

The ground controller cleared us to taxi to the active runway and said to call when we were ready to copy the assigned route. After writing down our designated airways, I informed the tower we were ready for takeoff. The controller responsible for takeoffs and landings came onto the frequency. Both Russ and I had great difficulty understanding her exceptionally strong Trinidadian accent. Doing our best to decipher her orders, we accepted the takeoff and departure clearance; our combined experience gave us a general sense of our flight path instructions. So off we went into the blue skies with our Boeing 757. The odd route required one big circle over the islands before heading toward Venezuela. I guess we did the departure correctly because we were never told otherwise.

* * *

There is a time every year when the pace of the islands speeds up. Not as famous as the Carnival in Brazil, Trinidad celebrates a similar holiday that is really an amazing party. During this non-stop festival, loud music is heard throughout all corners of the islands; people dance all night long. The steel drums always captured me as their beat seemed to be a perfect fit for the fun atmosphere. I could listen for hours. The Calypso music of Trinidad has a certain power to lift anyone's spirits.

The celebration acted as a change from the country's normal pace and provided an outlet for people to simply let go. With their rhythm, the drums remain a special part of the island's culture. A lot of the beat is quite relaxing, especially amongst the backdrop of the ocean and mountain echoes. Normally occurring in February, the festival made my stay at the upside-down Hilton that much more intriguing. The bird's special choirs at sunrise, the clapping of the afternoon thunder, and the reverberations of the steel drums throughout the parks and hills really made for quite a combination.

At the time I couldn't explain why but I actually liked Trinidad. It was the first time I had entered the Third World. I thought maybe I enjoyed it solely because it was new; yet there was something real that I liked about the islands, something about my experiences that lifted my spirits. In terms of the pace of my life, I felt like I had taken a giant step backwards. Many people might interpret that as somewhat negative. Normally I would have agreed but Trinidad gave me a new perspective.

I started to think I was running through life too quickly, that I might be missing or just not noticing a lot of my surroundings. If I incorporated a slower pace, might I absorb much more of what was important? My questioning was a touch ironic; after all, I was an airline pilot, and to go fast is baked into our job. Crewmembers live a fast-paced life on the go hopping from one city or country to the next. We even find ourselves eating quickly because of the rush inherent to our profession.

Having grown up in a major US city, I always accepted an accelerated daily routine as the norm. Run to catch a bus or subway; if time was tight, hail a cab; eat on the run and rush to appointments. But when I traveled to Trinidad, I was literally forced to slow down. The deceleration was not only physical. My mind was also much more at ease. In terms of taking this Trinidadian step backwards, I subconsciously began to recognize that maybe this style just wasn't such a bad idea.

The visits to Trinidad planted seeds of change, and slowly my life began to transform. It was as if I had just inhaled a giant breath of fresh air. Although I never forged any close or personal relationships in Trinidad, my frequent interactions helped me develop an awareness of the culture. What captured me were the kindness, peace, and a contentment among the people. They maintained a balanced level of simplicity attached to several aspects of their lives. The homes, cars, boats, stores and clothing were quite different. I was accustomed to modern residences, expensive cars, and fancy shopping malls with upscale department stores, all examples of what was considered to be progress.

Why then did I feel so comfortable in a place that seemed, at least on the surface, to have so much less? Or was it really a place that had so much less?

CHAPTER 5

The Strength of Straw

Proverbios en la conversación son antorchas en la oscuridad.

Proverbs in conversation are torches in the darkness.

After resting back home in Fort Lauderdale, I was anxious to pursue my new interest, flying south. When I was growing up, similar countries were dismissed as the Second and Third World. They were described as primitive and under-developed. In fact, I don't recall very many positive comments about life south of our border. But something made me want to go back. I wanted to experience more.

I requested a schedule that would allow me to layover in Venezuela, and thus I soon worked my first flight from Miami to Caracas. Although I had previously landed in Caracas via Trinidad, I had never remained overnight. Venezuela sits on the northern edge of South America. It's a vast country that touches the Andes Mountains to the west and contains parts of the Amazon rainforest in the south. Several islands are located off its coast in the Caribbean Sea. The country sits on some of the world's largest oil reserves and also has an abundance of natural gas. Of course, Venezuela has been mired in political turmoil for the past several years. Despite its rich natural resources, the country's people have struggled with a difficult and strained economy.

Pulling into the Miami International employee lot, I collected my thoughts. I was trying to anticipate just what my stay in Caracas might entail. The airport wasn't exceptionally busy so after exiting the employee bus, I strolled up the short escalator to our pilot operations. My captain, Ellis, was early and already waiting. I immediately saw he was quite the prankster.

Ellis was filled with tales and a boatload of jokes. Very relaxed, he was an inspirational and happy man. My impression was that he would make any task truly fun. After peering through the usual flight papers, he mentioned that he had to make a few phone calls. I offered to walk ahead and meet him in the cockpit. It was a nice afternoon, and I casually walked around the plane's exterior. When I finished, the lead flight attendant offered me some coffee and the captain arrived shortly. With the passengers all boarded, we pushed back off the jet way and were soon airborne.

Captain Ellis had kept me in stitches the entire time. He was just a naturally funny person to be around and had quite the wit. Very personable, he liked to chat about almost any subject. When you work with such great people the job becomes extra fun; they can turn boring hours into a memorable experience.

It was daylight, and I soon looked down at the Caribbean Sea. What a sensational array of sights, even from such a high altitude. One could be hypnotized by the beautiful shades of blue contrasting with the different islands. The sparkling sea was nothing short of spectacular. I tried to imagine what the view would be from a low-flying seaplane or helicopter. Nature should be awarded countless medals for her ever-changing impressions and displays in the Caribbean. It's a stunning and unforgettable view.

Our flight made contact with the same air traffic control sectors that monitored our route to Trinidad. Each country has a designated airspace; therefore, you are specifically regulated when flying through each of these corridors. As we proceeded south, the Miami Air Traffic Control Center transferred our flight to Havana control. When we left Cuban airspace, we were then placed in sequence with the air traffic controllers in Port Au Prince, Santo Domingo and eventually Curacao. Finally, we were transferred to Maiquetia, the center responsible for Venezuela's air traffic control.

Maiquetia's radio frequencies are often very cluttered as its airspace is frequently congested. At certain hours, it's not uncommon to experience difficulty trying to get a word in with the Venezuelan controllers. The supervisors can communicate quite rapidly, so it's critical to listen carefully. When one replies, it's a good idea to return with a slow and methodical response. Their English is not often clear and concise, so it's important to keep the exchanges defined. Both sides want to avoid misunderstandings.

Interestingly enough, in many places of the world, aircraft are not under radar surveillance. It's possible to be talking with a controller who doesn't have the aircraft on a radar screen. This was a factor in parts of the Venezuelan airspace. Since we'd left Miami late in the afternoon, the sky was beginning to darken. The Maiquetia controllers instructed us to begin our decent into the Simon Bolivar International Airport. It was now nighttime, and to our left I could see some of the airport lighting. Planning to land to the east, we were ready to intercept the final course that would take us directly to the runway.

On our nose were some rather high hills completely void of lights. If a pilot weren't familiar with the surrounding terrain, it was possible to fly an airplane directly into these mountains, especially in bad weather or darkness. Now at the proper low altitude, we veered left allowing the east runway to be displayed at our twelve o'clock position. Following another safe landing, we were on the ground in Caracas, Venezuela. All that remained was a slow taxi to our assigned gate. The passengers deplaned, and Ellis and I made our way toward the terminal.

Once again, I couldn't resist stopping by an airport shop. The terminal area was open, containing rows of seats, and large glass panes that faced the runways. A string of small stores were located just a short distance from where we parked. One display caught my attention. In the window were several unique wooden carvings and woven designs that seemed like clothing. With my broken Spanish, I attempted to introduce myself to the lady behind the counter. Sales appeared to be slow, so she was anxious to gain my interest. She was young, very thin, and wore white jeans and grey flip-flops.

Although she was unable to speak any English, we managed to communicate. She was soft spoken but maintained strong eye contact; she didn't strike me as shy. She claimed that she had never been to the United States and was saving money for a trip. Her dream was to travel to Miami and visit some distant relatives. While glancing through the small shop, I was intrigued by some of the handmade figurines. Hand-knitted scarfs were displayed in an assortment of bright colors. It was good to browse but my time was limited. My fellow crewmembers were anxious to get to the hotel. Hurriedly, I bought a few postcards of the Angel waterfalls in Canima National Park. I wished the saleslady great luck in visiting her relatives.

At the outset I felt that the people of Venezuela were curious, outgoing and polite. Call it a gut feeling; I rely heavily on that emotion. It's a rudimentary way of measuring things but when one ducks into an airport shop, you get a hint of what might lie ahead. That's not to suggest that the first people you meet are the sole representatives of a culture; that would be far too simplistic. However, it is sort of an unbiased introduction. People who work at an international airport contact people from all parts of the world. They are very good at adapting to visitors from a variety of backgrounds. The way they adjust and interact can often be telling of what to expect during your visit.

I walked past more shops that sold clothing and jewelry as well as a large liquor store. After placing my luggage through customs, one of the flight attendants waved for me to come outside to the transportation area. I stalled for a few more minutes because I wasn't quite finished perusing. Similar to Trinidad, people were dressed far more casually than back home. Name brands were virtually absent; if one wore such clothing, he or she would certainly be out of place. I wanted to explore a bit more but my fellow crewmembers were getting impatient. My cruising came to a halt, and I tagged along to find our scheduled ride.

***

The midsized van waited to take us to the Sheraton. The weather was even hotter than I recalled back in the Calypso islands. Even though it was nighttime, the searing heat really hit me. Once again it was dark, so I couldn't really see much outside of the van's window. All I could see were a few smaller stores and supermarkets, anything with a lit display. After a thirty-minute ride, we arrived at the Sheraton Macuto. Known to supply rooms to several airline crews, the hotel was near the port town of La Guaira. Adjacent to the hotel is a small sandy beach, and in the opposite direction sit rather tall mountains.

The lobby was shiny clean, and we were met by a host from the hotel's staff. When I opened the door to my assigned room I was pleasantly surprised; the room had polished tiles that kept the space cool. A large and comfortable bed faced a decent view of the mountains. The bright interior colors were uplifting in contrast to places furnished with stained wooden furniture, murky drapery, carpeting and covers. An interior decorated with a dark theme just never inspired me. I always found it depressing. Bright whites, greens, turquoise, and varying shades of blue elevated my spirits. They brought to life the reflections of the ocean and tropics. This room at the

Sheraton suited me just fine! The room was so inviting I decided to settle in for the night and read.

The next morning, I could tell the day was going to be another scorcher. I put on some shorts and went downstairs to find the hotel's restaurant. I called Ellis to see if he wanted to join me but he politely declined. He said he would go for a short walk and wasn't really hungry.

Although it was early, the establishment was already packed. I sat at a small table and ordered a ham and egg omelet with some fruit. The coffee as well as the food was quite good. The servers were men who appeared to be on the quiet side; this was unlike Trinidad, which had mostly women serving out by the pool. I discovered that in many parts of Latin America, when it comes to employment, men get preferential treatment. I say this only as an outsider. Maybe there are just not enough jobs to go around, and the few that are available get awarded to the men. If my observation is even partially true, I am hopeful that over time this situation can be rectified. And to be objective, it's not as if my own country doesn't have room for improvement in that area.

As I ate, I started putting together what I had seen so far. Admittedly, I was overanalyzing and couldn't really explain what triggered me to revert to my pragmatic ways. Maybe I was so relaxed that the down time allowed me to piece together too much negativity. Call it a sensation but whatever it was, a certain heaviness had overtaken the moment. I suspected that within the beauty of the nearby ocean and mountains lay undercurrents of despair. Things were calm and everyone was cordial enough but something was out of place.

The feeling was similar to what I recently felt about myself: that all seemed okay but in fact many things were missing. For the moment I just needed to snap out of it and let my gloomy mood go. I was too new to the area and culture and didn't want any undue prejudice to tarnish my take on the country. But I simply couldn't wash out some of the initial sights or erase some of the truths about the poverty back in my own country.

Over the course of time, I saw firsthand that the South American nations displayed vast socioeconomic differences compared to the United States. Their economies were soft, and jobs were not easy to find, especially jobs that paid a decent wage. Venezuela was no exception. Various currencies could quickly devalue and added to insecurities. Housing and infrastructure were often inadequate to the needs of the population. Many felt uncertain about their future and were experts at masking their real concerns. It took me a long time to see through many of these dark truths. It's much easier to ignore a lot of the world's wrongs. It is painful to peel through the many layers of poverty and bear witness to all that it encompasses.

When I first came into direct contact with some of the world's poor, the aura hit me like a brick wall. It was difficult to recognize how few people had what I considered necessities. I knew the realities, that a majority had a slim chance of advancing their standard of living. Their choices were narrow because the immediate focus was on survival – earning enough to afford basic requirements like food, water, electricity and rent. Seldom was any residual income left to purchase much else.

In Latin America, because of the lack of disposable income, almost all luxury products can be purchased in installments. If an item costs fifty-dollars, one can pay a down payment of five dollars and over the next twelve months pay off the balance. It is similar to using a credit card but since many don't have any credit, this system allows for transactions. If this system were not in place, many would not be able to afford even a pair of pants. Throughout the world, including inside my own country, the uneven distribution of wealth remains problematic.

Although I have traveled throughout Latin America, I also frequented many cities throughout the States. During my stays in different US communities, I made a point of going outside what would be considered safe perimeters. I became keenly aware that poverty persisted right in our own backyards. I didn't need statistics to confirm what I saw—that we had more than our share of people living at or below the poverty level.

All too often I saw people living in difficult conditions and thought of just how fortunate I was. I should be grateful to wake up in a nice home with an abundance of decent food. Over the years I walked through many American neighborhoods where people struggled to make ends meet. When I saw so much inequality, I muttered, "There but for the grace of God I go." I was constantly reminded of just how fragile the line of inequality can be. As a friend in Peru once told me, "Don't ever allow yourself to become a horse with blinders on."

After reminiscing, it was time to explore. The hotel's giant pool was surrounded with guests on beach chairs getting in a morning's tan. A decent breeze blew in from the ocean, and that helped to make the outdoor rest tolerable. Then I walked to a small beach and went sightseeing. All types of clothing, hats, food and drinks were for sale. The salespeople appeared nice, and each one seemed enthusiastic about their merchandise. Venezuela, like most countries, had its fair share of poor people, and the economic situation was not good. Still people made the best of things and seemed to be relatively tranquil. Like Trinidad, the heat of Mother Nature was in charge and dictated that the pace was slow. The beach was filled with children playing, laughing and enjoying the ocean.

The day went by all too quickly, and I needed to prepare for the flight back. The sun can really soak up energy, and I needed time to rest. I went to back to my cool room and took an afternoon siesta. All too soon, my alarm clock signaled it was time to return to the First World. I would have preferred to stay a few more days but no such luck! The hotel van was waiting. I took in the sights during the ride to the airport. At the outset I witnessed some similarities to Trinidad. Many of the homes, buildings and roads were not in very good condition. The supermarkets were smaller to what I knew. Many appeared to be family owned and were not at all like the giant corporate chains.

I felt like I was in a different era, and once again I thought of my youth. Many family owned stores had operated in my neighborhood in New York City. Little stores where one actually knew the name of the pharmacist, butcher, cashier and manager. During that ride, I mentally joined some dots between Trinidad and Venezuela. The two places seemed very much alike in their simplicity and tranquility.

During my stay, I had again felt as if a weight had been lifted. The lifestyle in Venezuela led me to take things one step at a time, to conduct myself at a much slower rhythm. I found myself thinking more clearly and with less external interference. I didn't have a craving to purchase much. I was content to enjoy an inexpensive meal, great coffee, fresh fruit, and to practice my Spanish. I lost any desire to go to a shopping mall. However, I did crave good conversation and interaction. As was the case in Trinidad, the Venezuelan people were always nice. I was never allowed to feel pressured, rushed or awkward in any of my exchanges. Feeling hurried was commonplace at home.

We arrived at the airport and prepared for our flight back. Our passengers boarded and we taxied to the runway. The air traffic controllers cleared us for takeoff and we were on our way back to the States. Once at our cruise altitude, I did some more thinking. I compared my latest two experiences south of the border with life in the States. Much in my country was well structured and organized. If I needed to purchase something, it was normally readily available. Not only was it available, I could likely purchase it without suffering any real economic hardship.

I had a nice car and even a small boat that allowed me to escape and drift in the peace of the beautiful ocean. If I was ever in trouble, dialing 911 assured a police response within minutes. To be blunt, I always felt safe. I had a good healthcare plan and access to several choice doctors. My career was going well, I greatly enjoyed my profession. Because I had ample residual income, I could afford to frequent local restaurants. No one could argue that my life didn't seem to be complete.

Then my focus completely shifted. A man on the beach near the Sheraton Hotel in Venezuela had tried to sell me a straw hat. Appearing older than his actual age, he had no shoes or shirt to shield him from the baking sun. Standing close to him, I peered into his eyes. His stare was gripping, and I immediately sensed a lot coming from deep within his soul. His eyes communicated to me a complex mixture of despair, envy, acceptance, happiness and tranquility.

The aura he transmitted was captivating, and I didn't know how to sort it all out. The best I could do was purchase a straw hat. I knew he was telling me a great deal about himself . . . and also about myself. It wasn't the right moment for me to even begin to decode what he tried to convey. As I walked away, the hat would not be what I would ultimately wear. To this very day, I would wear the powerful impact of the testimony of his eyes.

I often returned to Venezuela, and over time recognized the difficult challenges most of the people faced. Life was not at all easy and was vastly different from my own. Yet through all of their struggles, they took an abundance of hardships in stride. The people I came in contact with were teaching me a great deal. Not only about their life but also about my own. The lessons seemed trivial at the time but I later placed them above any I could have purchased from a university.

I was keenly aware that these experiences were contrary to what I was comfortable with back home. Yet something kept drawing me back to that part of the world. With each return, I became more accepting of what was offered and what was expected. At the beginning, I had no idea of what might lie ahead. Ever so slowly I found myself adapting to a very different quality of life. It was too soon to tell where all this would lead but I enjoyed the ride. When I think of Venezuela, I always carry those special feelings carefully woven into that straw hat.

CHAPTER 6

Mystic Lima

La juventud es la intoxicación sin vino; la vejez, el vino sin la intoxicación.

Youth is intoxication without wine; old age, wine without intoxication.

At one point my company decided to extend its flying service to Lima, Peru. Having read a lot about Peru I was excited. The mysteries of the Incas and Machu Picchu had always been intriguing. Peru is bordered by Ecuador, Colombia, Brazil and Bolivia. The Pacific Ocean washes up against its western shoreline, and some of the high mountains of the Andes drape over some of its fascinating topography.

My first flight to the capital, Lima, would commence on a winter evening from Miami and was scheduled to arrive before sunrise. That evening I ran late. I called the crew facilitator and had her pass on to the captain that I would meet him on the airplane. I arrived at the employee lot and ran to catch the next bus before it pulled away. Briskly walking down the F concourse, I made it to the cockpit thirty minutes before departure. The captain, Jim, was very gracious concerning my delay. I dropped my bulky black flight bag on my side of the flight deck and ran down to do my exterior inspection.

Douglas Andrew Keehn

Once I was back in the cockpit, Jim handed me the flight papers and briefed me on what he had highlighted with his yellow marker—the forecasted weather, terrain along the route, aircraft maintenance history, and the estimated fuel consumption. Still out of breath and a bit behind, I took a moment to gather my thoughts. I then loaded the plane's computers with our estimated weight for takeoff and confirmed that everything was in limits for a safe launch.

Finally feeling caught up, I had a few minutes to walk to the back and introduce myself to the lead flight attendant. She was super nice but had her hands full as the passengers were still in the process of boarding. It seemed that one of our flights was late arriving from the west coast, so we were waiting for a handful of connecting customers. We would be a bit behind our scheduled departure time. So much for my rushing to the airport!

After an hour's delay, we finally pushed off the gate. The tower instructed us to taxi to runway 9. After following a few jets, we lifted off.

I had only flown with Captain Jim once before but I knew him fairly well from our talks during local pilot council meetings. A man of medium build, he was an interesting character. Jim enjoyed writing, politics, and solving problems. He'd suffered the loss of his daughter from a horrific car accident. Somehow, he handled his pain but he was scared. Who wouldn't be after such a devastating loss?

Upon arriving at our cruise altitude, we chatted about recently published books and some bullet points concerning our pilot contract. The five-hour flight sailed by, and we were directed to maintain a lower altitude to initiate our approach into Lima, Peru. As we advanced, we noticed a thick layer of fog covering the airport. Visibility was quite restricted, and the air traffic communications were not sharp enough. Fog can become quite dense in Lima. The reduced visibility proved quite challenging for takeoffs and landings at Jorge Chavez International.

At some of the world's airports, there just isn't much room for pilot error, and Lima, Peru fits into this category. Several mountains surround the airfield, which forces pilots to be keenly aware of the terrain. The high territory, dense fog, communication barriers, and the challenge of working all night requires extra vigilance regarding safety procedures. Jim briefed me on what to expect for a minimum visibility landing, and barely able to see the runway lighting, we safely touched down.

As we pulled into the terminal, the sun began to rise. I was very tired and anxious to rest. Many things at the airport appeared to be closed. We passed through customs and walked outside to the hotel van. Our driver was dressed in jeans, and with a cigarette dangling from his mouth informed us to expect a fair amount of traffic. He was cordial yet a bit stoic and somewhat fatigued. The van was small and not very comfortable; we felt every bump in the road. Because I was so tried, I didn't really expect anything much to capture my attention. Although my eyes were half closed, I slowly began to take notice of what we were passing.

Houses that resembled shacks; horses and dogs wandering unattended on the streets; small fires burning in open trash cans. Now awake, my eyes wandered. I kept my thoughts to myself as I noticed how different these people's lives were from my own. What were their daily routines really like? I felt sad as I was struggling to digest many of the sights. My coworkers were silent. Most of our crew was sound asleep. Two of the flight attendants were awake but I couldn't tell if the environment fazed them. Then our eyes met as if to communicate, *My God.*

A feeling of emptiness took hold. The ride seemed endless, and the poor living conditions appeared in waves. Confronted by people who appeared so disadvantaged, I did a bit of soul searching. My thoughts didn't consist of pity or of arrogance. Rather I felt a sense of helplessness. Unlike my previous rides to hotels, this time I felt uneasy. Knowing little about the Peruvian peoples, I tried to put aside the depressed thoughts. I needed to gather my composure.

The van finally arrived in the neighborhood of Villa Flores. I was sore from the jarring ride and needed to stretch. The doorman along with the people at the front desk offered a warm greeting; all were well-dressed, professional and courteous. At first glance, the hotel looked luxurious and modern. It stood in stark contrast to the last forty minutes. The experience was all quite humbling.

My hotel room was nothing short of spectacular, and was one of the best quarters I had ever been assigned. The contemporary style was akin to the setting of an upscale movie with large, comfortable beds draped in fancy pillows facing a high-end television. Next to the TV was a bar complete with a polished silver ice bucket and a special set of tubular liquor glasses. The open living room allowed easy access to a marble-lined bathroom; stunning track lighting shone on the shower's sliding doors and seamlessly illuminated its delicate frosted tint. The smooth golden racks were perfectly lined with artic white decorated towels. No doubt the elegance was meant to capture the imagination.

I quickly learned that Lima is noisy. The constant car horns were clear even from the top floors. I really wanted to sleep but I was restless. Curious about the neighborhood, I put on a pair of jeans and ventured outside. The streets were crowded with people beginning their workday. Men and women of all ages headed out to local offices. Some dressed in suits but the majority wore slacks or simple denim. The temperature was cool and required a jacket or sweater.

I stepped into a small café and ordered coffee and a sandwich. The café was crowded, and most of the patrons appeared to be on their way to work. My round table was small and barely had enough room for dining. At the counter stood several middle-age men and women sipping coffee; I imagined they were catching up on some morning gossip. Some of the ladies were well-dressed and had a Peruvian-style blanket draped over their shoulders. The blankets were red, blue or yellow and decorated with birds, animals, or symbolic Indian artifacts.

I felt the urge to test the waters and initiate a conversation. Without much effort, I found myself engaged in a dialogue with five people, all of whom seemed excited to have an American visitor. Three of the five had a fair command of English, which made things easier for me. Although my Spanish was marginal, I did my best to engage the pair that didn't speak English. The conversation was light, and there was a lot of bantering.

Of the five, only one was a lady. It just so happened that she had the best command of English. The four men all appeared to be in their mid-fifties. Dressed in polyester pants and button-down long sleeve shirts, all but one worked for a construction company. The other was employed by the government. The lady was older, perhaps in her early seventies. With her hair in a tight ponytail, she seemed wise and was at times pensive. Her hands were quite worn and shook a bit. She was fairly knowledgeable about Florida. Her name was Isadora, and apparently one of her daughters was studying medicine at a US university. Each time she mentioned her daughter, her faced gleamed with pride. Her daughter hoped to one day offer her practice to those in need.

Everyone in the group had known each other a long time, and at intervals they all spoke as one. After I finished my coffee and ham sandwich, I stretched my legs. Leaving my friends behind for a moment, I strolled to the cashier. Situated near a partially opened door, the payment area was a bit cold. Standing on a small wooden platform was a short elderly gentleman bundled in a torn hooded sweatshirt. Puffing on his cigarette, he grinned as he looked over at my friends.

When I handed him my bill, he waved his index finger sideways as if to say *no*. Isadora tapped my shoulder. With the rest of the group looking on, she informed me that they "took care" of my payment. I was humbled and at a loss for words. Taken aback by such an unexpected act, the best I could come up with was a hug and some firm handshakes. It was clear that I had some new friends in Lima. My head shaking in disbelief, I left the small cafe feeling exhilarated. In my entire life in the States, complete strangers had never bought me anything, never mind a meal! Already I had the sense that Lima was going to fit a special pattern, one that I noticed ever since traveling this part of the world.

After breakfast, I walked over to an area containing many small shops. One large arena with tables displayed Peruvian jewelry and clothing. Most of the tables were wooden and had white cloth hanging over their sides. The unique merchandise more than made up for the room's poor lighting. The salespeople were ladies of Peruvian/Indian descent. Most wore long colorful dresses adorned with items resembling their native jewelry. They were polite, knowledgeable, and always anxious to make a sale.

Piles of specially crafted blankets lay alongside makeshift racks stuffed with shirts and sweaters. Like the jewelry, the blankets often contained a panoramic representation of a sky, eagle, or any of a number of animals. The market was crowded, and often I saw several customers competing for a distinctive item. After some procrastinating, I purchased a variety of coins with the sun, a bird, or a pyramid engraved at the center. The coins were unique pendants composed of gold or silver, which was a great gift for Lindsey. Unlike what you might find in the large US retail chains, much in Peru was handcrafted, interesting and eye-catching. Sadly, all of the distinctive Peruvian presents were later stolen from her South Florida apartment. I found this a touch ironic because so many of my friends equated life in Latin America as being riddled with crime, yet these adornments were unlawfully taken right in the good old US of A.

Shopping in Peru is different than shopping in the States. The shop owners expect you to bargain, and they look at a transaction like a game of chess. I always kept the bargaining stress-free and positive. That way everyone wound up happy and the shopping remained a fun experience.

Feeling very upbeat, I wanted to experience more of the city. I walked to a corner and asked a taxi driver if he could recommend a place of interest. The middle-age man wore a mustache and a worn black wool sweater. His reply was, "Get in."

Taking a chance, I was driven to an area with narrow streets and governmental buildings. I often closed my eyes as he raced in and out of traffic. After an abrupt stop, the driver pointed at a structure. A bit woozy from the NASCAR experience, I stepped out and inhaled. Glad to be in one piece, I found myself in front of a museum. The street was jammed with people, so I asked a gentleman how I could get into the building. The slender elderly man escorted me to a window where I could purchase a ticket.

Included in the fee would be a scheduled tour. Without any idea of what the tour entailed, I joined a small group. The guide was a lady dressed in casual business attire who spoke Spanish speedily with a defining tone. The museum had large open areas and was several stories high. The interior was rather old, and the walls and floors were a combination of brick and concrete. I saw paintings, sculptures, and human bones stored in a dungeon. I did a lot of looking but admittedly understood little. My command of Spanish was not good enough to interpret much of the guide's explanations. Nevertheless, the tour was intriguing. It made me want to explore more about the history and culture of Peru.

At the end of the tour I met a European lady who introduced herself as Sofia. She noticed that I was also a foreigner. Speaking some English, she told me that across from the museum was a restaurant that specialized in ceviche, a delicacy for which Peru is famous. Well-dressed in a black leather jacket, blue pants and gloves, she had a high opinion of the restaurant. I asked if she cared to join me but she said was in a hurry to pick up her children from school.

Douglas Andrew Keehn

I ventured across to the bistro. The restaurant was small, noisy, and packed. I was lucky to be alone because only one small table was available. I waited patiently before I finally got a server's attention.

Ceviche is made of raw fish, and I wasn't particularly comfortable with the safety of that type of food. Nevertheless, I didn't think there was much risk in the delicacy. After about a twenty-minute wait, the dish finally arrived. The bowl contained a thick assortment of shrimp, octopus, white fish, corn and onions. The freshness of the blend was complimented with a light lemon-lime sauce. I could taste the distinct flavor of each of the ingredients. The delicate seasoning enhanced the special tang of the seafood.

Eavesdropping on me was a middle-age couple sitting across from my table. They knew from my broken Spanish that I wasn't from South America. Their interest was obvious, especially the lady's as she periodically glanced in my direction. The thin waiter, wearing a black bowtie, seemed anxious that I wouldn't enjoy the selection. After several bites, I could no longer contain my pleasure. With a smile, I gave the server a thumb's up. Some light clapping by the inquisitive couple followed the waiter's expression of relief. Everyone beamed as if my acknowledgment signaled a major success! I now knew why ceviche was a staple delicacy in the Peruvian culture.

I wandered back outside. The narrow streets were still crowded. The weather was overcast with a light drizzle. I had enough exploring for one day, and it was time to get a taxi back to the hotel.

That evening, I joined Jim for dinner at a nearby pizza place. Nothing fancy about the restaurant, as most of the tables were located outside with a canopy to provide protection from inclement weather. The meal was good, and our conversation consisted mostly of shoptalk centered on our company's operations. After a short walk back to the hotel, I turned in early to get a good night's sleep.

I was up at sunrise and walked to a different place for breakfast. I found an eatery with a rather old appearance. Looking thru the glass, I saw large tables and lots of open space. After entering, I was led to a spot by a large window. As was the case in the Venezuelan restaurant, the waiters were all male. Their ages ranged from the middle fifties on up; it appeared they had worked at this place for a very long time. The café was bustling, and with one hand they carried entrees loaded on round aluminum trays. The servers swung in and out of the kitchen trying to keep up with the orders.

While watching all this action, I was approached by an older couple. The pair seemed like they had been locked in love forever. They were both in their upper eighties, however neither looked a day over sixty. The man wore a straw hat similar to the one I purchased on the beach in Venezuela. He was thin and wore dark jeans with beige moccasins. His wife was elegant in a bright red down sweater adorned with an iguana pin. Her eyes beamed with enthusiasm. Their names were Eduardo and Angelica. Speaking some English, both were curious about my thoughts about Lima. I asked them to join me.

On some level, I must have seemed like a typical tourist. They were very interested to hear what was taking place in America. They asked about my job, social life, and what made me happy. They boasted about their boys, both of whom worked for engineering companies. The couple was very matter-of-fact and accepted the many difficulties within their country. We discussed the political situation and the socio-economic problems that continued to plague Peru. Our chat progressed as we enjoyed coffee and freshly baked bread.

Eduardo reached over and buttered Angelica's slice. When she finished, he took a napkin and wiped her lips and chin. Their care left little doubt that they were each other's king and queen. They were always smiling and constantly joked with the waiter. I imagined they had frequented this place on several occasions. Their wit was sharp. When we finished,

Eduardo pulled the chair out as his Angelica was slow to rise. He grabbed her left arm and patiently escorted her toward the exit. They insisted that I meet with them the next time I returned. On the way out, Angelica paused and with a larger than life smile gestured toward me with a kiss.

The interior and exterior of the restaurant would not lure one to frequent the place. But the architecture didn't matter; the company truly encapsulated the experience. The value of this connection was becoming more apparent with each passing day.

The elderly pair had everything they would ever need— the company of the other. The inseparable team taught me things I could never derive from any book. I would see Eduardo and Angelica from time to time during my subsequent returns. They were both golden people, and their intellect always made for an intriguing gathering. Later on, I was saddened to learn that Angelica passed away. I was unable to retain contact with her loyal prince, Eduardo. It was just exceptional fate that I was ever placed in their path.

Was my ease meeting new people in Peru just plain luck? Was it pure coincidence that this occurred twice in such a short period of time? I recalled that people in Trinidad and Venezuela seemed easily approachable and outgoing. This is not to say that in the States people were only introverted. But I was slowly beginning to notice differences in individual contentment. The men and women I came across in Latin America possessed a different degree of warmth. They gave a relaxing and inviting feeling that assured me I was always welcomed. Although this feeling was somewhat prevalent back home, it wasn't as common a feeling.

* * *

The temperature was beginning to turn cold and the fog quickly returned. The dampness in the air made it feel even cooler, and a light mist blanketed the city. I surrendered to the cold and walked briskly to generate body heat. Moving down a hill, I wound up near cliffs that overlooked the sea. Next to me were young policemen carrying automatic weapons. Dressed in uniform, they were stopping cars and checking people's documentation. One thing was certain; just the display of that type of weapon motivated quick cooperation.

I walked to the edge of the steep cliffs and listened to the waves crashing against the bottom. The combination of those echoes and the smell of the salt air was calming. I stood alone thinking about my time in Lima. I caught myself reflecting about more than just my stay in Peru. Something profound was taking place, and the more I reflected, the more I could feel something building inside of me; something real was happening. I just couldn't tell what it was.

The mist turned to a cold rain, so I jogged up the hill toward the hotel. I spent the rest of the day reading a book and relaxing in my room. It was still funny to hear the constant honking from the roads. The sound would make any flock of geese envious. The environment wasn't exactly ideal for sleeping.

Later that evening our crew gathered in the lobby. It was time to leave Villa Flores. We had the same driver, and this time my eyes were wide open. I sat silently as we passed people huddled around contained fires. I couldn't help but think of how difficult life was for so many. My mind drifted, and I thought of how trivial some of my problems were in comparison. Many people were forced to do without much of what I took for granted. I don't know how they managed but they obviously didn't have a choice. The difficult sights left me with several lasting impressions.

We arrived at the terminal, sorted out our luggage, and walked over to the company counter. The ticket agents were extremely cordial and directed us to the flight planning office. Very foggy conditions persisted as Jim and I carefully reviewed all the departure procedures. We walked out of the small office and passed the check-in podiums. The terminal was extensive and had a nice place upstairs to enjoy coffee, sandwiches or pastry. As tempting as that light cuisine was, we both opted to pass. Instead, we strolled over to our plane and periodically glanced at the articles in the shops. Once inside the cockpit, we commenced our trip back to Miami.

A few hours into the flight, I recalled my experiences over the past several months. So much had been new and foreign to me. I was climbing a ladder with each step taking me to a new level of understanding. Each plank helped build a foundation that made it easier to keep climbing. My hike was challenging, yet with each stage the process became more enjoyable.

The Miami air traffic controllers came onto our frequency. Their instructions were always welcomed as it signaled we were nearing the end of a long night's work. When we parked at the gate, I thanked Jim for a nice trip and wished him a safe drive home. The morning was beautiful in Miami, and I was ready for my short drive north. At such an early hour the roads are empty, and the commute to Fort Lauderdale is normally painless. I squeezed into my little black Mazda and headed for the infamous I-95.

Once in my comfortable bed, I closed my eyes and thought about my new friends in Peru and wondered if I would see them again. The three different cultures I had recently come to know held much in common with their attitudes to life. Their approach was unlike what I had grown to accept in my own country. Certain things seemed to come easier—laughter, contentment, personal interaction, care and relaxation. And I also had no illusions that many things didn't come easier—careers, income and purchasing power, just to name a few.

For me, there remained a lot to weigh. Within these countries extensive percentages of the population lived well below a level most Americans would consider acceptable. I asked myself how so much poverty could contain so many positive attributes. Many of these people's ways of handling things was readily different from the States; but was it better?

I am specifically not talking about their ability to do better with less. Candidly, that's too ordinary and simplistic. Because so many in the Third World are economically poor by any standard, it's understandable for many from the First World to assume that this is my theme. To take a broad brush and admire how the poor manage with so little completely misses the mark. Instead I am referring to a distinctive approach to life, a different approach implemented regardless of any socioeconomic status. It just happens that a majority of the people I met were void of any real economic wealth.

Over time, I began to see my faraway friends not in the context of "doing better with less" but rather in their ability of just being able to do better. The significances of "doing better" can be open and infinite whether the words are considered separately or combined. How we manage our lives, what we value, how we see, interpret and interact . . . all of this requires us to be honest with ourselves and to remain sensitive to what surrounds us. I was learning that to do better required a lot of openness, little fear of change, and the recognition of a desire to grow. Hopefully we like to construct and mature on a foundation of what we believe to fundamentally matter . . . what we perceive to be important.

Then, as is my habit, I began to question myself. Was I building myself, my own life, on a correct foundation? Was I even headed in the right direction? Was my slow change in fact really a change for the better? Coming from a different culture, much of my understandings and acceptances had been formulated atop a dissimilar platform. Could I have misinterpreted much of what I had encountered? Would I eventually fall off the ladder, become disillusioned or possibly hurt? I wanted to continue on my journey and had a feeling that I was heading toward an important crossroad.

CHAPTER 7

Switching Gears

Life can only be understood backwards; but it must be lived forwards. — Soren Kierkegaard

Arriving back from places such as Trinidad or Venezuela and Peru, I always found myself making personal adjustments. The United States is not only large in scope, it also does almost everything large . . . large highways, large buildings, large malls, large cars, even large meals. Unfortunately, we even have too many individuals who can be considered large. Almost anything one could desire is just a stone's throw away from a credit card. In my travels down south, that was not what I saw nor experienced.

I noticed myself looking at modernization and progress in new ways. Although this change was subtle, it nevertheless was a change. Before I began heading south, I was rather content. I resided in a nice neighborhood, had a nice home, furniture and car. I was fortunate to have special friends and some friendly neighbors. The Fort Lauderdale beach wasn't far away, and I could ride my bike on a path alongside the beautiful ocean. My life was mostly complete . . . or so I thought.

After I experienced my travels to Trinidad and Venezuela, I felt a notch less content about returning to the States. It was too soon for me to make sense of my feelings, so for the moment I just chose to go with the flow. I thought to myself that this was just a passing phase.

I moved to Fort Lauderdale because it fit what I was looking for: a town centered on the beauty of the ocean. Ft. Lauderdale is known for its great beaches, superb boating, and deep-sea fishing. Everything I enjoyed was right in my backyard. As I had been born and raised in New York City, I was looking to escape its stressful environment—the terrible traffic, the constant sounds of emergency vehicles, the rush to catch a bus or train—so much that I wanted to leave in my rearview mirror. I don't dislike New York City and realize that many consider it fantastic. It never sleeps and has cultural events, unique stores, nightlife, libraries, museums and restaurants. It's just that I was no longer intrigued by the everyday hustle and bustle lifestyle.

I have only good memories of my old neighborhood, Chelsea, which changed so much over the years. The rise in the financial markets boosted the city's economy, and many neighborhoods have been substantially upgraded. New shops, art galleries, restaurants and condos sprang up throughout the boroughs. I used to play stickball in an empty lot across the street from where I grew up on West Twenty-third Street and Ninth Avenue. Today the lot is occupied by a building.

The neighborhood's low-story walk-ups that were run down, cheap to rent, and infested with rodents are today prime real estate. My friends and I would go to the roof of some low-rise buildings to retrieve the rubber balls hit up there while playing stickball. I can still feel those worn-out wooden stairs that led to the roof; with each step I heard the loud creak of the buckling and warped flooring. Some of those buildings acted as shelters for stray dogs and for cats that were often chased by rats twice their size. The smell of urine was apparent throughout the buildings, and the walls were riddled with chipped paint, water leaks, and cockroaches.

Douglas Andrew Keehn

Today these buildings are for the well-to-do. Sadly, unable to keep up with the Joneses, the free-roaming dogs and cats have been gracefully evicted. Coveted by many professionals, Chelsea is likely one of the most improved neighborhoods in the city. While I was growing up, there were several mom and pop stores. I knew many of the shopkeepers on a first-name basis. Freddy was the butcher, Sam owned the local grocery store, and Lenny owned the nearby toy store. Sam was a tall gentleman who always had a pencil resting behind his left ear. As the owner, he made it a point to work at one of the two cash registers; I can still hear those old money machines as he totaled up the bill. Shopping was so personalized I referred to the stores as Sam's, Freddy's and Lenny's. Today, all of those shops have been replaced by much larger entities. A nametag might be as personal as one can get from this point forward.

Because of the popularity of Chelsea and the city's overall economic rise, the population has also soared. In turn the traffic, at least in the neighborhood where I was raised, has vastly increased. Chelsea is located between two tunnels that lead to the state of New Jersey—the Holland tunnel to the south and the Lincoln tunnel slightly to the north. Traffic around my block used to be difficult only around the morning and afternoon rush hours. Today, the flow of traffic remains clogged for much of the day and becomes worse at peak times. It goes without saying that since I was a boy, the many structural and cultural transformations have been truly remarkable.

It's often implied that New Yorkers are rude. Although I grew up in the city, I have traveled extensively and can be objective about this particular stigma. New Yorkers are normally willing to help; they quickly adapt, are direct, and yes, can speak a bit fast. The cultural diversity in New York City is something quite unique. Contrary to what many believe, the mix of people seems to work just fine. I guess that sometimes people interpret the New York Style of being direct as somewhat rude. It's a mistake to think that as it's just a cleaner way of getting to the point.

* * *

My close friend John and his first wife Maria moved to Fort Lauderdale in the early 1990s. John has been a dear friend of mine since I was seventeen years of age. We are so close that I often refer to him as my brother. Since I am an only child, he became the brother I never had.

We were very young flight instructors at Teterboro airport in New Jersey. He worked for a flight school located directly across from my place of teaching. Both the flight schools operated out of trailers, and had a fleet of Piper and Cessna planes on their ramps. In the late Seventies, Teterboro was a busy airfield swamped with a combination of general aviation traffic and corporate jet and turboprop planes. At certain times, the air traffic control tower would be so overloaded that lengthy delays become almost the norm. Teterboro was a great place to learn how to fly; the air traffic congestion ultimately forced anyone to become adept at handling a fair amount of stress.

The learning and teaching experience was quite different from that of schools housed out of small, quiet, isolated airports. The facility I worked for had a contract to fly film for the Kodak Company of Rochester New York. This was normally accomplished in the evenings, and flown in either a twin-engine Piper Aztec or Navajo propeller plane. To gain more of this complex experience, I would tag along as a co-pilot when my schedule permitted. It was a good way to learn while on the job, and at a young age I quickly got used to flying in inclement weather.

One day John and I agreed to meet for lunch. There began a long and lasting friendship. My close friend is as giving as any, the type who would literally give you the shirt off his back. We eventually worked together at several companies flying turboprop and jet aircrafts. Today John is also a pilot for a major US-based airline company.

One day John and Maria decided to build their dream home in Fort Lauderdale. Sadly, soon after they finally moved in, Maria was diagnosed with cancer. It was a hellish period for John and everyone within the family. The cancer had quickly spread throughout Maria's body, and she passed away at the age of forty. Just a couple of years earlier, she'd given birth to a baby boy, John Jr. Shortly after her diagnosis, she recognized that she wouldn't live to see her boy grow old; the reality was devastating. It took some time for everyone to adjust to her death. John eventually married a sweet Brazilian lady, Simone, and John Jr. recently graduated from law school. We are still the closest of friends.

Before Maria's cancer was detected, I followed her and John down to Fort Lauderdale. I wanted to find a place close to my special companions. The mid-sized city is located between Miami and Boca Raton; all offered lots of variety and were connected to the charm of the sea. A huge percentage of all boat sales in the US transpire in south Florida. Fort Lauderdale certainly is a boater's paradise, and since I loved boats, it seemed a perfect fit.

One day John took me over to a small community of townhomes located on a canal near the large 17th Street causeway bridge. The bridge towers over the intercostal waterway and connects the southeast side to the beach area. I immediately fell in love with one of the townhomes. The three-story home was roomy and had a deeded boat dock in back; the ocean was only a few minutes away via boat, making it a sought-after spot! Armed with a loan from my aunt, I made the purchase within just a few weeks.

I liked my little community as I could walk over to what was then the Marriott Marina hotel for morning coffee. Since I was not far from the ocean, the easterly breezes calmed the normal summer temperatures. At dusk, I would walk to the center of the tall 17th Street Bridge and look down at the boats and yachts passing in and out of the harbor. I would often dream that I was piloting one of those big Hatteras fishing yachts with the pelicans hitching a ride on the back. I couldn't wait to get a boat. I so wanted to be out in the ocean fishing the time away!

Over the years, Fort Lauderdale began to change. The changes began to take hold in the late 90s, and by the early to mid-2000s the modifications became noticeable. The beautiful beachfront became engulfed with condos, hotels, miniature malls, restaurants and nightclubs. Today, loud music often drowns out the ocean. People seem more interested in purchasing clothing than embracing the waves as they gently rub against the shore. There is a substantial increase in the population, traffic, noise, and pollution . . . effects of progress, after all. In the western part of Fort Lauderdale, everyone is now captive to the giant brick-and-mortar retailers; conglomerates stand tall as far as the eye can see. There are now more fast food eateries than there are grains of sand on the beach.

Yes, nature still has provided the towering palm trees and a glistening ocean's pristine, turquoise water. Today, however, so much of the innate beauty has been overshadowed by manmade projects. Much of what drew me to Fort Lauderdale, the natural beauty and tranquility, has been watered down. All too often money winds up being the driving force. At the end of the day, wealth ultimately prevails. So much of the natural splendor that was once abundant has all but disappeared. In a sense I feel a bit sad for the younger people and for those who have only been exposed to the landscape of progress. Despite all this, south Florida remains one of our nation's treasures. Many pockets of natural magnificence still exist, which is why it still holds a key place in my heart.

My recent travels triggered me to think more about what my own country might be forfeiting. I wondered if we were truly conscious of what we might surrender in the name of progress. Are we really progressing? I had witnessed the mom and pop stores and the personal connections vanish in my old New York City neighborhood. Now I saw so much of what made south Florida pristine slowly drift out to sea. Things just seemed to be so ordinary and all too impersonal.

As I drove around I would see the same brand stores and restaurants regardless of what direction I headed. It was almost like watching the identical movie over and over again. Maybe that was the answer. Perhaps I just wanted a ticket to a different movie and my travels down south gave me just that—a different movie with many different features. Was it that superficial? Maybe I was overthinking, and my attraction to Latin America was just the need for a change of scenery. And if I liked only the scenery better, well then, no harm done, right? After all, it's perfectly natural to prefer one beautiful place to another.

I quietly queried myself about these obvious questions. Again, my gut feelings nudged me as if something internal was tapping my shoulders saying, "Not so fast." For the moment I felt a bit frustrated, almost impatient. I always considered myself fairly pragmatic; if I thought enough about something then I could eventually figure it out. The problem was that I didn't know what I needed to figure out! I felt as if a rope had been wrapped around my body, a cord that was tightening ever so slowly. Something was bothering me on one end of the rope, and something very positive was pulling me on the other end.

Something was going on in my life but I didn't have a clue as to what it might be. One thought stuck in my mind: this inner feeling. That this cord would continue to get tighter until I would have to actually do something. Good thing for me that the increasing tension was gradual. I needed a lot more time to sort things out.

One lunch hour in Fort Lauderdale I decided to shuffle things around. I decided to mimic the break as if I were away in Latin America. What exactly was I trying to achieve? I didn't have any specific answers; it wasn't anything precise enough to jot down on a piece of paper. What I was after was actually something simple: a feeling/mood similar to what I had repeatedly enjoyed during my midday Latin excursions.

I wandered out around noon, this time I was "unarmed," void of any smartphone or computer. I felt a bit naked but it was the only way to prevent any temptation to cheat. Because I let go of some American cultural nuisances, I wasn't all wound up and driven to have a quick bite. Quite the contrary, I looked forward to being attended by an unhurried server and experiencing a leisurely meal. Although I was relaxed, I knew the sensation was artificially induced and not in a natural setting. Tranquility doesn't flow easily in this part of the world.

After selecting an old neighborhood diner, I sat at a counter crowded with truckers, machinists and handymen. I sat facing some tall coffee pots behind a white linoleum counter. A tall waitress dressed in black and white with a pencil behind her left ear came through the kitchen's swinging doors. The turkey club sandwich sounded good. Using a slight southern accent to repeat my order, she jotted notes on a small white pad. I politely mentioned that I was not in any sort of hurry.

After a moment or two I turned to a gentleman on my right and asked about his day. He seemed upset and his demeanor notified me that he preferred to be left alone. Sitting to my left was a gentleman in his mid-seventies. He appeared to be in strong physical condition and wore a dark green maintenance suit. His face was wrinkled by the sun, and *Frank* was inscribed in an oval patch. My initial impression was that he too did not want to be disturbed. I thought I was going to completely strike out in the conversation department.

Life can be full of surprises. When my sandwich arrived, the man to my left initiated a discussion. And as luck would have it, Frank turned out to be quite an interesting character. Apparently, he worked as an engineer on a yacht that traveled around the world. As a fellow boater, we did have some things in common . . . at the very least our enjoyment of being out on the ocean. He described to me in a deep and muffled voice the several ports he had been to in Europe and Asia. Decorating some of the harbors were old wine bars, and outdoor cafes. I tried to visualize the sights as he talked and used his hands to explain his voyages.

His true excitement became evident when he described his mechanical achievements. Evidently, he had a special ability to repair almost anything on board that yacht; all the electronic equipment including the radar, radios, and navigation instruments; engines, compressors, pumps, cooling systems; and any damage to any part of the yacht's hull. When nobody else could find a solution, they called upon his extensive level of expertise. His pride was obvious, and he wanted an ear to share some of his adventures.

I asked how he'd gained such a level of expertise. He told me that he had started out as a merchant marine when he was very young. He'd been a deck hand on a large container ship and had tagged along with an old and wise seaman. This older guy had been able to fix anything in the ship's engine room. After building some trust, he took Frank under his arm and allowed him to watch repairs. That experience lasted almost eight years, and working by that man's side had been priceless.

Frank's facial expression changed when he told me his mentor had recently passed away. A bit choked up, he then recovered and went on to praise him, emphasizing how much of an impact his hands-on teacher had had on his life. I wasn't in any rush, and I mostly listened and remained captured by his descriptions and undertakings. After about the fastest two hours I can recall sitting at any counter, he stood up and calmly walked toward the restroom. Remembering my experience at the café in Lima, I paid Frank's bill. When he returned, he looked at me in disbelief but I assured him that the pleasure was all mine. He firmly gripped my hands and wished me God's speed.

I might have been in a diner in Fort Lauderdale, but the spontaneous meeting, calm, and interesting conversation let my imagination place me elsewhere.

CHAPTER 8

Nossa

O pior cego é aquele que não quer ver.

The blindest of the blind is the one who does not want to see. Some people shut their eyes to the truth.

O sol nasceu para todos.

The sun rises for everybody.

After several months of flying to South America, it was time to venture down to Brazil. I had always wanted to see the famous oceanfront city of Rio de Janeiro. Many Americans are not very knowledgeable about this large country. Admittedly, I was naive about Brazil and had scant knowledge of its people, culture, economy, and topography. All I could envision was what I had read in some books. I had become increasingly comfortable staying in South American countries, and so my time in Brazil would be rather routine . . . so I thought . . . .

When a typical American is asked about Brazil, the normal response is, "Oh yes, I heard Rio is very nice," or, "Brazil, isn't that the place with the Amazon jungle?" or finally, "Isn't that the place where they have Carnival?"

Douglas Andrew Keehn

Brazil encompasses one of the largest and most important areas on our planet, and yet even today many Americans know little about our giant neighbor to the South. Brazil is the world's fifth largest country in size and population. Boasting the seventh largest economy, Brazil is known for its mining, agricultural and manufacturing sectors. It's by far the largest country in all of Latin America, sharing borders with every country in South America except for Ecuador and Chile. Brazil also remains the world's largest Portuguese-speaking nation. The combination of the huge rain forest, Amazon basin, extensive mountains, immaculate shorelines, and diverse wildlife make it an intriguing and unique place to explore; I was more than ready!

On my first flight from Miami to Rio de Janeiro, I was unfamiliar with the captain and the other first officer. I had never met either of them before. The captain was a tall, slender man called Dave or Davie. In the operations room, Captain Davie greeted me with a firm handshake. He seemed mild mannered, not one to get easily upset. Davie was the quiet type, low key, and a bit cautious. A relaxed man, he carried an air of confidence. The other copilot, Fernando, was a tall and classy Columbian gentleman with jet-black hair. He was sharply dressed, polite and professional.

Both Dave and Fernando had been to Brazil before, which put me more at ease. It's always helpful when at least one of the crewmembers has some familiarity with the route and the destination. Fernando had some lines of the flight papers outlined with his colored pens. I didn't see anything of concern, so I agreed that the planning looked in order. We walked down the F concourse and arrived ahead of passengers patiently waiting in the boarding area. Several Brazilian and Cuban flight attendants had been assigned to our flight. They all had been to Brazil on several occasions and were eager to begin their layover at the Sheraton.

Our flight to Rio departed Miami on schedule. Close to midnight, I began to think of what might lie ahead. At first,

I struggled to connect with Captain Dave and searched for a way to ignite a conversation. Working with so many different people from diverse backgrounds can make it challenging to find a mutually interesting topic. At times I felt like a safe cracker, turning a knob until I found the right combination.

While in flight, Davie and I exchanged some small talk followed by a lengthy period of silence. After recharging my conversational battery, I finally found the code that worked — fishing. When I mentioned my boat and that I loved to fish, Dave's eyes lit up. For the next several hours we exchanged fish stories as if we were long-lost comrades. On this particular flight began a long and special friendship. Over the next several years, I flew countless trips with Captain Davie, mostly to Brazil and other destinations in South America as well as within the United States.

When Davie went on his break, I chatted with Fernando. He was also calm and confident, the type you would want to be with if something ever went wrong. He was also quite thought-provoking and asked about my interests, which books and periodicals I gravitated toward. He mentioned that he and his family came from Colombia. I asked what his life was like there. He said that although he enjoyed the stability the States offered, he missed a lot of the fun, food, and natural beauty of his country. He described some of the unique beaches that touch the Caribbean Sea between Cartagena and Santa Marta. Some of his relatives still resided in Colombia, and he always looked forward to visiting them from time to time.

The night sailed by, and then began the rise of the sun. After we were transferred to the Rio approach control, several mountains came into view. They appeared covered in a perfect coat of dark green, aligned as if they were to guide us to the airport. The approach corridor took us between the mountains, and from a distance identified the active runway. The airport sits on a wide bay that funnels out into the Atlantic Ocean. As we came in for a landing we flew low over the water; the sights and sounds of our large jet frightened a flock of airport gulls directly in our path. They scattered and disappeared into the morning sky.

After we landed it was a rather long taxi to where we needed to park. Finally, at the gate, I shut down the engines and finalized our checklist. Following Fernando, I entered the terminal at Galeao International Airport in Rio de Janeiro. The décor seemed ordinary and the temperature was uncomfortably hot. We worked our way toward the crew checkpoint and in short time were released through Brazilian customs. The loudspeaker made announcements in Portuguese, a language that I had not experienced before.

I placed my bags in the customs machine and handed over an informational entry form. We took an escalator up one level, passed a café and a store selling an assortment of sports shirts. A large bus was parked curbside waiting to take us to our hotel. Before boarding we encountered *Doleiros*, people who change currency, waiting for us to exchange US dollars for Brazilian reals. Their exchange rate was always more favorable than any bank or hotel, and we were happy to do business with them. This did not exactly turn out to be the proper procedure, and after a few months the police made it clear this practice would no longer be tolerated. Subsequently we changed our money through normal channels.

Before getting on the bus, we were greeted by our company's station manager Geraldo. Born in Rio, he was a large man, tall and stocky with short black hair. Dressed in brown pants and an open jacket, he walked over with a great smile and introduced himself to the entire crew. For no apparent reason, he immediately struck me as a fun person. I'll have to chock it up as another one of my intuitive feelings. Geraldo asked if everyone was happy and if there was anything he could do to help. He corralled a few of us and began to tell us jokes. He was well versed at maintaining people's interests.

Over time I would get to know Geraldo as he became the company's manager responsible for both the Rio and

São Paulo International Airports. Contained within his large frame was a large heart, and he was a very caring and gentle man. I jokingly nicknamed him Tiny. Outgoing and easy to approach, Geraldo had an extensive knowledge of the intricate politics involved in managing our company's operations within the confines of the Brazilian laws, which was no easy task.

Along with being jovial, he was also smart as a whip. He could size up anyone or any situation as well as the best. He often reminded me of the TV character Columbo, the lieutenant detective played by Peter Falk. Columbo would come across as funny, sloppy, and having average or below-average intelligence; he lulled people into thinking they were smarter or that he was naive. All along he held his thoughts private, intentionally keeping everyone off-guard. Ultimately Columbo was always a step ahead of his suspects and fellow detectives in solving the most complex of puzzles. With the exception of his size, Geraldo fit this character to a tee. He is a remarkably funny and interesting man, someone whom I learned never to underestimate.

With the bags now loaded, we needed to leave behind many unfinished jokes and stories. I got on the bus and waved a special goodbye to Geraldo. At the time I didn't know it but his relaxed, joking and outgoing demeanor would ultimately set the tone for my encounters during my stay in Rio de Janeiro.

The bus was comfortable and had air conditioning, which was fortunate as the outside temperature was exceptionally hot. I purposely situated myself upfront to capture a panoramic view. Before long we found ourselves in the middle of an extensive traffic jam but eventually we crawled toward the hotel. The slow ride gave me ample time to take in the views. Unfortunately, much of what I saw was not good. Many neighborhoods consisted of door-to-door shacks and homes that had been quickly pieced together with electrical wiring dangling from the roofs. Stray dogs and horses ate whatever they could muster in large empty lots. Children playing in dirt fields seemed numb to their surroundings.

Admittedly my first impression of Brazil was disappointing, and I felt empty witnessing so much poverty. Sitting next to me was a flight attendant of Brazilian descent. She whispered that many of these communities were called *favelas*, a Portuguese term used to describe a slum. Why she pointed this out without my asking was puzzling; perhaps it was my body language or a painful look on my face. Either way, she seemed genuinely concerned.

With a lot running through my mind, I watched in silence as we drove by several *favelas*. Then my curiosity got the best of me and I turned back to her. The flight attendant was quite familiar with some of the realties surrounding these neighborhoods. Apparently, their history goes back to the 19th century when the shacks were developed by soldiers and eventually utilized by former slaves. Over time, many of Brazil's poor also began to occupy areas that lacked any infrastructure. As the decades passed, the rise of these rudimentary homes grew as population of the poor expanded.

She explained that Rio has more than its share of these slums, and that the government has made different attempts at improvements. I continued peering through the windows. She told me that as dreadful as some of them looked, in some instances their utilities and structure have been improved; that seemed hard to believe. I tried to image what they might have looked like before. Finally, she mentioned that drug traffickers ruled some of these *favelas*, and that there was an inherent "understanding" about their governance. These areas indeed seemed to have a complex history and an improvised structure with no easy solutions.

I thanked her and remained a bit subdued. These sights were not easy for me to digest. The van eventually left these areas as we steadily drew closer to the ocean. A beach packed with sun worshipers came into view. The bus driver shifted gears to proceed up a steep hill; I saw several boys surfing near some very large rocks. These rocks were quite a distance from the shoreline, so I had no idea how they managed to get there. The rocks were constantly pounded by large waves that seemed to make the area quite risky. For the boys, the fun was probably in defying the danger.

Off to our left, some fishermen stood in front of a ledge. Their rods were exceptionally long to allow them to cast their lines far from the cliff. Next to them stood several food stands surrounded with people talking. We finally arrived at the Sheraton located at the top of the hill in the neighborhood of Leblon. The building overlooked the ocean and some small islands on one side; the other section faced some mountains and buildings down the hill. Captain Davie tipped the driver on behalf of the entire crew; the flight attendants were speechless. I never encountered another captain who had ever entertained the thought of such a noble deed. His unpretentious gesture was another hint of his very special character.

The hotel lobby was modern, complete with a bar and an upscale jewelry store. The flooring was marble and well-polished. I went to my room and was taken aback by the fantastic view of the ocean. From my balcony, I could hear the waves splashing against the shoreline. With the terrace door open, the echoes of the waves lulled me to sleep. My room was medium in size with some tile flooring. As was the case in Venezuela, the tiles helped keep a comfortable room temperature.

In the center of the living room was a glass table with frosted edges supported by a crafted stone block. A small couch and some tall lamps were situated in the corners. What really made the stay special was not the décor; it was the great views, sounds and smells of the ocean. When I finally woke up, the sun was at its peak. I got dressed and wandered around the hotel. On the ground level was a large pool surrounded by reclining beach chairs.

With parents looking on, children filled the pool. Their excited splashing and laughing was occasionally overshadowed by the sounds of the ocean. Near the pool were large cages containing beautiful toucans; their diverse mixtures of blue, red, white, and yellow were striking. Often vocal during feeding time, they squabbled and ruffled their feathers. During my return trips, I often watched them and was intrigued by their organized social hierarchy. I began to learn which of the birds was in charge.

Adjacent to the pool and the toucan cage was an outdoor pizza shack. It was shaded by large trees and had several small tables where customers could enjoy good brick-oven pizza. I met Dave at the pizza hut for an early lunch; he relaxed with a cold glass of his favorite vodka. The stray cats that lived by the pizza place always looked forward to his return. They knew when Davie was around; if they were patient enough, they would be rewarded with a handfed gourmet meal.

Dave owned an antique store located in the Homestead section of south Florida. Every once in a while, he needed to restock his store with birds carved from stone. The birds, mostly toucans and parrots, were handcrafted out of beautiful Brazilian rocks. They really stood out displayed in his store's window. The yellow, pink, blue, green and jet-black colors made the statues seem lifelike. He purchased these birds at a store in Rio far from our hotel. To get to the store, he summoned Dario, his "personal" cab driver, to pick him up in front of the Sheraton.

With a joke every step of the way, Dario was always full of energy. A gentleman in his thirties and of medium build, he couldn't speak a word of English. How Davie was ever able to direct him was a mystery. Davie couldn't utter a single word of Portuguese. Yet one thing was for sure; you could always count on Dario to never show on time.

After lunch I decided to accompany Davie on one of these excursions. Dario's cab had torn seats and a stale interior. The tires looked as if they hadn't been changed in a decade. The drive took us along some winding narrow roads that funneled between large cliffs. Dario was not afraid to go at . . .

well, let's say a faster than normal pace. The shocks were so worn I could feel every bump and hear the squeaking of the springs.

During the drive, Davie was his normal relaxed self. I, on the other hand, held onto the seat for dear life. Recognizing my fright, and at the same time joking with Davie, Dario turned to me and said, "Don't worry, be happy." Sweat pouring down my face, I politely answered, "Okay." A ride on a rollercoaster would have been a nonevent compared to this little jaunt. I thought that he must have gone to the same driving school as his peers in Lima!

When we eventually made it to this special store, the display of unique stone birds was overwhelming. Entire floors were filled of carvings, and large rocks made of pure crystal and amethyst were for sale, things that were uncommon back in the US. I purchased as much as I could carry back and prayed they would survive Dario's Indy 500 race back to the hotel. Somehow surviving years of Dario's skills, Davie would make it a point to bring him numerous gifts from the States. Dario was quite a colorful character.

* * *

Upon our return to the Sheraton, there was still plenty of time for me to stroll down to the nearby sands of Ipanema. Reminiscing about the bus ride, I wanted to retrace what I had seen along its route near our hotel. To get to the beach, I had to walk down a steep hill, squeezing my way through a narrow passage. On the right side stood an iron rail and some homes with guard dogs overlooking the ocean. On the left side was the winding road in front of a steep hill. About halfway down, the iron rail gave way to solid stone walls that protected against accidental falls. The ridge dividing the walkway and ocean offered quite a drop; any stumble could result in a serious injury.

Watching my balance, I encountered the fishermen I had seen during the ride. Their morning's catch was openly displayed in buckets. One of the anglers, an older man, proudly held up one of his catches as if it were a trophy; his smile could have lit up the sky. Without knowing any Portuguese, I used the universal language of laughter to initiate communication. The man and his friends were relaxed and easy to get along with. Their darkened skin had been hardened by years of exposure to the sun. Not wearing any shoes, they had on some torn shorts and were shirtless. Their equipment was antiquated, and I could tell the lines were frayed and needed replacement. Nevertheless, they managed to make the best of what they had.

I tried to describe some of my personal fishing equipment and the type of fish I was used to catching. The exchanges were interesting, and I gathered that the elderly man might have been the leader of the group. I eventually understood his name to be Luiz, and that some of his friends were, in a fun way, mocking my efforts to communicate. Admittedly they had every reason to, as at times I paused and laughed at myself. After about twenty minutes, I firmly shook Luiz's hand and waved goodbye to his company.

Eventually I entered the beach of Leblon. Parallel to the beach was a path constructed of black and white stones. It served as a busy highway for joggers and cyclist. The beach functioned as a giant playground for people of all ages; several games of volleyball were underway, kites sailed high in the sky, and soccer games dotted the shoreline. Walking toward Ipanema and Copacabana, I tried not to interfere with the serious athletes. The makeshift soccer games, volleyball nets, runners, bicycles, kites and dog walkers made for one big obstacle course. I thought this was organized and well-accepted chaos. People had so much fun and adapted to whatever surrounded them. I never saw any arguing or complaints as one fun activity flowed into the other. The fun symphony was invigorating; the atmosphere of the beach was electrifying. Everything around me was a shot of pure energetic fun.

Where Dolphins Walk

Along the beach path kiosks offered condiments. The kiosks were basically wooden shacks, and from the ceilings hung bananas and green coconuts. They also offered smoked sailfish, French fries, and a variety of sodas. One of the local favorites was *agua de coco*, pure coconut water. The man behind one counter was short, stocky, and of dark complexion. He had on a light blue shirt with half the buttons missing. I ordered the local favorite and watched as he used large machete to cut the top off a large green coconut. I was handed the fruit with a straw stuck inside. Now I was feeling very Brazilian, and had no time to reflect about any worries at the beaches of Rio. The aura was too uplifting, and there simply wasn't space for an ounce of sadness. I was enjoying every moment of my walk. The sights were a people watcher's dream.

Another person of interest was a dark-skinned man who seemed a bit out of place. Shirtless with some paintings on one arm, he stood alone in the middle of the beach; a red and white bandana was draped around his head and neck. His only clothing consisted of a pair of unevenly cut brown leather shorts; some beads and strings dangled down the side of one leg. He was obviously of Indian descent, and likely from somewhere deep within the interior of the country.

I went closer. He was selling what appeared to be a bow. It was a bent piece of wood with a single string attached from one end to the other. Attached at one end was a hollow cup carved out of a piece of dried fruit. I had absolutely no idea what he was selling. I didn't see any arrows, and the dark-stained cup did not seem to belong. Then a tall lady with light brown hair stopped beside me. My curiosity must have been too obvious. Tugging the leash of a large dog, she wore a red bikini and a new pair of Nike sneakers. Fortunately, she spoke some English and quickly volunteered that she was a nurse.

Paula was kind enough to explain exactly what he was offering. The object was called a *berimbau.* Paula told me that a *berimbau* is a single-string musical bow used in conjunction with *capoeira*, a Brazilian form of martial art. Apparently the bow's sounds were the musical foundation for the many defensive and aggressive movements associated with the unique dance of *capoeira*. She also said the Indian man was from far away, and that he was a master and teacher of the Brazilian art.

The teacher seemed as interested in me as I was in him. He looked at me in a focused way, and I sensed that he was trying to tell me something. Paula's erratic and energetic dog became still. The man's positive calm reminded me of the Venezuelan man. His relaxed and confident mannerisms were eerily similar to the straw hat salesman. How many interesting stories this teacher must have, and how much wisdom he likely had stored within. He wanted to convey so much but even though Paula could understand most of his thoughts, he just couldn't find the proper words. It didn't really matter; the energy and power radiating out of his silent look more than made up for anything words could possibly have delivered.

Like the salesman on the Venezuelan beach, was he trying to tell me something about myself? I wondered what he was thinking. Did he feel something about my future? Could he sense the pulses of my past and present stories? Paula gave me a gentle nudge. Overly pensive, I decided not to purchase the *berimbau*; too much was racing through my mind. Pulling myself together, I turned and thanked the master. He smiled and outwardly signaled his happiness over our meeting. In all my years of walking along the South Florida beaches, I can't say that I ever bumped into this type of mystical individual; it was an experience to remember. Ironically, several years later, my close friend John would actively participate in *capoeira* lessons offered in a small Fort Lauderdale auditorium.

Paula asked if I would accompany her to meet some friends. She was on her way to another kiosk located only a few minutes closer to Copacabana. The dog was a beautiful and powerful black Labrador. Paula handed me his leash and asked if I would take him to walk by the water. Because of his strength he was difficult to control, and in reality, it was I who was being walked by the dog. Adding more fuel to his fire was a couple throwing a Frisbee; he happily dragged me from one of the couple to the other. His frenzied activity helped me shake loose and awakened me from my reflections.

Then it dawned on me why I had been volunteered for the walking assignment. Paula was in need of some relief and was laughing at my inability to control her big Lab. She then took the leash and released the dog; he bolted toward the ocean and plunged fearlessly into the waves. After the dog had his fill of the ocean, he charged in my direction. Apparently, I was his new best friend, and he made it a point to shake water directly onto my shirt just in time to meet Paula's friends.

The group was rather small, consisting of about seven people, three men and the balance women. They all wore beach attire, and some had a bicycle by their side. After being introduced to the group and soaking in the doggy's saltwater, I became the object of a barrage of jokes. Slightly embarrassed, I took it all in stride; in short time I was made to feel as if I was a special part of the gang. Some spoke in a broken English, so I caught the gist of what they were communicating.

I was invited to many different homes that afternoon, so many in fact that I felt overwhelmed. Flattered, I decided to visit a couple, Karina and Ramon, who both worked in the medical field. They asked me to join them in the evening for a *churrasco*, a Brazilian version of an American barbeque. Both in their mid-thirties, Karina and Ramon seemed very much in love. They remained close to each other's side and often embraced. Karina was short and fit and had long, dark blonde hair. Ramon was much taller, clean cut, and was also in good physical shape. They gave me their address and suggested that I arrive around 9 p.m.

Douglas Andrew Keehn

Their home was relatively close to my hotel, and they mentioned that they were special friends with Paula. I stayed with the group for another hour but was beginning to run low on energy. If I were to meet them in the evening I would have to return to the Sheraton and rest. Happy and armed with my invitation, I jogged along the beach path and back up the hill to my hotel.

With my balcony door opened, the sounds of the waves once again made it easy for me to relax. When I finally woke it was early in the evening. I made it a point to call both Dave and Fernando to tell them I had made plans. I put on some jeans and walked downstairs to have a taxi take me to Karina and Ramon's home. And unshaved thin older gentleman with grey hair and brown pants occupied the driver's seat. The interior of the taxi was a mess with ripped seats and holes in the cloth roof lining. Once I had handed over the street name and number, the driver nodded. He slammed on the gas pedal, and away we went speedily down the hill. This was going to be another one of those interesting rides.

At the bottom of the hill we made a left turn and then headed toward the area of Lagoa, an upscale neighborhood that faces the Rodrigo de Freitas Lagoon. The heart-shaped body of water has a path along its shore, which is normally occupied with morning and afternoon joggers. The driver slowed but didn't stop for several red lights; apparently a red light was only a suggestion that we come to a halt. After a long fifteen minutes we pulled up in front of a home. I gladly got out and paid the driver while brushing dust off my jeans.

When I arrived, at least twenty people had gathered for dinner. The two-story home was constructed of wood, and surrounding its yard were rows of thick green bushes. Inside, the furniture was old and of antique style. Two cats and a slobbering and huffing bulldog patrolled the kitchen. I peeked into some of the rooms and noticed they were quite small; they had ceiling fans, ordinary dressers and nothing larger than a queen-sized bed. Most of the activity was taking place in the yard.

Karina greeted me as Ramon was busy entertaining his close friends. I quickly learned that Brazilians often ate at late hours, and more people kept arriving as the night progressed. There was Brazilian *bossa nova* music, laughter, and great food; plenty of baked chicken, fried fish, and some Indian rice. The attire was low key, and the guests were devoid of fancy clothing or jewelry. Brand labels seemed unimportant; what was important was who could tell the best jokes and create the most laughter. I never realized so much fun could continue all day and last until the end of night. How were these people going to wake up for work?

My American way of thinking had to go through a quick adjustment. I realigned my thoughts and decided to go with the flow—to just relax and enjoy the night. Fortunately, enough people had some command of English so that I didn't feel so out of place. Around 10 P.M., Paula entered dressed in high heel shoes and white jeans. I was happy to see her. She talked to me at length about Rio, and gave me a list of restaurants and piano bars in close proximity to the Lagoon.

She introduced me to several people. There was quite an assortment of guests: doctors, lawyers, businessmen, stylists and federal workers, just to name a few. Admittedly, after time, I was exhausted. I wanted to leave the party around 4 A.M. after being boosted by some of life's most important ingredients: good friends, good food, wine, music, conversation, and an abundance of laughter. All of this seemed so simple. Maybe that was because it was designed to be simple.

I was literally dizzy from having met so many different people. My head spun and I could barely recall the many names. Never in my life had I attended such an electric party. Karina, Ramon and Paula insisted on driving me back to my hotel. I got into the back of a silver Chevy and, with Ramon steering, was chauffeured to the Sheraton. They were exceedingly gracious, and I couldn't find a way to thank them enough. I kept in contact with Paula until she relocated to a city far in the interior of the country; she needed to move to care for her elderly mother. Karina and Ramon eventually sold their home and moved to the coastal city of Natal, located far to the north.

Despite slowly losing contact with the three, I never forgot how they indoctrinated me into Rio's culture. When we'd first met I had been a complete stranger, yet I had been treated as if I had known them for years. Little would they ever realize how much of an influence that evening would later have on my life. I came from a structured society and discovered I had a lot of pent-up energy. That evening in Rio I felt as if I was a wild tiger that had just been released from a cage. Of course, I came from a country that valued freedoms, and I never felt as if any of my liberties were ever held in check; I loved the freedoms that my country offered and proudly protected. But it wasn't those autonomies I held internally.

As an American I would have stopped and not ignored a red light, I would not have driven so quickly, and probably would have set the party's music at a lower volume. I also would not have stayed out until 5 A.M. knowing I had to report for work in a few hours. Yet back home, I had never been accepted so readily by a group of people whom I'd never met. Maybe in my culture there was too much mistrust? Americans, myself included, were normally more reserved.

Just what was it that I had found within that evening in Rio, the feeling that when released allowed me to feel so elated and liberated? It was the one of the most basic of human desires—the craving to simply have some unrestricted fun. To just let go in every sense of its meaning. When it comes to inexhaustible fun, the people of Rio are the masters of the world. Yes, maybe they overdo it, and at times they push the limits nearly to the wild and lawless side. But the formula of fun was liberating and mentally balanced my regimented American expectations.

Why shouldn't a weeknight be as much fun as one over a weekend? Do we have to only have fun one or two nights each week? Are we subconsciously crossing out certain days for socializing? Trying to strike a reasonable balance, I came to my own conclusion. I noticed that I was overly focused on their behavior, concerned that the Brazilian way of festival was simply too crazy. I was looking at the boundaries solely from an American perspective. The question I should have asked myself at the outset was not are they having too much fun but rather are Americans having enough fun?

* * *

I awoke slightly after noon. I was craving some of that great Brazilian coffee. The weather began to deteriorate as many clouds darkened the sky. Coincidentally I met Davie in the lobby, and we agreed to have coffee along with something to eat. As he had during the flight, Davie carried his gentlemanly manners outside the cockpit. We chose the outdoor café near the pool and were protected from the rain by a wooden canapé. He explained how he was going to need help lugging some of those stone birds back to his store in Miami. Seemed he had done this a few times before and knew precisely what was required.

Time was ticking by and it was already late in the afternoon. We both adjourned and went back to our rooms for some final rest. After sleeping for a short while, I packed, showered, and put on my uniform. With the rain strengthening, our crew met in the lobby; in the dark, off we went to the Rio airport. The bus ride was again long as the soaking rain stalled the traffic. I couldn't help but once again focus on what was outside. After enjoying such a super time, some stark realities were again entering my thoughts.

Under the surface of all the fun and relaxation were sobering reminders that all was not well. Despite the inclement weather, I again saw children, barely clothed, playing alongside malnourished horses and dogs in trash filled lots. Obviously, for a large portion of the native people, life was diffi-cult. Rows of abandoned buildings and plenty of dilapidated houses were in evidence. Many tourists preferred to block out these images and not allow certain realties to interfere with their stay. I always thought this approach to be an awful mistake. Compassion for those who are struggling is a must; I never allowed myself to treat my stay in any country as if its neighborhoods were simple playgrounds.

My recent travels were forcing me to come to grips with many diverse truths. I was slowly being taught to look past a lot of pain and focus on the hidden beauty that lies within. People often do a poor job of understanding much of what they fear; poverty, hunger, sickness and the like . . . not con-necting with any sort of mess was certainly more comfortable. However, my ongoing experiences taught me that I would be haunted if I chose any path that led to selective blindness. Pain is real, and to mentally place a Band-Aid over it only covers the wound for so long.

Still fighting a rainstorm, our driver did an excellent job of returning us to safety at the airport. Davie told Fernan-do and I to go ahead, and that it wasn't necessary for us to meet him in operations. He instructed us to go directly to the plane where he would meet us about thirty minutes prior to departure. I thought it a bit odd, and he looked as if he was hiding something. Nevertheless, he was the boss and we had no problem bypassing the normal routine.

The process of clearing customs went smoothly. We again met Geraldo, or Tiny, before boarding the flight. He was his normal carefree self and offered his assistance to expedite our departure. Davie then entered the cockpit carrying a small beige animal cage. Soft whining emanated from behind its aluminum bars.

"Davie, what in the hell is this?" I asked.

"Sheraton and Rio, two cats I am rescuing from the pizza shack," he said. "Don't worry, be happy."

He then assured us that they had both been armed with the proper shots and immigration papers. Fernando and I laughed. These two had just hit the cat jackpot. They couldn't have found a kinder owner!

Luckily, by the time we departed, most of the rainstorms had dissipated. With our checklists completed, Davie, Fernando, Sheraton, Rio and I were set for the flight home. Our route would take us over the Brazilian cities of Brasilia, Manaus, and Boa Vista, then over Caracas, Venezuela, the Caribbean, and finally into Miami. Much to Geraldo or Tiny's delight, we departed on time and were quickly in the air headed northbound. Off we went with our two novice passengers.

It was a long flight, and the trip included a fair amount of protesting from the feline section. With no inclement weather anywhere along our course, the lights of Miami came into view about thirty minutes earlier than scheduled. We landed, and Captain Davie taxied the plane to the F concourse. Sheraton and Rio both recently passed away; each lived into their early twenties, well-loved in their charmed home in Southwest Florida. I would continue flying to Rio de Janeiro for many years to come.

Rio, situated along the southern Brazilian coast, is surrounded by an array of beautiful mountains. Over time, I would come to know Baha de Tijuca, Lagoa, Leblon, Ipanema, and Copacabana. The green mountains, active blue oceans, unique rock formations, and lagoons make Rio's topography dynamic. Although famous for its celebration of Carnival, I always thought the city shone all year around. It an energetic place with wonderful people, great views and a nightlife one can never forget.

I also had some interesting experiences during my stays at our layover hotel. One such incident was a bit unnerving and at the same time revealing. Located just to the right of the hotel entrance was a tiny cubicle where a policeman would normally be stationed. Because there were some rough neighborhoods, specifically a large *favela*, nearby, safety was always a concern.

I was relaxing in my room when loud popping sounds caught my attention. I walked out onto the balcony to find a single policeman with an old pistol blindly returning fire into the nearby hill. I couldn't tell what he was aiming at but lots of bullets flew everywhere. The policeman was alone, and apparently, he was frantically trying to make a call from his booth; it seemed that he did not have a radio. Not only did he not have a radio, he was also very much outgunned. His pistol was no match for the rapid fire coming his direction.

It was too dangerous for me to remain on my terrace, so I went back into the room and waited for the gunfire to cease. After several minutes, the shooting stopped. I went back outside and was happy to see the policeman was okay. As unbelievable as it seemed, he was still trying to call for assistance. Finally, after about twenty minutes, help arrived. Honestly, I have no idea how he hadn't been struck. I don't even know why the shooting took place.

I went downstairs and was elated that none of the hotel workers had been hurt. And even more interesting was how fast life in the lobby returned to normal. The doormen and clerks acted as if nothing had really happened. I scratched my head, and a bit befuddled took the elevator back to my room. I guess they probably had seen this script a few times before and were accustomed to dealing with sporadic violence. Although they might have seemed unfazed, I needed a scotch.

The shooting bought to life the intricacies of Brazilian society. So much fun, care, beauty and tranquility were at times overshadowed by extreme violence. Not that there wasn't plenty of violence in my own country, but I felt more vulnerable in Rio. If the police were vastly outgunned and had difficulty calling for help, what could I expect for my own security?

Over time I became keenly aware of the many problems Rio faced; the social and economic difficulties were all too real. Yet despite many extreme hardships, the people remained positive and made the best of each and every day. Without much effort, I could always count on making new friends there; the ease in the way friendships developed is a quality that makes the city so special. The managers, doormen, taxi drivers, fishermen, waiters and medical professionals all provided me with new ways to approach life. The kindness of the *cariocas*, the people from Rio, was genuine. In all my stays, even though I came from the First World, I never felt a shred of resentment. Never was I portrayed as having more or being superior.

Oddly enough, it was I who often felt inferior as I was secretly becoming envious of their lives. I was learning that life in Brazil, as in other Latin American countries, was often unstable. Currencies could wildly fluctuate, and sweeping governmental policies could be unexpectedly implemented. The bottom line was that the people learned to live with a fair amount of instability.

My travels challenged me to constantly check myself; to reflect on what actually captured my imagination, enthusiasm and interest, and to realign what I considered priorities. I was slowly recognizing that many people outside my country adapted to various crises in amazingly different ways. Because of the volatility affecting their lives, they were often forced to confront a continuous barrage of unexpected circumstances. Yet because so many positive qualities were rooted in their upbringing, they managed to overcome a vast amount of difficulties; they rode life's unpredictable waves like a professional surfer. Their family ties, friendships and outlooks were part of a solid foundation that secured their survival through almost any disaster. To endure any tragedy, I learned that it was necessary to confront it and not to ignore its gravity. In comparison, too many of my compatriots turn away from abstract and distant problems as well as from each other.

Obviously, stability is beneficial in our lives; it's a quality we universally try to achieve. However, I was seeing that in order to feel stable, I needed to be comfortable with managing instability. People who daily faced enormous uncertainties quickly adapted; because they faced so many barriers, they were well-equipped to steer through almost anything. Yet at home in my own backyard, I knew many who became rattled by even the slightest change, some of which I didn't even consider necessarily bad. I again wondered about my lifestyle. I found myself uncomfortable with being so comfortable, and questioned if my protected life made me vulnerable. My parents grew up during the Great Depression, and I compared their expectations, needs, and abilities to adapt to my own.

Then the expression *"nossa"* came to mind, an expression the *cariocas* used meaning, "Wow."

My times in Rio highlighted several questions. Did stability really enhance stability? What exactly was living in the First World supposed to imply? I felt puzzled. In the strange, complex and wild city of Rio I had always felt happy and tranquil, as if I were at home. But I wasn't at home . . . or was I?

CHAPTER 9

Sampa: Many Bright Shining Moments

Pimenta no olho dos outros é refresco.

Pepper in someone else's eye is refreshing. It is very easy to make light of someone else's suffering.

Soon my travels continued in Brazil. The next new destination on my wish list was the giant metropolis of São Paulo. I had heard a lot about this city from several coworkers, and I arranged my bid to increase the probability of a São Paulo layover. Shortly I received news that I would be flying there for the bulk of the following month.

To simply say that São Paulo is a big city would be misleading. São Paulo isn't just big, it's enormous. Located in the southeast part of the country, it's less than an hour's flight to the south of Rio. Brasilia, located in the central western part of the country, still remains the nation's capital but São Paulo is the country's business hub. Its stock exchange, the *Bovespa*, is the second largest in the world.

São Paulo is the name of both a city and state. Approximately forty million people live in the state, and about eleven million reside within the city. The neighborhoods house a diverse population that includes a substantial number of people of Italian, Japanese, and Arabic descent. In fact, the country of Brazil is home to the largest Japanese population outside of Japan, the bulk of whom reside within the limits of São Paulo. This major Latin American zone is now considered a key junction in the new global economy.

My first flight to São Paulo included captain Davie and first officer Charlie, both of whom I had worked with in the past. Charlie originally came from Eastern Airlines. After their default, our company hired approximately eight hundred of their pilots. Charlie was a bit short and stocky with dark black hair. Mostly the quiet type, Charlie was very intelligent and had an in-depth understanding of finance.

Davie had already flown to São Paulo on several occasions; he was familiar with the route, radio frequencies, and approach procedures. And more importantly, he picked up some Chinese food for us. Whenever I flew with Davie, I could always rely on him to pack some great food! Even if the departure was in the morning, he would rustle up a home-cooked omelet.

Most of the flights to South America departed Miami around midnight, and São Paulo was no exception. After the normal review of the flight papers, we were all set. Before most of our flights left Miami, Dave and I met some of the workers from the ramp; most were responsible for handling the checked baggage. Their office was at the bottom of the F concourse where most of our jets parked. When we met, it became customary for this group to taunt us with relentless, "The pilots are this, and the pilots are that."

Some of the workers were built like bricks as they routinely managed large containers and heavy pieces of luggage. Arm wrestling with the pilots always served as their rallying point. Needless to say, I lost my matches most of the time . . . okay, all of the time. But interacting with the ramp guys was always uplifting. I think it was one of Davie's secret ways of relaxing people before they began a night shift; he used it to set a positive tone for the rest of the evening. The joking and laughing placed everyone at ease, and served as a perfect complement to the seriousness of our job. Davie knew all too well that laughter was a powerful formula for success.

Finished with our briefing, we entered the plane and were met by Ted, the most senior flight attendant. Soft spoken and tall, he coordinated information that pertained to the flight with Dave. We received the confirmation of our route from the Miami traffic controllers, and with all the doors closed, began our push off from the jet way. We steadily taxied to runway 30 where, after a standard takeoff, we were on our way to São Paulo, Brazil.

Although I had never been to São Paulo, I was acquainted with the route. It was nearly identical to the track I had piloted to Rio de Janeiro. This highway in the sky would have us pass over Haiti, the Dominican Republic, Curacao, and then enter the northern part of Brazil via Venezuela. On these southern courses, the weather could be problematic. Storms that formed near the equator often forced us to deviate. It wasn't unusual to encounter a storm that exceeded an altitude of 40,000 feet. The intensity of these storms required us to maintain a minimum separation of twenty miles.

Thankfully on this night, the weather was good. The flight was smooth and we encountered little turbulence. Dave was his usual relaxed self and talked about his new cats; seems they were getting along fine with his dog Gypsy. After about three hours, Charlie returned from his break and sat in the captain's seat. This allowed Davie to get some rest. Charlie talked of the possibility of placing his South Miami home up for sale; he was ready for a change. We chatted about the stock market and some different political ideologies. Around 5 AM. we were both feeling the effects of the night shift, and I was ready for my break.

I returned from my light snooze about two and a half hours later. Davie had already begun initiating our change to a lower altitude. The sun was beaming through the cockpit windows, so I donned my sunglasses. Continuing our descent to Guarulhos International, I saw farmland and houses sprinkled throughout the rolling hills. A ridge or mountains and some radio towers initially shielded the view of the runway's approach path. Then, as if a curtain had been lifted, the city of São Paulo came into view. The sheer scope captured my attention; buildings of all sizes extended as far as the eye could see. At first glance, the structures did not seem to form any pattern. Mixed in height, shape, and color, their display seemed anything but cohesive.

Guarulhos International is located close to Congonhas, a smaller yet busy airport located on top of a hill. The hill is situated in a densely populated area, and is literally surrounded by buildings. There is little room for error flying in or out of Congonhas. If you ever fly out of this airport, your experience will be memorable. Close to the city's downtown district, Congonhas primarily serves jets flying routes within Brazil. Due to the close proximity of both these major airports, the air traffic can become congested, particularly when the weather is marginal.

This morning the weather was holding, and without any delay our flight was given a clearance to land. Passing a small ridge, we made a left turn and joined the final approach course leading to runway 9R (right). After Davie's smooth touchdown, the ground controller cleared us to cross runway 9L (left) and directed us to proceed down the parallel taxiway to our assigned gate. The large airport consisted of several remote (off gate) parking spots and lengthy concourses.

The passengers began to disembark. I packed up my flight bag and followed the rest of the crew for the long walk to exit the concourse. I carried my luggage down a flight of stairs that lead to the federal police and customs booths. With my passport stamped, I walked by the baggage claim area and out to the main terminal. The architecture of the airport was not sophisticated but its layout offered a seamless transition between the airlines. The design helped passengers make connections. The building had three levels, each containing a variety of shops, restaurants and cafes. There were even banks and pharmacies.

Passing through a crowd greeting arriving travelers, I was finally at the exit. Outside and to my left was the giant bus that would take us to the hotel. In front of our bus were several boys waiting to shine shoes for US dollars. Not even in their teens, the tan and dark-skinned boys were playing a cat and mouse game with the airport police. The officers constantly chased them away. I and other crewmembers allowed them to polish our shoes. Ironically always barefoot, none of the boys had a pair of shoes or even sandals. Later, I would occasionally try to bring sneakers as a gift.

Dressed in torn shorts, skinny, shirtless and covered with patches of dirt, I think they enjoyed their little hide-and-seek match with the local police. It struck me that our routine welcome from the boys represented a realistic introduction into Brazil with its stark divide between the haves and have-nots. Obviously, our greeting wasn't the red-carpet treatment but it was a solid reality check. Those few moments with the boys was an indication of what might lie ahead.

Their body language and stares weighed on my thoughts as if they had something to tell me . . . perhaps a story, their reality? Either way, I was affected. The entire exchange placed my reflections right back on the beach in Venezuela. Once again, I saw the straw-hat salesman peering directly at me. For a moment I felt immobilized, and bowed my head as if to cowardly avoid the boys' expressions. With my hands in my pockets, I just felt empty and didn't know how to react. I was uncomfortable; I felt torn because we had to leave; I knew as soon as I got on the bus I would be detached from the boys until the next return. But I simply couldn't shake off these emotions.

Oddly enough, when I went to buy new clothing or shoes back home, the presence of the boys or the Venezuelan man would be rekindled. If I were in a store when this occurred, I would often reverse course and return what I had been about to acquire. My change of heart wasn't a case of feeling guilty about having the ability to buy something someone else couldn't. It was more a matter of the practicality. Just how much did I really need? For example, in most malls scores of places sell sneakers. If I already own two pairs, why do I need another? And so, when I thought of the man or the boys, their images acted as a self-check. It was not a case of doing more with less. It was simply a case of, do I really need more? This was likely only one of many messages they were trying to convey.

Their silence was anything but insignificant. They made me think about certain aspects that have taken hold within my own culture. The bareness of the boy's possessions made me recall what I had desired at their age. Of course, it goes without saying that my youth was in a much different era. Today, with such tremendous technological advances, there is a huge leap in what is offered for sale. Yet one thing seems to remain on par between these boys and my youth; the craving to accumulate remains balanced. When I think of what this gang strove for and what I desired when I was younger, a dramatic difference arises compared to the current expectations of my friend's children.

How much stuff they accumulate even before they are in their teens: several electronic games, computers, a television, smartphone, and a wardrobe of upscale clothing; all these examples are quite common. The list of possessions was extensive, and when given some thought, I found it remarkable in the sense of what so many, especially from outside our culture, manage to do without. It wasn't simply the age and ownership of such luxuries; the frequency of cravings was disturbing. I've had the disadvantage of never having parented and therefore am not professing to be an expert. I admit that my travels both local and abroad have influenced the way I look at many realities.

From my perspective, I find that the word "no" is lacking in our vocabulary. Adults often seem conflicted on how to combat this thirst for extravagant belongings. Today it's not uncommon for both parents to be feverishly working because of life's economic demands. A persistent desire to own expensive items gets thrown into their laps, placing a tremendous amount of undue pressure on the entire family. The burden can be overwhelming.

Every parent wishes his or her children could have a better life. But when I engaged with so many who had so little monetarily, I began to question if the quenching of this thirst to accumulate was preparing younger privileged individuals for a better life. I wondered if in fact we were truly creating a better quality of people—people who should be focused on giving, sharing, and being compassionate. My concerns were clearly driven by what I learned from my travels. I came in contact with scores of kind and gentle young people, people who would never think to afflict any unnecessary materialistic pressures on their parents or relatives.

The boys at the airport may have not been fortunate in the context of owning very much, but I felt deeply privileged in having had the opportunity to be in the presence.

On subsequent trips, I always looked forward to the boys' brief company. If they were absent, it signaled the nearby presence of the police. In my mind, they were ever-present. Like my exchange with the Venezuelan, there wasn't much verbalization but their silence was captivating. They might have thought their work was only passing and insignificant but to me they presented many bright shining and lasting moments.

* * *

Our hotel, the family owned Maksud Plaza, was located in the heart of São Paulo just off of the Avenida Paulista. (A *paulista* describes someone who was born in the state of São Paulo.) Similar to my experience in Rio, the density of traffic was enormous. I doubted the infrastructure was meant to handle the demands of the trucks, busses and cars that engulfed the roadways. Looking outside, it became apparent that São Paulo, like any large city, had its share of diverse areas. Our route passed through neighborhoods that weren't well manicured. I did see an interesting array of people. Some wore business attire and others appeared in torn shorts and barefoot.

Reminding me of Santiago, lines of city buses assigned to numerous destinations hinted at the extensive size of the city. Looking up to the skyline, the air was layered by a grey cloud of smog. Pollution emanated from numerous factories and vehicles. Looking back with a grin, the bus driver took note of my curiosity. The bus was large, yet the driver was able to maneuver through narrow streets without difficulty. He made it all seem so easy as he wove the big rig through the dense traffic. At our hotel, one of our flight attendant translators offered my thanks to the driver. He was thin and wore a pair of dull grey pants. Accompanying his freshly lit cigarette was a big smile; the driver was humble and seemed content with his accomplishments.

I had our translator ask the man about his work schedule. He said he worked long hours six days per week, often well in to the night. Hmm, interesting. Not his answer but the way in which he answered. Despite his grueling schedule, his manner and tone were devoid of discontent. He seemed to accept his situation and wanted to make the best of the workload. At the moment, I didn't give this exchange much thought but it might later add up as another meaningful message.

Once again, Davie tipped the driver for everyone on the bus. The flight attendants who didn't know him were befuddled.

The front of our hotel appeared ordinary with a tall doorman named Chavez guarding the entrance. Over time Chavez became a friend of Captain Davie, who was a quick study of what people liked. The doorman loved to read and could count on a new book from Davie upon each of his returns. Needless to say, Davie had some books in hand to transfer as soon as we arrived.

The layout of the lobby was typical—a restaurant, gift shop, and jewelry store occupied the ground level. On the left was a restaurant that normally offered both breakfast and lunch buffets. The floors of the hotel wrapped around its center, leaving an interior view of levels spiraling all the way to the roof. The personnel behind the front desk were cordial and professionally dressed; over the years I would get to know them well. One of the clerks, Marcelo, told me his commute entailed taking several buses each way; the round trip added up to many hours and he routinely worked six days per week. The extent of his travels was a forced sacrifice due to the lack of available jobs. His salary was low, yet when all was said and done, I couldn't think of a moment when he displayed any sadness or signs of fatigue. Again, I tried to a see through a fog that masked many of Brazil's difficult realities.

Because of the age of the hotel, my room was a bit outdated. The twin beds had sheets designed with flowers, and a thick TV sat atop a long wooden dresser. The lighting was dim, hiding the bland condition of the off-yellow carpet. Curiously, the room lacked a clock. Maybe it wasn't so crucial to know the time.

I opened the drapes and viewed the adjacent street; not much to see other than a row of parked cars. The tile bathroom had an old white sink where I washed my hands and decided to change into jeans and then go for breakfast. Davie was tired and passed on joining me. A few blocks from the hotel on Alameda Santos, I found a place that reminded me of a small diner. Located in front of a counter were revolving torn red seats. Occupying the café were several people starting off their workday. Most were regular customers who knew the servers on a first-name basis.

The attendants wore white smocks and different colored caps. Constantly moving around and taking fast, none spoke a word of English. Using my subpar Portuguese, I somehow ordered an omelet. There was a lot of laughing, and I found it a super way to begin any day. I had the impression that foreigners didn't frequent this café and imagined some locals thought I might be lost.

My server was a short man with a mustache. A white towel hung over his left shoulder. He really got a kick out of my presence. Underneath his mustache, he just couldn't contain his smile. I knew the customers were talking about me and that I must have stood out like a stray lamb. Overall, I was sure the private joking was innocent. I was just a new beach ball for the seals to play with. Even though I didn't understand their language, I went with the flow; I nodded and laughed with a few of the people prodding me. It was all silly and harmless; after all, a good sense of humor is universally understood.

Interactions with the locals was a recipe no chef could prepare. It wouldn't have mattered if the food had been marginal. The spice of the people would have compensated for any bad ingredients. I thought of how much more fun I had with a simple two-dollar breakfast compared to my expensive dining experiences back home. Décor has its place but the real beauty lies in the people who can make any occasion fun.

On my walk back to the hotel, I again pondered the values of simplicity. How uplifting and reassuring life can be when people can just be themselves. Stepping into my room, I pictured my time at the counter with all the faces and the clowning. I laughed myself into a dream recognizing that good company is priceless.

* * *

After a solid sleep, I arose in the mid-afternoon. I was ready for a walk. It was lunch hour, and the streets were flooded with taxis and buses. I walked alongside the busy two-way Avenida Paulista. On both sides, skyscrapers, banks, and an array of shops paralleled the avenue. Ready for a bite, I went into a large restaurant that offered grilled foods. Located on the bottom of an office building, it was furnished with rows of long cafeteria-style tables. Several groups were eating, conversing and telling jokes. I was reminded of my breakfast that morning and of my times in Rio de Janeiro; the fun and relaxed Brazilian culture was alive and well in São Paulo.

I got on a line and ordered some cooked meats and a scoop of white rice. After lunch, I enjoyed some coffee that packed quite a punch. When I strolled over for a refill, I was invited to sit by a small group on a separate bench. A conversation quickly ensued as we talked about the States and the variety of nightlife offered in their city. But they seemed distracted and more focused on some sort of personal prank. All were well-dressed, and at times they laughed so hard they might have been watching a comedy.

A tall and thin cleanshaven fellow appeared to be the leader. He was the type who could inspire anyone to laugh. His name was Nicolas and he spoke English rather well. I asked Nicholas why there was so much hysteria. The group had played a trick on some coworkers; apparently the hoax had worked better than expected. They had been led to believe that a man watching them work in the morning was a high-ranking executive. Well-dressed in a pinstriped suit, he was merely Nicholas's cousin.

I guess the two cooked up the idea of having him stroll around pretending to be someone of importance. Whatever the plan, it seemed to have worked like a charm. Lunch hour was not just about lunch; it was about having fun. I shook the hands of Nicholas and his cousin and congratulated them on their successful prank. Laughing and shaking my head, I paid the check and went back onto the wide avenue. Giggling to myself, I must have appeared a bit strange to other pedestrians.

I hiked by several hospitals, schools, supermarkets, and malls, sites expected in any large city; the atmosphere was like that of Manhattan. After an extensive walk I felt fatigued and hired a taxi to take me to the hotel. The driver immediately asked my nationality. When I told him I was from the States, he came to life. He seemed to have a high opinion of

Americans, and he enjoyed listening to my English. Despite the language barrier, we made the best of our communications. The middle-aged man's relaxed demeanor was accompanied by a reassuring tone; his approach would have made any customer feel welcome. I thanked him for his kindness and proceeded back to my room.

As evening approached, our crew agreed to meet for dinner. Because I was unfamiliar with the city's nightlife, I thought it best to let our native Brazilian flight attendants take charge. They suggested a nearby Italian restaurant called Lellis Trattoria located at the bottom of a hill. When we arrived, there was a long line extending out the door. Inside wine bottles decorated the walls and hung from the ceiling. The tables were large and covered by white cloths. The atmosphere was noisy enough that I needed to raise my voice.

The kitchen was open, and I watched the frantic pace of the waiters flawlessly carrying large bottles and plates. How they never ran into each other or dropped anything was always a mystery. The chefs tossed dishes in huge pans alive with fire. The client's anticipation was excited by the aromas coming off the high-flamed stoves. A well-dressed older gentleman stood in front of the kitchen. Wearing a pair of glasses, he had his hair neatly combed back and wore a pressed light brown jacket. It occurred to me that he might be the owner.

I asked him if my intuition was correct. In fact, by sheer luck I was right. He asked if this was my first time at his place. He grinned and promised that I wouldn't be disappointed. He gestured for a server to bring a complimentary bottle of wine to our table. Seeing he was busy, I was just happy to have made his acquaintance. I shook his hand and returned to the table. At first our group enjoyed some vintage red while flipping through an extensive menu. We agreed to order some fish with a side of pasta; everything that came was mouthwatering! The pasta had a perfect blend of garlic that was in a league of its own. The codfish was cooked in a butter sauce and could only be described as superb. After my first bite I understood why there was such a wait to get seated. All around us groups of all ages and nationalities, couples, and families engaged in laughter and conversation. The meal was another home run, and I envisioned myself returning many more times.

My evening didn't end with dinner. I had jotted down a place recommended by another crewmember. I asked if anyone wanted to join me but there were no takers. Davie went back to the hotel while Charlie wanted to go to a popular tavern. I hailed a cab outside Lellis, climbed in, and handed the driver an address. After about twenty minutes I was released in front of an elegant hotel—the Hotel Unique.

The lobby was simply astonishing with an ultramodern design, light brown marble flooring, a large skylight, and art deco furniture. On the roof was a bar and restaurant called Skye. I took an elevator to the top and felt like I was on another planet. Skye opens with sensational views of the city. On my left was a long sushi bar, and to the right were tables filled with couples. Then came a few small couches and another small bar that led to a large terrace.

I ordered a glass of wine and took in the electric atmosphere. I chatted with a few people out on the balcony, and absorbed the energy and lights glowing off countless buildings. I talked for a while with a lady named Patricia who was studying to become an anesthesiologist. She was very excited about her future. Having long blonde hair and professionally dressed in black slacks, she was quite attractive. As the early morning hours approached, I wanted to return to the Maksud Plaza. Patricia accompanied me to the lobby and, after flagging down a taxi, we embraced and said our goodbyes. We agreed to stay in touch, and did so for a while via the Internet.

Waking late in the morning, I decided to get a haircut. I walked a few blocks and found a big modern salon. Upon entering I was greeted by a stylist who penciled in an appointment. With two levels, the entire place carried the heavy smell of hairspray. Thank goodness my wait would be only minutes. The barber was a short man named Rudolfo. Pictures of his children stood in front of a large mirror. He had a large family; the many photos were evidence of his love for his children. Unable to speak a word of English, he signaled that he was ready. This was going to be interesting.

Before the haircut began, I was given a quick massage and offered a cup of coffee. This custom is common in the salons of São Paulo. Rudolfo asked what I wanted. Using my hand to simulate a pair of scissors, I sat in a large winding chair and muttered, "Snip, snip." Despite my rudimentary description, he gave me a great haircut. I retained Rudolfo as my barber for the next ten years. Always happy, he loved to talk about soccer, soccer, and more soccer. My "snip snips" were always fun . . . I just needed to brush up on my knowledge of soccer and be certain to root for his favorite team.

Eventually I would travel to São Paulo hundreds of times. The vast city brims with a charged lifestyle. Some malls I frequented in the neighborhoods of Iguatemi, Ibirapuera and Higienopolis were complete with modern stores. In the shopping Higienopolis, it was permitted for people to bring their pets. It was not uncommon to see shoppers and their dogs weaving in and out of the many shops. The city has a multitude of cultural centers, and offers quite a diverse nightlife.

São Paulo basically has two different types of train service. One is the subway that normally travels within the confines of the metropolitan area. The other is the train whose routes branch off into neighborhoods outside the main areas of the city's limits. My experiences with each were quite different. For the most part, the subways were kept fairly clean; as a frequent passenger, I normally felt secure.

My experiences on the train were educational. The cars were often crowded, not very clean, and people sold items as they walked between the cabins. In some cases, it felt like a carnival atmosphere on tracks. At night I felt especially vulnerable on the train or waiting at outlying stations. But in order for me to truly experience a different side of the city, I needed to take some chances. After all my times on both the rail systems, I never once experienced any problems.

Having grown up in Manhattan, I felt myself to be somewhat street wise. In many of São Paulo's outer areas, my internal caution flag was periodically raised. I needed to be vigilant and exercise commonsense. Of course, I was careful not to carry an obvious wallet nor wear any jewelry that would catch attention. My visits to the outer boroughs allowed for definitive glimpses into the lives of many who couldn't afford the city's better neighborhoods. In time I managed to make some acquaintances in the outer areas, and despite all of their difficulties, I was always met with and treated with complete respect. Just like New York City, São Paulo has pockets that are riddled with crime. But within every dark cloud are pockets filled with positive energy. You just need to turn on your radar to find them.

* * *

After traveling to the city for some time, I began to see a lady who went by the name of Marta. We dated on and off for about a year. I met her one afternoon as she worked in a jewelry store in a large shopping mall. Marta was pretty; she had dark black hair, olive skin, and an athletic body. She was quiet, exercised often, and ate only healthy food. Later I met her brothers, one of whom played the guitar. They both lived far outside the metropolitan area. Marta and her brothers had been raised on a farm well to the north.

When we saw each other, I would stay in her small rental residence. The unit was tiny and resembled a New York City studio apartment. In the summer she left the window open as she didn't have any air conditioning. The view offered a sliver of the nearby buildings and the dimly lit street below. Nevertheless, Marta was comfortable with what she had.

I recall a moment where I was telling her about some money I had recently lost on a bad investment. Not fluent in

English, Marta struggled to tell me, "Doug, you don't need to make much money."

Without thinking, I abruptly answered, "Marta, I do need a lot of money. Don't you?"

Marta explained that she had grown up in an area where it didn't take a lot of money to survive and to be happy; her lifestyle was not complicated, and she was truly content. Continuing in a low-key way without defiance, anger or jealously, she calmly exclaimed, "Doug, I don't think so much about making money. I think Americans think too much about making money."

Those words came out ever so softly and were straight from her heart. It would take several years for Marta's message to rise up from within. The accident in Fort Lauderdale somehow rekindled her words and gentle purity; I finally began to awaken to what she had struggled to get across. I wondered if that accident hadn't been an accident after all. Maybe we had been hit for a reason. Maybe I desperately needed a jolt, and the attorney and his companion were just unwitting messengers.

Although my car had been struck from the rear, maybe I was as distracted as the couple. Could it be that I held many similarities to the attorney and the lady, that my concerns were too fixated with the allure of wealth? At the time of the accident, had I been at a certain critical juncture and needed to be awakened? It would take Marta, and people as genuine as her, to remove a mask that had blurred my concepts of what to truly value.

Still on my initial flight to São Paulo, it was time for the ride back to the airport. The large bus pulled in front of the Maksud; Chavez was there to hold the doors and guide the driver as he backed into the confined space. Davie, Charlie, and all the flight attendants were on, and away we went again. The ride to the airport that evening was very long; it took hours. A hard rain had flooded the highways and the traffic slowed to a crawl. By the time we arrived we were exhausted. Well, no sense complaining, as we needed to take a full load of people to the US.

We weren't alone in our tardiness. The flooding placed scores of travelers behind schedule, and the jammed customs lines only added to the evening's delays. It was going to be one of those long nights. Wanderley worked our flight operations; he handled the planned runway and airplane performance calculations. Also, on duty was Joselito, an experienced and very capable mechanic.

Joking and taunting were routinely integrated into the flight planning ritual, allowing the Brazilian fun to continue up to the very end. Charlie went out to the plane to do the walk around, and I wandered outside on the ramp where I chatted with Joselito. I had known him for many years and before my flight, if time permitted, we would meet for coffee. On this evening, coffee in hand, we stood to the side of a door leading to the flight planning and operations room. Our position was hidden, so if someone exited the room, they would not be aware of our presence.

My flight was to depart in about an hour, and I had already reviewed the flight papers with Davie and the other first officer. Out came Captain Dave briskly walking onto the noisy ramp. Engaged in our conversation, neither Joselito nor I were focused on him. Our plane to Miami was parked at a jet way directly in front of us. Near the plane, standing alone and not attached to anything, was a set of portable stairs—an apparatus that is wheeled to a plane's door to allow passengers to either exit or board when a fixed jet way is not available.

Our passengers were patiently waiting inside the terminal, and through its large windows, they could see everything taking place outside. Joselito, a tall, thin man in grey mechanic's attire, tapped my shoulder and hollered, "Look at this!"

Out of the corner of my eye I saw our fearless leader, Captain Davie, walking up some stairs. Under normal circumstances this wouldn't require a second look. But good old Captain Dave, dressed in full uniform, was on his way up the portable stairs that led nowhere. In plain view of the passengers. Joselito and I couldn't control our laughter. Imagine what the passengers must have thought! There was the captain, who couldn't even find his way up to an airplane. Was he blind? Poor Davie, finally realizing his wrong turn, glanced back at terminal. He knew he was the star in the middle of an unrehearsed comedy. It was just too funny!

With everything completed, I made a point to escort the boss up the proper staircase. We were now waiting for the many late passengers. Despite the stresses presented by the heavy rain, our customers took it all in stride. They didn't appear the least bit upset by the lengthy delay. Finally, in the early morning hours, Terry released the brakes and we commenced our flight back to Miami. We took off to the east, and after we had enough altitude to safely clear some mountains, we made our left turn and headed northbound to America. Exhausted, we arrived back in Miami about three hours late.

I always felt a bit empty departing São Paulo. I so easily connected with the doorman, clerks, bus and taxi drivers, barbers, shop owners, waiters, and our company employees. I missed their positive attitudes and the constant clever clowning. During each visit, I took a subconscious snapshot of all they had to offer. Through all the lightheartedness, I knew there was suffering. Yet I remained inspired by the way they dealt with so many real problems. It was a movie I had seen before in my travels to South America, a movie worth repeating. How to so consistently turn a bleak situation into something positive was a process I needed to build upon.

I again did some soul-searching and reflected on my life. I thought of my own interactions at home. Ever so slowly I recognized that to be in the presence of those who have so little can be priceless.

* * *

The morning after returning from São Paulo, I woke up shortly before sunrise. I was restless and felt like taking in some fresh tropical air. I put on some jogging shoes and walked toward Fort Lauderdale beach. Soon after I arrived along the shore, the skies opened up and it began to drizzle. As the rain grew stronger, some image stopped me in my tracks. Instead of running for shelter I stood still and faced the ocean.

I was numb to the downpour, and with the incoming tide surrounding my legs I just stared beyond the waves. Lightning flashed in the distance followed by visions of the Latin straw hat salesman. I closed my eyes to refocus and turned my head from side to side in an attempt to snap out of it. But my mind would not let the mirage vanish. My concentration forced me to wonder if it just a coincidence that I had purchased the straw hat in Caracas. Was my draw to that man just by chance?

I carried that hat while walking the sands of Fort Lauderdale. As a strong wind blew, I took off the hat and let the rain soak my hair. When I turned the straw hat around, I noticed that it resembled an empty nest. Maybe one of the messages the Venezuelan man was trying to signal was that life is fragile, and that I should be careful in how I was building my own. That with all I had, perhaps my nest, my perceived triumphs, were empty?

Still focused on the water, my thoughts deepened. Could it have been that when our eyes connected that day, he saw things in me I was not consciously aware of, that so many accomplishments if attained or handled improperly will turn out to be shallow, that I would need a new direction? I thought about my exchange with the *capoeira* master in Rio. Had that been just another happenstance? Exactly what was it that he had been able to see? What had he so eloquently been trying to deliver?

These reflections built inside of me. I just couldn't ignore their hidden significance. Covered with water, I took a deep breath and felt as if I had awoken from a dream. An almost surreal peace took hold. With a profound level of clarity, my mind was now directing me to dig further into my analogies. My introspection broadened, and then a few revelations came into focus. I sat down in the wet sand with my arms wrapped around my knees and started a self-analysis. What was I really trying to comprehend? Why now?

Then as if a curtain was being lifted, I began to put some pieces of a complex puzzle together. It dawned on me that I had met both the Venezuelan salesman and the *capoeira* master on the same grounds that I currently occupied . . . a beach . . . a place adjacent to the realm of the dolphins. Many of my most striking hints and realizations came together when I was either on the ocean or by her side. Mirroring the dolphins, the men were wise, kind, confident and mysterious; they seemed content with what they had. Through their silence, each was trying to convey a special message, as if to push me onto a different path. When the dolphins surrounded my boat, I always felt they were silently watching and skillfully trying to guide me. As was exactly the case with the salesman and the teacher. Their presence would always leave a lasting impression and subconsciously incited some much-needed changes.

After what seemed like endless hours, I jumped up feeling somewhat triumphant. I wondered if some links of a valuable chain had at last come together. The clouds were dissipating, and the rain gave way to a rainbow that arched over the Lauderdale reefs. I stretched, brushed the sand off my legs, and peered out at the ocean's horizon. Slightly offshore and directly in front of me were two large dolphins. It had been a while since I had seen any, and it was beyond odd that they appeared at that very moment. Not one to believe in miracles, I couldn't help but to imagine their appearance was symbolic, a type of reinforcement. Their timing was simply uncanny. I stepped backwards trying to keep the dolphins in sight but they vanished. Feeling stunned, I slowly walked back toward the 17th Street Causeway Bridge. I wanted some private time in my townhome; there still remained a lot for me to digest.

My interactions during my travels confirmed what my parents had tried to teach me all along: many of the best forms of personal creation evolve out of selflessness. And I was ultimately beginning to recognize the many dynamic powers contained within the codes of silence.

CHAPTER 10
Beyond the Andes

El que a buen arbol se arrima, buena sombra le cobija.

If you are near a good tree, good shadow will protect you.

Surrounding yourself with good people will bring you good luck.

Every month most airline pilots have an opportunity to bid a particular schedule. I wanted to travel to Santiago, Chile. To get on that route required a solid seniority number; trips to Santiago were a top choice for many of my peers. Normally schedules are awarded in order of a pilot's seniority. A pilot's years of service are critical because it determines the seat position (captain or first officer) and which aircraft they can select.

It is not uncommon to have a situation where a captain can have a lower seniority number than a first officer flying together on a particular pairing. This happens because the first officer remains in his position to keep a high seniority number. A high seniority within a rank allows for superior schedule, so one can more frequently enjoy certain days off. What it often boils down to is a quality of life decision, a tradeoff between earning more money and retaining good control over monthly assignments.

I want to point out that first officers (also referred to as co-pilots) are required to go through the same intense training as captains. They normally fly the airplane, take off and land as often as the captain; and in most cases are required to have the same level of skill and proficiency. By choice, I remain a first officer so I can better manage my yearly schedule. I never chased the money. Because of this sacrifice, I was ultimately able to fly to Chile and other destinations while maintaining a decent schedule.

* * *

At some point in 1997, a notice was issued that our Miami base would soon receive some new Boeing 777s. At the time, the 777 (Boeing triple seven) was a state-of-the-art jetliner; I was excited about any opportunity to fly a premier machine. It was clear the airline would utilize this larger jet to service most of the Deep South destinations. As I was currently flying the Boeing 757s and 767s, I swiftly entered my request to transfer to the new 777.

Within a short few months I was awarded the change of equipment. This entailed that I return to the Midwest training center for over a month. Just like my previous experiences, the school would encompass everything one needs to know when learning to fly a different aircraft type. The process consisted of computer-based and classroom training, written and oral exams, and guidance and testing in a simulator. Fortunately, my examination went well, and I had finally completed everything required to serve as a 777 first officer. The program is inherently stressful, as it's purposely designed to test one's abilities under a certain degree of pressure.

At this juncture I was exhausted and was more than ready to go home for a few days. I wanted to reconnect with the serenity of the ocean. Taking advantage of a warm summer evening, I found some quiet time on my small ocean master boat. The sun was waning as I was quietly drifting along the shoreline of Fort Lauderdale. The burdens of the training center now behind me, I had the opportunity to just kick back and float on the clear turquoise water.

A large sailboat came close to my side with its majestic white masts capturing the light easterly breeze. It was a ketch; its large main rectangular mast towered over the smaller mizzen mast directly to its rear. On its stern was an American flag, and the sound of it flapping carried across the surface. The waves gently rubbed my bow. I welcomed the solitude of the moment. With a warm breeze blowing off the ocean, I thought of the flag's connection to my freedom.

I thought of my dad's bravery and the sacrifices of so many that afforded me so many great opportunities. Thanks to exceptional men and women, I could experience countless extraordinary times knowing I was kept out of harm's way. My travels taught me that for too long, I had taken many items of luxury for granted. The flag waving in the wind reinforced that I shouldn't make the same mistake concerning my freedoms. Reflecting off the waves, its overpowering bright colors conveyed that I should never lose sight of how my liberties had been won. I knew I was in a special place and in a special country. The flag trailing the small mizzenmast of the passing ketch, the independent feeling that comes with sailing and boating on safe open waters, the sounds of clanging buoys pushed around by the strong currents brought home the very essence of what I owed to so many . . . and what it was truly like to feel so completely free.

As darkness began to set in, I entered the port of Fort Lauderdale. Docked alongside the Marriott hotel was a large yacht owned by one of the world's leading software companies. Its 007 design and sheer length was eye-catching. In the harbor, I placed my engine in neutral and sized up the solid dark hull. I couldn't help but notice the beauty and complexity of such a daunting machine. Large round and oval radars were mixed with different antennas mounted high atop the pilothouse. What other country in the world could ultimately give rise to such opportunity and wealth? Where else could the mind of a Bill Gates or Steve Jobs flourish? What other nation's freedoms, protections, possibilities and stability could lay the foundation for such amazing ingenuity? What nation has always been the pioneer in aviation?

While it is certainly true that brilliance stems from all corners of the globe, it's not by accident that so many transforming marvels were created right in our own backyard. And like the ketch's ability to sail free of harmful waters, their success, our success, is once again tied directly to the many who served and continue to serve our country. This blinding dedication preserves and has allowed for a creativity that has far outshone any other in the history of mankind. The combination of sacrifice and innovation allowed me to absorb the beauty of the Florida coast, and to pilot the jet of my dad's wildest dreams.

* * *

As luck would have it, my first trip out of training was to Santiago, Chile. As in my previous first-time travels, I had no preconceived notions about what to expect. I arrived at Miami Airport around 9 PM. I often tried to arrive early to enjoy some Cuban coffee. One's intake of Cuban coffee needs to be managed with care; if you're not accustomed to the drink, the effects can be potent. I have read articles explaining ways to better cope with graveyard shifts and to lessen the impacts of jet lag. Personally, I have made little progress in adjusting to either one. As strong as Cuban coffee can be, it's not a panacea for fooling one's body clock. We are just not meant to be awake all night and to constantly cross a multitude of time zones.

Soon after I finished my coffee, I met the captain and other first officer in the flight operations room. As required by FAA regulations, we take three or more pilots on longer flights to allow for alternating rest periods. Having reviewed the route, weather, maintenance issues, and numbers impacting the aircraft's performance, we began the walk to our Boeing 777.

The captain, Al, was a tall gentleman with a large frame. He was polite but he was somewhat regimented. Dressed well, his uniform was neatly pressed and his shoes shone from a new polish. All in all, he seemed like a decent person, and I was confident I could find a way to connect with him. The other first officer, Ray, had been called at the last moment; the scheduled pilot had likely fallen ill. Around my age, Ray was a short and stocky Latino. He was jovial and filled with a boatload of jokes. Totally the opposite of Captain Al, Ray's shirt was partially untucked, wrinkled . . . and his shoes? Well, let's just say they could have used a cleaning. I never met either of my coworkers before this flight but this was not uncommon. We met the flight attendants, some of whom were originally from Chile and fluent in Spanish. They were all quite polite, relaxed, and seemingly quiet.

After completing the normal preflight checklist, we were delayed due to severe weather just south of the airport. A few tropical storms that would likely pass. Obviously, we would not arrive in Santiago on time. The wait was rather lengthy but the passengers took it in stride. They were mostly relaxed, and didn't appear concerned about the delay. I often saw how anxious many from my own culture became at the slightest hint of an interruption. For the moment I brushed this comparison aside. But I didn't underestimate its importance.

The storms eventually passed, and we were cleared for takeoff. Destination: Santiago. The first part of the flight was routine, crossing over the many Caribbean countries and boundaries that had become familiar. Later, just south of Colombia, we entered a communications blind spot where we couldn't communicate with controllers for more than an hour. We would fly through more communications blackout areas as the night progressed. It's quite safe; there are simply sectors in the world where, due to several factors, pilots and controllers are unable to stay in touch.

While Ray was on his rest break, Al told me stories about his brief encounters with Albert Einstein. It wasn't every day you met someone who came in contact with an individual of that caliber. My colleague was like many others I would grow to know. He had an interesting history and some fascinating stories. On some of these long flights, I felt as if I were in a library receiving private tutoring from a variety of wise professors.

The highlight of the flight came as the sun began to rise. Although it was uncomfortable to have the sun directly in our eyes, especially after being awake most of the night, what lay below was truly spectacular. The Andes Mountains was another sight I had never before captured. The peaks and valleys were remarkable, the heights nothing short of astonishing. From our altitude, I could see snow covering many of the mountaintops with its white contrasting designs like those of a zebra. When the clouds allowed, I saw the sun's rays reflecting off parts of the peaks, highlighting the clarity of the layers of snow. What a fantastic painting, a true gift from nature that took my breath away. I could have circled for days, never growing tired of its indescribable diversity.

As our destination drew near, we contacted Santiago air traffic approach control and began our descent into the Chilean Airport. Similar to Lima Peru, Santiago has many high mountains close to the airport. Fortunately, the weather was good but it was not uncommon for problematic fog to form. When that happened, poor visibility required flights to divert to a different airport. Mendoza, Argentina, an airport close to Santiago, frequently served as a good alternate. When this situation occurred, it really made for a long night; while waiting for the fog in Santiago to lift, our plane would need to be serviced and refueled. A new route and flight plan would have to be filed, and all the procedures associated with the new flight would need to be reviewed.

This particular morning the fog did not develop. Both the approach and landing were routine. At first glance the terminal in Santiago appeared modestly modern. The shops were clean, well-lit and decorated, offering products ranging from perfumes to handbags. Mixed between the shops were cafes selling patties, juices and coffee. Although I didn't have an opportunity to explore any of the establishments, I could sense that Chile might be a reasonably developed country.

Chile, with its defining pencil shape, borders Argentina to the east, and Bolivia and Peru to the north. The Republic has a long and vast coastline that stretches nearly 2,700 miles from north to south along the Pacific Ocean. The supreme mountains of the Andes shelter the country along its eastern borders. And because of its long and narrow shape, the width only expands approximately 200 miles when traveling east to west. The Chilean economy has probably been the most stable of any in Latin America, containing a vast amount of copper and other precious minerals in its northern sectors.

After stopping at a cubicle and handing my passport to the customs agent, I followed a crewmember toward the airport exits. A corridor opened up to the outside, and I just continued to tag along. Off to my left a small van waited to take us to our hotel. The minivan was similar to the Volkswagen Kombi used for some of my prior transportations. The exterior was green, and I noticed a fair amount of rust around the passenger doors. The interior was a bit gloomy; it was damp enough that the wet seats required a towel. The driver was very young and wore a green buttoned-down army style vest. His brown pants were wrinkled and long enough that the hems continuously scraped the ground. Not exceedingly talkative, he offered to take my suitcase and place it in the trunk. Having inspected the general condition of the van, I reluctantly stepped inside.

Initially the drive took us past several small farms with horses and livestock. The farmland scenery was nice, with lots of tall green grass parallel to the road. Comprising of two opposite direction lanes, the paved path was narrow. To pass a vehicle, you had to accelerate into the oncoming lane.

This maneuver was not simple, especially when you're in a vehicle that doesn't exactly have much horsepower. It's not uncommon to try to pass more than one vehicle, making the experience tricky.

The first time we crawled by a car my heart raced. Our weaving in and out of the opposite lane was a scene out of a horror movie. I thought that I wasn't getting paid to be a stunt man. This made my taxi ride in Lima seem mundane. The driver was calm and completely unfazed by even the large trucks heading directly for our van. It was as if we were playing a game of chicken. Privately gripped in fear, I prayed to arrive at the hotel alive.

During the rather insane ride, the driver acted as a tour guide. The quiet and reserved guy seemed to open up a much more personable side. His quiet manner at the outset had been deceiving. In reality he was quite kind, talkative, and cared a great deal about making sure we enjoyed our stay. But the truth was I had my hands on my lap and was gripping my legs. I just wanted to be done with this phase of the journey. I was shaking and laughing to myself in the back, just laughing about how routine this terrifying ride was to our subdued driver. How naïve of me to think the driving experience in Miami was ever dangerous.

When the doors of the van finally opened, my heart was still racing. I was the first to exit. As I walked to the rear of the Kombi, I felt like kissing the ground. The driver gave me a look as if to say, "Hey, what's your problem?" My expressions of relief might have been overly apparent. While handing over a tip, I shook his hand and told myself it was a fee for a different brand of roller coaster ride.

As I entered the hotel lobby I muttered, "And people think flying isn't safe?"

Over time, I would adapt to a very different driving culture.

The hotel was a tall building in front of a busy two-way avenue. A great deal of traffic carried more busses than anyone could imagine; so many that at times it appeared like they were attached. Owning a car is a luxury in South America, and large parts of the population rely on buses for transportation. The street was noisy but after my experience in Lima I had become more accustomed to that sort of distraction. The hotel seemed fine; the lobby and front desk had a rather bland design. Speaking with a soft Spanish accent, the clerks greeted us warmly. Dressed in suits, they were disciplined and provided exceptional service. Our introduction was friendly, and I looked forward to some rest after a long night in the skies.

Like the lobby, my room did not carry any special décor. The carpet was light brown and visibly worn. The bed was fair, marginally comfortable, and the bathroom rather typical. One small bar of soap rested by the sink, and a minimum assortment of ordinary white towels was on offer. But it wasn't a bad place; it was clean and had a bird's-eye view of the busy avenue. After several hours of quality rest, I showered to jumpstart some energy.

Seemed like a nice day, so with much anticipation, it was time to explore. At the front desk I asked for a map of the city but unfortunately none were available. The concierge then mentioned a nearby metro station, and that the trains traveled through several neighborhoods. As I was eager to see parts of the city, I took his advice and walked down a flight of stairs towards the platform. After a short wait, a train roared through the tunnel. I boarded a car and rode about six stops. The trains and stations were quite safe, clean and comfortable. Because the morning rush hour had passed, the short commute was mostly absent any crowds. Eventually I got used to the system, and I found it a convenient way to travel throughout the city.

A short walk up the stairs from my stop, I found myself in a rather nice area. Enjoying the morning's breeze, people were dressed casually in a variety of lightweight clothing, I walked past a small park fitted with a few wooden benches and noticed several couples passionately kissing. Apparently, my presence was not the least bit distracting. This same outward show of affection occurred at other parks in close proximity to our hotel. It seemed the Chilean ladies loved to kiss and were quite comfortable openly acting out their feelings. This public display was refreshing, and it appeared to be readily accepted within the culture.

Lunchtime was approaching, and the area was busy and alive. I stepped into several places to get a gauge on which restaurants seemed popular. Noticing many people dressed in business attire, I followed a small group into a place with a large buffet. Apparently, I was in the midst of a financial district. The restaurant was two stories high, and the corridors were narrow enough to make maneuvering difficult. Fortunate to have found an empty seat on the second level, I eased my way into a long line and selected from an assortment of appetizers. The trays offered a variety of cold meats, vegetables, broiled fish and chicken. There was also a separate island displaying a decent assortment of salads.

After filling my plate with mostly rice and fish, I walked back to my small table and relaxed. I sensed the people surrounding me knew I was American, and some of them looked at me curiously as if wondering if I was lost. A well-dressed middle-age woman approached and asked where I was from. She wore a bright yellow shirt accompanied by black slacks and high heels. Her dark black hair was short, and her nails displayed a perfect French manicure. As it turned out, she had been educated as an engineer in the States. Upon completion of her degree, she returned to her native city of Santiago. Her name was Marina, and she was now working for a large multinational company.

Marina emphatically explained her attachment to Santiago, and said she wouldn't think of living anywhere else. She was in her mid-fifties and had an astonishing command of the English language. We talked for some time, and she told me how much she adored the people, cafes and restaurants. She was delighted to describe her travels to the mountains and beaches. As a skier, Marina portrayed the slopes as beautiful and challenging. She talked of the snow and its formations between the tall trees. Even during the summer, she loved hiking the trails while anticipating the echoes of numerous birds. She portrayed what it really felt like to absorb the stillness of the forest during sunset.

Apparently, Marina had not been in the States for a long time, so she was curious to hear any American news. We talked for a bit longer, and afterwards we stayed in contact via postcards. A later year her company transferred her unwillingly to Europe. They were eliminating several positions and left her little choice. When I last saw her, she wished me luck with my future stays in Santiago and offered prayers for my safe return back home.

Alone again in the restaurant, I summoned a waiter for a cup of coffee. Behind me was a group in which everyone seemed to know each other. They were dressed in business apparel, and I was curious whether anyone spoke English. It reminded me of the five people I'd met that day in Lima. Again, I was in luck, as one of the younger ladies and her gentleman companion were both proficient in my native language.

Julia, a woman in her late twenties with long blonde hair, wore brown pants and low black shoes. Estefan was in his forties and wore a grey business suit. Searching for a quick conversation starter, I asked if they were enjoying their food. At first, they seemed a bit reluctant to engage in a conversation. I had the feeling they wanted to be polite but at the same time wanted to keep some distance. After several minutes I was fortunate enough to have gained their trust.

We talked for a short time about our respective countries, their company, and about their immediate concerns. They both specialized in computer programming, and mentioned that this particular skill was very much in demand. Appearing somewhat short on time, Estefan handed me a business card and mentioned that the entire group worked for a nearby company. He asked me to call the next time I was in Santiago so I could again meet with the group for lunch. I thanked everyone for their hospitality. Embarrassingly I somehow managed to lose his card, and upon returning to the same cafeteria I could never find either Estefan or Julia. I was saddened and careless. No doubt I had squandered a special opportunity.

Upon finishing three cups of coffee, I was wired and gained a second wind. Continuing on my walk, I quickly passed through a somewhat modern shopping mall. The quality of goods on display was similar to what I would find back home. At the moment, I just wasn't in the mood to shop. Wanting to spend more time outside, my stroll took me in the direction of the hotel. Eventually I stumbled upon a long path that paralleled a winding river. The water was muddy and shallow but its natural beauty enhanced the scenery that surrounded the neighborhoods parks.My first contacts with the Chilean people indicated that they seemed more cautious than the other cultures I had recently experienced. Though somewhat reserved, the people I had met so far were polite and educated.

After completing a long walk, I returned to our hotel's lobby. Over in the lounge was a couple holding several cases of luggage. They had an interesting piece of baggage. Seemingly out of place, it was a large cage that contained two small birds of yellow and green coloring. Even from a short distance, I noticed the birds never left each other's side, which I had never seen before. When one bird moved, the other moved right alongside as if they were attached.

Slowly, I drew myself a few steps toward the lounge to get a closer glimpse of the birds. I couldn't resist asking the owners what type of birds they were. Speaking in a broken English, the lady first told me that she and her husband were from the northern part of Chile; they were staying in Santiago for business. Carolina told me they would never leave their birds at home alone. I mentioned that I found their close attachment interesting. Laughing, she told me they were Chilean love birds and that they were truly committed to each other. At first, I thought she was playing a joke on me but then I felt she was telling me the truth.

As it turned out, there is such a thing as Chilean lovebirds. It was great just watching them interact, each one knowing what the other expected. The couple, also well-dressed and seemingly educated, chatted with me for a moment. Roberto, in his forties, was clean cut and even had cufflinks on the sleeves of his white tapered shirt. He was tall and maintained an almost perfect posture. Carolina was much shorter, and wore a light blue dress designed with horses. She was quite talkative. Wishing them all the best on their business trip, I moved toward the elevators. Carolina asked if I could join her and her husband for dinner. Without hesitation I accepted her offer. I had secretly hoped to spend more time with them; this was their country, and it was likely they would know of a good place to dine.

We agreed to meet at 10 PM in the lobby, as it's common for people in South America to eat late. The evening was rapidly approaching, and after a few hours of sleep and a relaxing shower, I was ready for a night out. Meeting promptly downstairs, the couple asked me if I would enjoy seafood. I answered with a positive yes, and they had a place already picked out. Carolina, with her short brunette hair, was wearing a long white dress and a pair of brown cowgirl style boots. Around her neck was a gold and silver pendant of an eagle. Roberto was dressed casually; he wore blue corduroy pants along with a white long-sleeve polo shirt. He wore a pair of short beige cowboy boots.

Outside of our hotel, a doorman wearing a red coat with gold buttons hailed us a taxi. My escorts gave the driver the address, and it wasn't long before I found myself in a stadium-like atmosphere. The restaurant, *Aqui Está Coco,* was overflowing with people. Large groups stood around and a long line extended from the entrance to around the block. The entrance had a palatial appearance and I gathered I was about to experience a popular and historic place. People of all ages were there along with families and couples who were neatly dressed.

Noticing that I was a foreigner, the host asked if I would like a tour. I couldn't remember ever having a tour of a restaurant before. My answer was a reluctant, "Sure," and with the blessing of my laughing hosts, I was escorted through the establishment. Following the young lady, I was led down a flight of stairs as if I was entering a large cave. The décor was perfectly lit with brick walls decorated with various cultural paintings. Couples were closely seated enjoying wine and sharing their affection. Thick candles on the tables shone on the bottles of wine and the elegantly styled glasses. The atmosphere was hypnotizing and lulled people into their most romantic feelings. I passed by many tables filled with an unbelievable variety of specialty dishes. The smells made me impatient, as I wanted to immediately partake in the dining experience. Not overpowering, the garlic, cooked wine, and spices flowed perfectly through the air. Apparently, I was in the midst of a place renowned for its diversity of seafood.

The hostess was gracious, and asked if I had enjoyed my private journey. I nodded my head and thanked her for such personalized treatment. She then returned me to my friends. Finally, we were seated, and I couldn't wait to order. Our table was of medium size and had a white tablecloth draped over the top. My good sense told me to let the couple do the ordering. It took them about two minutes to make a selection, and they did so with a great deal of confidence.

While waiting, we enjoyed some mellow Chilean wine. I was curious about how they had arrived in Santiago and the effect the transportation had on the lovebirds. Roberto told me they traveled a long distance from the north in a large SUV; it was currently parked in a garage adjacent to the hotel. Apparently, the birds faired quite well during the journey and were not intimidated by the traffic. He chuckled and made a point of telling me the birds could never survive in the cargo bin of an airplane. Since Carolina was so attached to the pair, flying has simply been eliminated.

I wanted to know more about their work and community. With both of them offering enthusiastic descriptions, it became clear they were both ranchers. They owned large acres of farmland and were in the business of raising cattle and horses. Most of their excitement, especially Carolina's, centered on the stallions. She had two favorites and bragged of her love of caring for them. Roberto was more pragmatic as he stressed the responsibilities of owning such a large piece of property; he talked of the costs of feed and the amount of hours required to run such a business. From what I understood, they lived in a sparsely populated area and were surrounded by dirt roads and green acreage. Although not an easy life, they both truly enjoyed their seclusion and attachments to their animals.

Complementing the cattle, horses, and lovebirds were several sheepdogs, roosters and chickens. I could only picture the complexities attached to taking care of all that agricultural and livestock stuff on a daily basis. Since I was born and raised in a major city, any sort of farm talk always captured my imagination. I asked if they had any help with the chores. I was met with a quick "of course," as they employed a husband and wife team as full-time workers. The couple lived in a small home attached to a barn and were instrumental in relieving many of the daily work-related stresses.

With our waiter approaching, the conversation shifted back to the dinner. Proudly the lady explained that Chile was famous for its seafood restaurants, and in their opinion this was one of the best in Santiago. All the seafood that touched my palate that evening was fit for a king. The appetizers consisted of freshly breaded crabmeat sautéed in a fish broth. The meat melted in my mouth and the taste was nothing short of outstanding. Two separate fish entrees followed the appetizers; one was a baked red snapper dressed with lightly fried calamari, the other was codfish served in a wine sauce stuffed with wild rice. They both were cooked to perfection, and I can't say I would ever be able to duplicate their incredible flavors.

The couple was elated that I was enjoying their selections. Lasting for hours, the ambiance combined with the excellent dishes exemplified what dining was all about. The evening was super, and after a great meal I suggested we walk before taking a taxi. According to the couple the neighborhood was safe, so we went for a midnight stroll. The streets were mostly quiet but some police were out carrying machineguns across their backs. Like the police in Peru, the officers appeared to be very young. I doubted if they were a day older than twenty. I asked my new friends about the need for the police to carry such advanced firearms. They nonchalantly replied that this type of weaponry was common amongst the authorities.

I remembered the history surrounding General Pinochet, and the US involvement in the military coupe. That dark period consisted of pain and suffering for the people of Chile. Then it dawned on me; this history might explain why the people in the group had been hesitant to talk with me. Gathering my thoughts, I got the courage to ask my hosts.

They confirmed that Americans were not exactly held in the highest esteem, and because of the agony of the era, it would require time to heal the many wounds. This probably explained some of the reasons why others approached me with a certain level of caution and apprehension. Yet I never felt any animosity from either of the couple; on the contrary, I was treated as if they considered me a close friend. I was finding the Chilean people to be welcoming and humble. Understandably, it just took a bit of time for them to feel comfortable with an American.

It was getting late, so Roberto suggested we catch a taxi back to the hotel. It wasn't difficult to find a cab, and so we quickly arrived in front of the hotel's canopy. The evening was great, and I was sad to see my friends depart. They both were remarkably wonderful people, and I hoped that one day I would have the opportunity to extend the same kindness and consideration they had offered me. Because they didn't reside near Santiago, I felt that our paths might not cross again. I wrote to both Carolina and Roberto, and received some letters back. But admittedly over time the correspondences slowed. For me, it was a night to remember. And of course, I also wished the lovebirds safe travels.

The new day came fast, and I was up bright and early. I hadn't slept well and kept thinking about my fantastic night. It was a dreary morning with an overcast sky and a light rain, a good opportunity for breakfast. A small cafe close to the hotel was known to open early. I sat at the counter and ordered scrambled eggs and coffee. One very noticeable thing about this café: the waitresses were beautiful! They wore short skirts that enhanced the ordinary breakfast atmosphere. Frankly they were so gorgeous I could barely focus on my food. I wasn't alone in my inability to concentrate; plenty of men starting their day's work overly enjoyed the ladies' personal attention. Let's just say the morning's meal more than exceeded my expectations.

It then began to rain hard. Drenched, I returned to the hotel and hurried up to my room to dry off. When a lull came in the downpour, I returned downstairs to a store selling a variety of newspapers and magazines. All the periodicals were in Spanish but I wasn't deterred; on the contrary, I specifically wanted a traditional Chilean magazine to get a flavor of current events. I thought this could help me to learn about the city's culture.

While the writing was in a foreign language, I still found it useful to get a pulse on what affected the local population. I always thought it important to find out what really mattered to the locals to make conversation possible. Knowledge is key for making icebreakers a success. The rain was again heavy, so I purchased a few periodicals and wrapped them in plastic. I hustled back to the hotel and arrived soaked. I would take the magazines to the airport and ask our employees to help me in understanding some of the highlighted stories.

Before leaving for another night over the Andes, I felt like getting in a condensed workout. I was told there was a small fitness room on a high floor. The gym equipment was old, rusted, and not well maintained. Nevertheless, it was sufficient to accomplish what I needed. It felt good to activate the endorphins before traveling all night.

The evening rolled around and our crew met in front of the hotel. Apparently, everyone had enjoyed their time in Santiago, and on the ride, I listened to many uplifting stories. The drive returning to the airport was as nerve-wracking as it had been going to the hotel. Who would ever admit that the most dangerous part of our trip would be the van ride to and from the layover hotel? Standing in front of the terminal, I felt my hands shaking. I was elated to be out of that flimsy contraption and headed toward my nice luxurious jet!

I hastily tipped the driver, and the captain Ray and I went first to enjoy a cup of coffee. We had long night ahead of us. The airport had plenty of places for warm drinks, pastry, or just some light sandwiches. After reviewing all the required papers associated with our flight back to Miami, we reinforced our awareness of the high terrain near the airport in case anything went wrong and we needed to return to Santiago.

Our takeoff was uneventful. Upon reaching our cruise altitude, I reflected on how fortunate I was to have had the opportunity to experience so many faraway places. Many people never have a chance to venture far from their neighborhoods. So many new interactions were coming at me in a short time.

I traded jokes and tales with Ray as it was the captain's time to rest. It was a clear night, and we experienced a brief period of turbulence as we approached the equator. After Havana Center handed us over to the Miami controllers, we knew it wouldn't be long before we would land. I called the lead flight attendant and asked her to wake up our commander for the approach. I could see the glow of the downtown buildings from a distance. Well rested, Al arrived and took control of the plane. He greased the wheels on the runway and followed the taxiway lights back to our parking area.

I often used my drive home in my little black Mazda as a time for reflection. The morning offered a perfect time for me to gather my thoughts while my retention remained fresh. Now I was back again in my own country and my own familiar settings. The predawn hour and the cultural comparisons allowed me to reinforce some observations. I was always able to relax on my drive home.

I retained the lion's share of every moment of my trip, even miniscule ones. It seemed this storage was becoming more deliberate but I still couldn't explain why. And I was taking more notice not only of my trips but also of the environment within my neighborhood. I enjoyed the contrast of my experiences in South America to those in the United States. With each step, I felt the people of South America to be genuine. The South Americans were able to adapt and enjoy life to its fullest with fewer if any luxuries. Undoubtedly, I had more investigating to accomplish but their formula for living, as far as I could tell, seemed at odds with a wide variety of what I had grown to accept. Even casual conversations were becoming easier to ignite with people whose primary language wasn't even my own.

I parked my car in front of my townhome and left the engine running for a few minutes. I just sat in the low seat and thought about the city of Santiago. How it was filled with positive energy, eccentric restaurants, and a distinctively romantic aura. The people were generous and always willing to help. I found the Chileans to be exceptionally warm and outgoing despite my country's controversial involvement in their past political affairs. If the people of Chile could forgive and move beyond such a history of injustice, then why did there remain so much polarization within the confines of my own culture? It was just another thought that came to me out of left field, another small piece to fit into my ever-changing personal puzzle. I turned off the ignition and steadily walked up my stairs. Like any good recipe, I just wanted to let things settle for a while. As my Trinidadian thoughts dictated, it was a good time to unwind and take a step back.

CHAPTER 11
Midnight in Recoleta

Sin calles ni atardeceres de Buenos Aires, no puede escribirse un Tango.

Without the streets or dusks of Buenos Aires, a tango cannot be written. —Jorge Borges

Although I enjoyed returning to the places I had already visited, I had a stronger urge to fly to new destinations. My company only served a limited number of places in South America. Upon hearing so many positive comments about Argentina, I placed myself on a request to fly to Buenos Aires. After several days my computer alerted me that I had been awarded a trip to Argentina.

I met Captain Dave Dryer for my usual pre-all-night coffee jolt at the Miami airport cafe Versailles. I was a bit subdued because my good friend was getting ever so close to his retirement. At the time, one was not allowed to fly for a US airline past the age of sixty. The time for my partner in crime to leave drew closer by the day. Admittedly, I was anxious about his departure. I was masking my sadness and trying my best to make the best of the inevitable reality.

The Cuban coffee electrified my system. The Miami evening was beautiful with a full moon and a crystal-clear sky. A full moon lights up the sky and often helps us see storms that might otherwise be masked by the darkness.

Meeting in operations, Dave and I, along with the other pilot Mike agreed that the flight papers were in proper order. We made our way down the concourse to gate F-8 where our Boeing 777 was parked. Mike was a tall Latino, even taller than Dave. He was slender, handsome, and a magnet for the ladies. Relaxed and with good sense of humor, I found him very easy to get along with. After completing the required checks of the aircraft systems, we were ready for pushback and taxi.

The flight attendants were the normal diverse group. They were a mix of American and Latin backgrounds with some fluent in Spanish. All were quite nice, and treated Dave, Mike and me quite well. The airport traffic was lighter than normal, helping expedite our taxi time to the departure runway. We were number one in sequence for takeoff and were airborne in just a few short minutes. Because of the unrestricted visibility complimented by the moon, Miami's skylight was in plain view. The different blue and white lights emanating from the skyscrapers made for a magnificent photo. On a clear night, the reflections of buildings towering over Biscayne Bay decorate the water.

An hour into our assigned cruise altitude, Dave and I talked about his family, our company, fishing, and other assorted subjects. The full moon lit up the islands of the Caribbean. With its special glow, a full moon can place a unique shine on the scattered clouds and open terrain. From our altitude, the reflection drew the islands much closer than they actually were. Highlighting the special treasures of the islands was this powerful yet subtle radiance. At night and out of reach, I was always drawn to the mysteries of the Caribbean.

During the early morning hours, I was alone in the cockpit with Captain Davie. The other pilot was in the cabin taking the first of three rest breaks. At three o'clock in the morning, Davie appeared concerned. Somewhat startled, my initial thought was that something was wrong with the airplane. Davie forcefully patted his shirt. In a tired and crackled voice he proclaimed, "Doug, I can't find my glasses, I can't find my glasses."

Gathering my thoughts, I stared at him for about thirty seconds until he regained his composure. Then I calmly broke the news. "Davie, those glasses," I paused. "You're wearing them."

There was a moment of silence before he answered in typical Captain Dryer fashion, "Oh, okay."

At that moment the air controllers were trying to contact us to pass on a new radio frequency. I was laughing so hard it took me an extended period of time to finally acknowledge their transmission. I looked over to Davie and joked, "Oh, those tricky glasses. How could they have been so elusive?" The flight continued without further emergencies but my laughter wouldn't abate for a long time.

The remainder of the flight was routine. We enjoyed our crew meals and completed our rest breaks. After more than nine hours we were finally within striking distance of Buenos Aires. Soon the Cordoba air traffic controllers would guide us to the final approach into the Buenos Aires Ezeiza International Airport. While descending, I could see a great deal of open green farmland. I could even discern livestock wandering about in various lots. The Argentine landscape was vast, consisting of farms for as far as the eye could see. The boundless greenery was beautiful and reminded me of the heartland of America. I was amazed by the bright clarity of the contrasting greens. Ranches were boarded by perfectly defined dirt roads; at times I envisioned the countryside as one giant colorful chessboard.

Located in Southern South America, Argentina mostly sits alongside Chile to its west, and borders Bolivia and Paraguay to the North. To its northeast are parts that touch Brazil, and to its east it borders Uruguay and the cold South Atlantic Ocean. Argentina has over the years developed a large industrial, manufacturing and agricultural base, and remains one of the world's leading exporters of beef. For a long time, I anxiously awaited to see what life was like in the streets of its largest city.

With the airport clearly in view from several miles out, the tower controller issued our landing clearance. We touched down on the Ezeiza runway on schedule and taxied to our assigned gate. Once we had passed through customs, the terminal opened up to a wide area that led outside. Small stores, cafes and kiosks surrounded the extensive area. Before exiting, we worked our way past crowds of family members waiting to embrace loved ones. A small Mercedes Benz van waited outside to take us to the downtown hotel. The young driver, dressed in black slacks and a brown cowhide jacket, placed our bags in the back. The outside air was much colder than anything I had previously experienced in South America. I hadn't anticipated this low temperature, and the wind added to the chill. For the moment, I would simply have to make do with my light jacket.

The drive was quite tranquil compared to my earlier transportation experience in Santiago. We passed many small farms and communities. I finally had a close-up view of parts of the beautiful chessboard. The farms were well-manicured, and groups of cattle grazed behind white picket fences. Leaving a toll plaza, the drive transferred onto a highway that funneled into the heart of Buenos Aires. The highway passed many buildings, and some of the neighborhoods were a bit run down. In all fairness, because of our proximity, it was difficult to tell in any detail the true condition of the structures. The highway was well offset from the various neighborhoods, and we were traveling at a relatively high speed.

As we approached the area near our hotel, the neighborhood seemed to improve. We arrived at the hotel lobby about an hour after we landed. The Sheraton was an upscale hotel with a large modern lobby and several shops scattered throughout the main level. The floors were of spotless beige marble, and brown and black designs had been perfectly etched into the tiling. The clarity of the main floor windows was such that they appeared almost invisible.

One level up was a narrow glass corridor that led to a contemporary health club. I peered inside and saw a small indoor pool that was overshadowed by a much larger pool outside; both were pristine. The outdoor pool's blue tiles made it glisten in the morning's bright sun. The gym's treadmills faced the pool, so one could people watch during any virtual run. Because of the cold temperatures, the pool area was mostly empty. The gym had a wide selection of cardio machines and free-weights. Lighting up the interior were large bordered windows installed on the ceilings, making for a remarkable skylight. The gym even employed personal trainers responsible for individual instructions for paying members. Also attached to the club was a large terrace with a view of the surrounding neighborhood.

The employees at the front desk greeted our crew with enthusiasm. After assigning our rooms, they directed us to the correct towers. I pressed the button on one of the elevators and waited for the large stainless-steel doors to open. Davie and I agreed to meet in a few hours for a late breakfast while Mike chose to catch a good day's rest. Situated across from the hotel was a park with an old bell tower built out of stone. The tower was close to one side of the hotel, the side I happened to be facing.

Once in my room, I brushed my teeth and crawled into bed. About thirty minutes into a deep sleep, I was awoken by an odd noise. I was groggy and began squinting while trying to figure out the source of the sound. Then my focus was drawn toward the foot of my bed. And there it was, a bat, sitting on the edge flapping its boney wings! Pointing directly at me were a pair of rat-like ears and dark, beady eyes. Initially I thought it was just a dream but then reality took hold. The Halloween image sent a chill up my spine.

For a moment I was paralyzed. And then . . . all I can tell you is I never knew just how fast one could transition from a bed into a hallway. I darted out of my room in Olympic time. With the door now open, out came the bat, wings spread, loyally following me down the hallway. His flying skills were far superior to my own. There I was, a grown man in the middle of some hotel hall wearing only a pair of underwear. Watching the entire fiasco was an older lady who quickly went back into her room and hastily bolted her door. The episode, starring the bat, must have scared the hell out of her.

Embarrassed, I went back into my room and put on some clothing. With my adrenalin still pumping, I went banging on Dave's door. He was on the same floor and only a few rooms away. Startled and half-dressed, he reluctantly unfastened his lock, stepped out and calmly asked, "Aren't you very early for our meeting?"

I told him I had been chased out of my room by a prehistoric bird, which gave him quite the laugh. Shaking his head, he suggested that I try to get another room. I facetiously replied, "No kidding," and I told him I would call when I was resettled. To level the score, as I turned away I asked about the whereabouts of his glasses. Of course, he slammed the door. I didn't have a clue of just how to explain this event to the hotel personnel on the phone, so I went downstairs and searched for a representative.

Finding an impeccably dressed concierge, I described what had happened. To my surprise, his reaction was completely nonchalant. He seemed quite familiar with the bat complaint. He calmly explained that bats congregated in the tall bell tower outside my window. If my window was even fractionally open, a bat would find its way into the room. Apparently, a bat can make itself quite portable to squeeze through almost any tiny opening. Almost invisible, they would silently hang on the curtain rods. Their color blended perfectly with the drapes.

Whatever the case, I wanted out of that room. Without hesitation, he agreed to switch my room to a section on the

other side of the hotel. For certain I was obviously not interested in anything that faced the bell tower. I never considered
myself to fear change, and in this case, fear quickly drove me
to change. No cardio exercise was necessary for the rest of
this layover.

The entire bat episode reminded me of a trip I had flown
one afternoon out of the Philadelphia International Airport.
The captain Steve and I were in the cockpit of a Boeing 757
while the passengers were boarding. Our destination was
Chicago's O'Hare international airport. While still parked at
the gate, a flight attendant entered the cockpit and mentioned
that an unclaimed piece of luggage was located in the first
row's overhead compartment. At the moment the problem
didn't strike me as being of much concern.

I got up to check it out. The luggage resembled a bowling
bag. I thought okay, I'll just open it up and take a quick look
inside to reassure the flight attendant that everything was
perfectly safe. With the eyes of every passenger glued to me,
I placed it on the floor. Then I calmly unzipped the bag. No
more than a nanosecond later, a large black snake, obviously upset, raised its scaly head. His flat-ironed skull, blinking
eyes, and thin tongue became quickly focused on my nose.

Just as during the bat incident, I momentarily froze. Then,
in full view, I ran like a track star off the plane. Suffice it to
say my expeditious retreat was quite embarrassing, and the
removal of that unhappy passenger was left up to the local
authorities. With a bit of coaxing, I swallowed my pride and
returned to the cockpit. I'll never forget that delightful afternoon at the airport in the city of brotherly love.

Time quickly passed, and with little sleep, I called the still
chuckling Captain Davie. I threw on another pair of jeans and
went down to the lobby. Dave was hungry and was anxious
to get something to eat. Because it was so cold outside, I wanted to purchase something to keep me warm. We walked to
Avenida Florida, a famous part of Buenos Aires that is quite
extensive. Within the avenue are rows of attached stores that

are packed with shoppers as soon as they open. We entered a shop with a good selection of winter clothing. The number of jackets and sweatshirts on display was mesmerizing.

I wasn't looking for anything special; an ordinary sweater would suffice. Quickly, I selected a red wool sweater of decent quality. The saleslady was quiet, and basically standoffish; nevertheless, I was happy wear something warm. The payment was only a few dollars, and then we continued the hunt for a place to eat. A strong wind whipped around us. My new sweater did the trick, as I was comfortable and shielded from the cold. My lightweight Floridian clothing was no match for the winter-like temperature.

Several eating establishments were spread throughout the area. Dave was the boss, and since I had never been to this city, I couldn't really make any recommendations. He chose a rather large place on a busy corner. It turned out to be a good choice. Large windows shielded the café on all sides. Our table offered an unrestricted view of an active intersection. We sat and watched how people dressed and interacted.

Numerous men wore business suits; their ties were blown back over their shoulders. Others were bundled up in long pants, sweaters, and leather jackets. Argentina is world renowned for its fine leather materials, especially coats. The quality and the designs are capturing. Several shops in the area specialized in leather goods. Crewmembers often purchased hand-tailored jackets for their distinctive quality. The styles seemed to be a mix of what I had seen in Venezuela, Chile, and back home. The attire was low key, yet proper.

The morning's chill was obviously expediting people's pace; they were forced to cope with some punishing gusts of wind. Dave was happy, as he could now eat and enjoy a late-morning beer. Displaying little emotion, a tall waiter with a thick mustache came to take our order. He seemed very matter of fact, and I struggled with my mediocre Spanish attempting to order correctly. As a backup, I pointed to some of the choices on the menu. Fingers crossed, we waited for what we believed to have selected: ham and cheese sandwiches with a side of French fries. By sheer luck, that is exactly what arrived.

Fortunately, the simple meal proved to be more than sufficient. Dave and I didn't do much talking that morning as we were both still recovering from the all-night flight. He was still ribbing me about my trials and tribulations with the damn bat, even suggesting that I should investigate moving into the bell tower! He really got a kick over my almost naked exposure in the hall, and even accused me of chasing after the elderly lady. I took it all in stride as I knew he was just messing with me!

Our restaurant was crowded, and there was plenty of conversation to be heard. Although the place did not have a special décor, the atmosphere was fueled with the chatter and laughter of customers. The upbeat mood of the people lifted the restaurant out of being just another ordinary dining experience. Once again, the atmosphere was lighter than what I would normally find at home both in terms of the pace and the temperament of the people. The dining experience was geared toward fun, companionship, and relaxation. Our appetites satisfied, we paid the check and explored different shops. After about an hour we both surrendered to the biting cold and briskly strolled back to the hotel. We agreed to meet later in the evening for dinner.

When I arrived in my room I got a second wind and wanted to do more sightseeing. I put on a warmer pair of socks and was now better prepared to combat the chill. Close by was the well-known neighborhood of Puerto Madero. The community was situated along a waterway with some interesting ships docked alongside the riverbanks. Some resembled old pirate ships, similar to what I had seen at the port in Trinidad. They had tall masts with large rectangular white sails. Tied to the docks with thick worn ropes, their wooded hulls squeaked as they rubbed against the concrete walls.

When I went close to the side, I could smell the mildew of the cabins, their odor transmitting decades of their connec-

ne seas. Protruding over the river was a bridge con-
bright white concrete and steel cables; it reminded
_ _ _niature version of San Francisco's famous Golden
Gate. Its design was unique, as the combination of the solid
material and cables took on the shape of a large modern harp.
The river had several restaurants located on one bank of the
waterway. I thought of this as "restaurant row" because the
sequence of eateries extended for several city blocks.

The area was constantly alive with people. The views offered by the river only complimented any dining experience.
Superb meat and seafood dishes were offered in countless
restaurants; cafes, bars, steak houses, seafood, Italian, and
Japanese restaurants lined the riverfront. Looking through
some of the windows, I saw brick ovens slowly cooking a
variety of meats pierced on skewers. Later I would frequent
many of these bistros and unwind while watching boats pass
in the night. The combination of extraordinary food, passing
boats, and lively conversation all made for fun and memorable times.

Eventually my company would switch our hotel to the
Hilton situated in the heart of Puerto Madero. The change
ultimately placed the river and all of the fun establishments
right in our own backyard.

Having walked a long distance, I was tired and thought
it time to return to my room. So far, I really was enjoying
Buenos Aires; along with its friendly people, the city seemed
both interesting and exciting. I looked forward to a late afternoon's rest. My medium-sized room was clean and comfortable. The two queen beds were covered in soft cotton sheets.
Although the television was modern, I didn't have any real
interest. There was too much on my mind, and a lot remained
for me to see in the nearby neighborhoods. As I was on a high
floor, I had a good view of a wide avenue with an endless
array of small cars making their way toward the center of the
city. The bathroom had shiny tiles and the décor had a Euro-

pean flavor. Modern polished faucets complimented beautiful towels etched with floral designs.

Even though my room offered plenty of comfort, I remained a bit restless. I had trouble trying to sleep and periodically opened my eyes to make sure the coast was clear; I was still haunted by the bat. Eventually I rested. Hours later, trying to wake, I splashed some cold water on my face. After a quick shower, I was ready to meet Dave in the lobby. We tried to locate Mike but it seemed he might have made other plans. Dave asked the concierge to recommend a good steak house. Buenos Aires is famous for having some of the world's finest steak restaurants.

The concierge suggested El Establo, which was within walking distance. We strolled over and waited inside to be seated. The restaurant seemed old and possibly historic. On the walls were paintings of bulls, mountains, and Argentine landmarks; the flooring was black and white tile. The large windows that encased the eatery were partially draped by white curtains. Formally dressed in a fitted jacket, the maître d escorted us to a large table. Our waiter wore a white button-down tapered shirt with a black bow tie. With his help, we ordered the house specialty, steak and potatoes.

While waiting we enjoyed some smooth and dry red Argentine wine. Several large families were seated throughout the restaurant. The waiter said the families included parents and children, cousins, aunts, uncles and grandparents. I saw that same phenomenon during my stays in Peru, Brazil and Chile but did not yet recognize its implication. It wasn't often that I saw an entire family unit dining together in my own country. In fact, I couldn't remember the last time I had seen that type of gathering back home. In South America, these large reunions seemed somewhat commonplace. I began to realize there might be some lessons in these close family ties.

Our meal arrived, and with my first bite I could taste this experience was going to be a home run. My steak cut as if it were a bar of butter. The seasoning and flavor were nothing short of remarkable. I can't remember eating a steak that literally melted in my mouth. Freshly prepared and sprinkled with salt, the potatoes had been baked to a perfect crisp. Remembering my dinner in Santiago, I again felt as if I were eating a meal fit for a king. The atmosphere was more subdued and it was rather easy to decipher nearby chatter. A few tables over some young children played with their grandparents; constantly giggling, they took turns hiding underneath an extended bench.

Dave and I spent hours savoring the exceptional combination of food and wine. We agreed it was certainly a place worth frequenting. Because of his nature, Davie insisted upon paying the bill. Despite my battle, he remained determined and I eventually surrendered to his unparalleled kindness.

It was eleven o'clock in the evening, and we both chose to walk off our meal. We went over to Recoleta, another area known for its clubs, bars and outdoor cafes. The temperature had warmed up, so we decided to sit outside and enjoy the evening. The weather was odd because as the sun went down, the outside temperature rose. It was now midnight and we were sitting outside, watching people and enjoying fine coffee. At midnight, the nightlife is just beginning in Buenos Aires. We found ourselves surrounded by conversation and laughing. So many people of different ages, clothing and nationalities continuously filled the area. Nobody dressed formally; it was exciting just to be in their presence.

At nearby tables, people spoke a variety of languages including Portuguese, German and French. At any café in Buenos Aires, one can order a single cup of coffee and sit for hours without being pestered. Never did I feel rushed or pressured to order or hurried to pay a check; flipping tables is simply not in the culture. The experience of late night dining, enjoying great cafes, and being able to truly relax . . . I thought that I could get used to this lifestyle. Imagine moment eating, drinking and enjoying a conversation without feeling as if you are holding up some sort of line. What a nice concept.

Sitting quietly, Davie and I took in the endless stream of late-night activity. Morning was approaching, and I was thinking of how to outsmart Davie so I could finally reciprocate. I faked a trip to the restroom and handed our waiter enough money to cover the bill. I returned and said to Davie, "Let's go." He knew what I had done, and swallowing his stubborn pride, he gave me a big pat on the back. With the evening winding down, Davie and I stood on a corner and hailed a cab back to the hotel.

Recoleta bustles with nightlife. The positive energy of the neighborhood will lure almost anyone into its shops, restaurants and cafes. The pace of the services act as a counterbalance to what I encountered back home. One could enjoy a nice dinner and not have a tab arrive before the meal was finished. Places offered music and cocktails, and were solely centered on providing one with a soothing night on the town. Not many places in my neighborhood, if any, were open at such late hours. Places that offered superb pastries and coffee where one could sit for hours and bond with family, friends, or just take in the sights. The eclectic choices offered in Recoleta, when mixed with the personalized service, make it a fantastic place for anyone to kick back. It fit perfectly with what I had seen on my Latin travels, and I privately wished the same flow and diversity was more prevalent back home.

Later that morning, I went downstairs to get breakfast. Some type of disturbance came from outside the hotel. After I finished my coffee, I walked across the street and noticed that traffic was at a standstill. Scores of cars, trucks, and lines of taxis were piled tightly together. The blocks surrounding our area had several police cars with their lights flashing overhead.

Unfortunately, the economic situation in Argentina was not good, and crowds were protesting. I was not privy to the specific details of what had caused their anger; I only knew it was generally about certain government policies. The protesters were mostly young, seemingly in their twenties and some in their thirties. They were indeed organized yet obedient as they marched on. As was the case in other countries, the demonstration reminded me that life in Argentina was not all fun and games. I took this reality to heart and returned to my room. I didn't want to mix into the crowd.

With my head down, I slowly walked back to the hotel and stood alone in one of the many elevators. For the first time during my visit, I turned on the TV to search for coverage of the rally. A news station showed pictures of what was transpiring right outside the hotel. But because the language was so quickly spoken, I just couldn't understand the commentary. After some time, I saw that the crowd was starting to disperse. Argentina, like any country, had many wounds that still needed to be healed. Today the economy remains severely strained, and there has been political strife concerning different leadership policies. As I do with some other countries, I pray the governing situation in the capital finds some workable median, and that in the near term the economy will reverse its losses.

A bit subdued, I remained in my room until showtime, the time our crew was to meet in the lobby. Everyone was prompt, including the van driver, and off we went to Ezeiza Airport. Mike told us he had joined a few of the flight attendants the other night and dined at another great restaurant. Some of our female flight attendants had gone shopping and were comparing bags filled with shoes and assorted clothing. Everyone seemed to have enjoyed the stay. I was sitting alone preoccupied with a prank; I wanted to even the score with Davie for his relentless teasing about my bat retreat. The ride back to the terminal was fast. When I exited the van, I felt emboldened with a foolproof plan I had concocted.

A light mist fell at the airport and visibility was marginal. The weather was not bad enough to be of any real concern, and we were told by our operations people not to expect any delays. In a small operations area with winding stairs, Dave, Mike and I reviewed the flight papers. One working computer up on a counter was used to print out the required documents. Arriving upstairs, I noticed our plane didn't have a single empty seat. Our manifest indicated that our cargo bins were fully loaded. Dave taxied the plane down to a dark and secluded corner where our takeoff runway was located. It wasn't long before we took off into the friendly skies of Argentina.

Once level at our cruise altitude, I mentally reenacted the scheme I had developed during the van ride. I waited patiently for the right moment. After Davie had a few cups of coffee, it was time to make my move. I asked him if I could have a bathroom break knowing he likely needed one as well. Given the okay, I went into the lavatory directly behind the cockpit. Nonchalantly I returned to the cockpit, and it was now Davie's turn.

No more than a few seconds after he left, I heard roars of laughter. Apparently, the passengers were ecstatic about something. As soon as our captain had opened the washroom door, a roll of toilet paper unraveled all the way down the cabin aisle. Davie returned with a red face. In his typical fashion he calmly sat down and whispered, "Very nice." Of course, I denied any knowledge of what he was referring to. After all, I said, "I was just in the same john and everything was in proper order." I added, "I can't imagine who would perpetuate such a sophomoric act." Davie, staying on course, shook his head and took it all in stride.

Other than this untimely event, the rest of our flight back to Miami was mostly uneventful. We headed over the many hidden mountains and watched the partial light of the moon try to uncover the mysteries of the night. Approaching the equator, we encountered the normal tropical storms; their lightning dispersed in all directions. Knowing that nature was always in charge, we steered well clear of the massive cloud buildups. The light shows were always unique, powerful, and capturing. If for only seconds, the entire night sky could be lit up as if it were noon. The dominance of the storms was sobering, and was more than worthy of our utmost respect. At times blinding, the bolts of lightning reminded me of an animal protecting its territory. I could hear them say, "Don't dare come near." With admiration and anticipation, I looked forward to the next light show. After all, I always had a seat in the front row.

With the storms well behind us, we passed over the Caribbean. Entering a nice morning in Miami, our plane's wheels touched the Florida runway right on schedule.

* * *

Over the next few years I made it a point to incorporate Argentina into my flying schedule. On subsequent visits, I found places where people danced the tango, a colorful ballet famous throughout the country's culture. On one evening I stumbled upon a crowded ballroom hosting a dance competition. The competitors were impeccably dressed with men wearing perfectly tailored jackets and women looking nothing short of astonishing. Their sparkling makeup and soft red lipstick captured the imaginations of all who stood on the sidelines.

Simply put, the ladies were always "dressed to kill." Their bodies were in pristine condition, and I watched as their dances flowed in a perfect harmony. Watching them up close was nothing short of exhilarating. The sounds of their shoes echoed off the floor. At times I could feel a breeze forced off by their winding movements. The combination of their movements and their body language translated into a ballet of intense passion; at times just the sheer gymnastics hypnotized me. The ballroom had one very large open chamber with beautifully laminated wooden floors and soft lighting, a perfect setting for experiencing the tango. When I had the opportunity, I returned to this special ballroom or attempted to seek out another show. Any place a tango took place, I watched in awe.

During the drive home on I-95, I thought about my time in Buenos Aires and how much I wanted to return. I loved the energy of the city and its peoples. The Argentines struck me as a focused people, people who were proud of their country and of their culture. All were easily approachable and always made me feel welcomed. Despite many economic hardships, the people seemed to remain positive.

This upbeat attitude was appearing more common amongst many of the individuals I had met. Through their energy, I was gravitating ever so slowly to a new and promising level, a more stress-free and happier state of being. When I got to my house in Fort Lauderdale, I sat down and thought before I fell asleep. I felt as if I was being prodded by memories, hinting that I should pay more attention to both obvious and subtle experiences. Experiences that, with each trip, subconsciously whispered in my ear. The voices told me that I might want to rethink many aspects of my life.

That evening in Florida as the clock struck midnight, I was completely tranquil. Overcome by a sense of inner peace, I dreamt I was relaxing in Recoleta.

CHAPTER 12
A Hidden Gem

No estoy particularmente interesado en ahorrar tiempo; Yo prefiero disfrutarlo.

I am not particularly interested in saving time; I prefer to enjoy it.

— Eduardo Galeano

In the early 2000s, my company chose to shut down the Boeing 777 base in Miami. This meant the 777 pilots who wanted to remain stationed there had to transfer back to the smaller Boeing 767. I definitely wanted to stay, which meant I would have to be retrained to fly the smaller wide-body jet. Since I already had extensive experience flying the 767, my training time in the Midwest school would only be a few weeks. So, I packed my bags, took a deep breath, and readied myself again for the educational environment.

By then I had become more acclimated to the daily stresses and routines associated with the training schedule. My own training from traveling abroad allowed me to more readily handle the constant pressures. The weeks quickly passed, and I was once again requalified to serve as a Boeing 767 and 757 first officer.

Douglas Andrew Keehn

Upon my return to Miami, I began to fly the route from Buenos Aires to Montevideo, Uruguay. The flight in the B-767 was short, and we had only an afternoon layover in Carrasco, a town adjacent to the airport. The purpose of this flight was to allow a plane to be positioned in Montevideo to take passengers to Miami via one stop through Buenos Aires. The captain and I would simply fly to Montevideo and return in the early evening to Buenos Aires. We would fly the trip back to Miami the following evening.

I met Captain Ed in the lobby at the hotel in Buenos Aires. Because the flight between Argentina and Uruguay was so quick, it only required two pilots. Ed was quite young and a relatively new captain. He was of larger build and stocky. It was early in the morning, and we got into the van that transported us to Ezeiza International Airport. Like myself, Ed was tired. We didn't talk much along the way, only sporadically about local sports teams and how their seasons were transpiring.

We arrived at the airport about twenty-five minutes early, and agreed to enjoy a cup of coffee. We sat down in some plastic seats at one of the few airport cafes. After placing our simple orders, we took a twenty-minute break to get ourselves reenergized. The airport was moderately crowded, and we watched the travelers pass. Once we both felt alert, Ed went to the operations to gather the papers. I walked directly to the gate to prepare the plane for departure.

Uruguay is the second-smallest nation after Suriname in South America. Located in the southeastern part of the continent, it is bordered by Argentina and Brazil. The Atlantic Ocean lies to its south and southeast. It boasts advanced container terminals in Port of Montevideo, and is one of the world's largest producers of soybeans. It's basically a peaceful country with more than 90% of its population claiming to be of European descent.

Ed met me in the cockpit and briefed our flight plan. The weather forecast was nice, and we soon completed all the required checks. The flight attendants came from another destination that morning and were transferred over to our short flight; they were tired but cordial. We didn't have many passengers as our trip was a scheduled continuation flight originating from the US. Ezeiza control confirmed our route, and we were shortly on our way. The scheduled flight time was approximately forty-five minutes and involved a simple crossing of a wide berth of the Rio De La Plata River, the waterway that slices between Argentina and Uruguay.

Our cruise altitude was low, and before I knew it the shores of Uruguay came into sight. The captain landed the 767 and taxied to our assigned jetway at Carrasco International Airport. The terminal had a modern white dome draped over rows of glass. It reminded me of an open clamshell or possibly an oval spaceship. Once the aircraft was parked, the flight attendants remained on board until all the passengers deplaned. On this afternoon's layover, they would not stay in the same hotel as Ed and I.

A small car was waiting, and we were welcomed by a polite young driver. Dressed in an old pair of black slacks and shoes, he took our bags and placed them in the trunk. Because of the hotel's proximity to the airfield, our ride would be fast. The route took us past some forests and older homes that decorated the tops of small hills. Without encountering any traffic, we arrived promptly at our offbeat lodging. When I stepped out, I wasn't sure that we were even in the right place. The structure resembled a multilevel home; one would never know from the outside that it was in fact a hotel.

The center portion was painted a light blue with a V-shape structure defining the roof. When you first enter the lobby, the check-in counters are immediately to the right. Because we had to wait a few minutes, I took a fast tour. Past the counters the main floor opened up into a wide area with two older brown couches. They were separated by a Persian rug, and white lamps rested on wooden end tables. The walls were decorated with framed paintings of landscapes, and tall potted plants filled the corners. The flooring was tiled with black and brown squares, and toward the rear was a small outdoor pool and patio area.

The hotel didn't have many floors. A winding staircase was situated near the elevators; it really was not a strain to walk up to a room. I walked down to a lower level and entered the eating area. The unique walls were formed from large stones neatly fitted one top of each other. Wine bottles were displayed on light wood ledges, and the wooden tables and chairs had been stained brown. I walked back upstairs and retrieved my keys. The clerks were professionally dressed and quite polite. They were knowledgeable about the community, and were always eager to provide suggestions and directions.

Ed and I agreed to change and meet back in the lobby; our stay was short and we didn't want to squander the opportunity to see the neighborhood. I took my key and walked up two levels to my room. I was struck by the sheer size of the quarters. I had a large bedroom and an extensive living room. I laughed because such sheer dimensions weren't necessary for a quick rest. The rug was blue, and the walls had been painted a combination of light blue and white. The furniture was wood, and a medium-sized television sat atop a dresser. The bedpost was also wood and the mattress was comfortable; my quaint place would more than suffice for an afternoon's stay. I found the soft coloring and simplicity of the rooms along with the lobby's decor made for a calming feel. To some extent, the accommodations reminded me of a New England style bed and breakfast. A cozy ambiance was distributed throughout.

Now dressed in grey shorts and sneakers, Ed waited in the lobby. Accompanied by some perfect weather, we ventured out into the neighborhood in search of lunch. The small town of Carrasco is located on the Rio de la Plata River, the same river we had seen on our approach. The suburb was sprinkled with nice homes, supermarkets, cafes and stores.

A handful of restaurants close to our hotel offered a wide variety of Uruguayan foods; unique dishes of meat, chicken, or fish were often mixed with an assortment of vegetables.

Ed and I walked for about fifteen minutes and then selected a large restaurant with indoor and outdoor seating. The temperature was too nice to remain inside, so we chose an open-air table facing the street. All of the waiters were male and wore black pants and white shirts. The menu resembled that of an American diner; it was extensive, and we were overwhelmed by the choices. After some deliberation, the moment of truth arrived; it was time to be brave. I tried some lightly fried fish cooked in a lemon batter with a side of Spanish rice. Ed chose breaded chicken accompanied with potatoes. Both meals turned out to be nothing short of superb.

I not only found the cuisine to be excellent but because I never felt rushed, the lunch hour became more than just a lunch break. The midday meal in Carrasco transpired in a relaxing dining experience, a welcomed contrast to what I was accustomed to back home. In Trinidad, Venezuela, Peru, Chile and Argentina, and now Uruguay, I felt a much different stride in daily routines. On the surface, its significance might have seemed trivial but the change was anything but insignificant. I used to hurry many of my meals; half the time I didn't notice or even care what I was eating. I was so focused on the time element, the rush to get through the lunch hour (or half hour) that the act of eating became just another rote procedure. It took me some time to finally appreciate the absurdity of wolfing down a meal.

As Americans, in many parts of our country, we find ourselves almost unwittingly forced into a habit of rushing. No doubt I was stepping on a brake pedal and slowing my routines. I noticed that with this deceleration came a domino effect of rewards. For example, during lunch, I was truly able to relax by placing any time constraints on the back burner. I actually tasted my food and could focus on a good conversation. Now of course I realize that there are situations that can influence us to eat expeditiously. And that for much of the world's population just finding a simple meal, let alone trying to enjoy one, is a daily struggle.

However, I am also not suggesting that my personal approaches changed at the speed of light, that I just flipped a switched and all of a sudden became a new man. Nor am I naïve enough to think that all circumstances can be molded to fit a single category. To assume that one size fits all is just plain foolish. What I began to absorb was a certain awareness, a recognition there were times when I could incorporate new and better ways to function within an inherently fast-paced culture—the American culture.

Our slow lunch was concluding, and Ed informed me that he would return to the hotel and read. I remained sitting alone for a few minutes and absorbed the moment. I closed my eyes and thought of the thousands of fast food establishments and restaurant chains thriving throughout my country. It began to dawn on me just how much originality has vanished over the years. The conversions weren't restricted to restaurants. When I was a boy, many distinctive shops had covered my neighborhood. Today some can still be found but many have been replaced by the cookie-cutter entities.

In all fairness, perhaps some of the transformation was for the better. But change often comes with a price, and although I admittedly thought I liked some of the changes, my travels had me periodically questioning if the price was simply too high. How much individuality had been thwarted? I opened my eyes to find my waiter and three other waiters standing by my side. They were all waiting for me to wake. For a brief moment I returned to my PS -11 helicopter days; their gazes rekindled my music teacher scolding me for daydreaming and not paying attention. Slightly humiliated, I asked for my check. I paid and then quietly stepped over the outside platform hoping I hadn't made a complete fool of myself.

* * *

Over time I worked many flights between Buenos Aires and Montevideo, and became comfortable with the neighborhood of Carrasco. Often instead of taking a nap after lunch, I walked around the community. I explored a few small clothing shops, went into smaller supermarkets, and at times watched as people passed by on horseback; yes, people actually rode horses around the streets.

One afternoon I strolled by a luncheonette filled with teenagers. The restaurant was on a corner, and appeared to be a meeting place for local students. The teens sat together talking, laughing, and enjoying their lunch hour; apparently a school was close to our small hotel. I entered into the cafeteria and walked over to a large table occupied with several students. As soon as the opportunity presented itself, I asked if any of them spoke English.

Not only did most of them speak English, but they were also fluent in Portuguese, German and French. When I was a teen, the importance of foreign language proficiency was not well enforced. Some languages were offered and taught during my pre-high school years. Yet foreign language skills were not adequately tested as their relevance simply wasn't stressed. If one could speak enough rudimentary words and get by, that seemed to suffice. In retrospect, I now know this mentality was a mistake, especially since the world today is more connected than ever before.

The students began to ask in-depth questions about the political situation in the US. They had an extensive knowledge of US history, a far greater understanding than many of their American counterparts. I found their level of curiosity and education to be an eye-opener. It revealed how substantial a portion of my own culture was falling behind. The students were not only educated, they were inquisitive, well-mannered, and cared about their appearance. I had a good conversation with many of the teens and was sad that it could not have lasted longer. Their classes normally started shortly after lunch.

Douglas Andrew Keehn

Here at this unpretentious luncheonette, groups of young people relaxed and engaged in smart conversation. Their activity was complemented with healthy and refreshing food. I admired their curiosity and their closeness to their families. The level was very different than what I recollected from my teenage years. Sometimes when I sat at the corner luncheonette, I had flashbacks of my adolescent experiences. Bleak memories of my gathering with friends inside the school lunchroom. The food was awful. Large aluminum garbage pails were filled with untouched meals. The quality of food was so poor I often didn't bother to eat; I just waited for dinner to be served at home. But at least I knew I could count on having supper; some of my friends from poorer backgrounds weren't always so lucky.

The conversations we had in the cafeteria were often mundane, impersonal, and short . . . but not short of complaints. I never shared this part of my history with the Uruguayan teens. Perhaps that was a mistake. Maybe I was selfishly absorbing their positive energy and using it to replace some of my mediocre recollections. Either way, I took to heart their formulas for how they tackled life and inserted some of their joy into my more developed life.

Although I was older, I learned a great deal from the South American teens. I listened attentively to their concerns; they frequently inquired about the advances taking place within the electronic/Internet community. I also found their determination to protect a simpler way of living revealing. They seemed content with their pace of education and were careful not allow the title wave of technology to overshadow what they considered important—mainly family and friendships. Their ability to stay focused on the core qualities of life was refreshing. They balanced their thirst for knowledge in a way that afforded ample time for fun with family and friends.

On subsequent returns to that luncheonette, I never heard a single complaint from any of the younger people. Their positive outlooks and upbeat vibrations always made me feel so alive. Even to this very day, I can still hear their loud laughter resonating in that ordinary cafeteria; I can envision the many faces filled with promising smiles.

With our short stay now winding down, I showered and dressed in my uniform. Ed was in an optimistic mood, and handed me a picturesque magazine of some Uruguayan beach communities. La Pedrera, Atlantida, and the summer resort of the famous Punta del Este were highlighted with astonishing photos. No wonder he was so happy. He probably was dreaming of basking in the sun at those places. Well, it was back to reality, as we needed to focus our attention for the return to Buenos Aires.

A car similar to the one we had taken in the morning waited outside. This time we had a pretty lady for our driver, definitely an eye catcher. Young, fit, and with straight long black hair, she chauffeured us back to the airport. This was one of those rare times I wished the ride was longer. In about ten minutes we were back at the terminal and were delicately handed our bags. Ed and I waved her an extra warm goodbye and checked in at the small operations area. With the weather remaining clear, our journey to Ezeiza would be routine.

One modern duty-free shop close to our gate sold a variety of liquors, perfumes, clothing and the like. I strolled through the aisles on the way to the plane. Already becoming dark outside, it was my turn to fly back to Buenos Aires. After rejoining our flight attendants, we were soon headed southwest across the Rio de la Plata River. In short order, we were on our final approach to the well-lit, active runway at Ezeiza. After completing the landing, I handed the plane over to Ed and we received clearance to taxi to our assigned gate. After a full day of venturing around Carrasco, I was ready for some rest. I looked forward to getting back to our hotel in Buenos Aires. Late in the evening I found time to unwind by the beautiful riverfront of Puerto Madero.

My personal radar told me that Uruguay was a good nation that consisted of a culture mixed with loyal and hardworking people. They seemed friendly, relaxed and content. In a certain way my time in Carrasco reminded me of Trinidad; it was a place where I could shut down and feel a total sense of peace. I always felt that Carrasco had a very soothing aura. The small family owned shops, cafes and restaurants, people riding on horses, the sights and sounds of the Rio de la Plata.

I was fortunate enough to have captured these aspects of the city, and combined they presented a particular feeling of comfort. Back home, I would have to venture far offshore, as only the solitude of the ocean could compete with the serenity in Carrasco. I always thought of Uruguay, and specifically Carrasco, as a hidden gem, a place that would forever shine in my memory. My stays in Uruguay might have been short but the valuable lessons were everlasting. Those lessons helped clarify the ways I should look at my life and the lives of others.

In reality, it was I who had been the student in that ordinary yet extraordinary luncheonette.

CHAPTER 13

The Magic of Floripa

One day you will wake up and there won't be any more
time to do the things you've always wanted. Do it now.
—Paulo Coelho

Unfortunately, in 2004, my company decided to close our Miami crew base. As a resident of Florida, this had a dramatic impact on the quality of my life. I would have to select another domicile to begin my monthly trips. Since my company did not have another crew base in Florida, the closure forced me to join the ranks of commuters.

In order to begin a shift, many airline employees travel from places within and outside the US. The majority of the commuters are pilots and flight attendants. The company doesn't mind where its employees reside as long as they promptly show up for work. Eventually I decided to fly out of the Chicago hub. In contrast to Miami International, Chicago's O'Hare International is one of busiest airports in the world. It would take some adjusting to get used to the airport congestion and to survive the punishing Midwestern winters.

Why did my company make such a decision? September 11th had a tremendous negative impact on our profitability. We were bleeding cash at a rate of approximately $2 to $20 million per day. This scenario lasted for a substantial length of time and ultimately forced the airline into bankruptcy. Our bankruptcy was no different than most as the ensuing impacts on the employees were life-changing: massive layoffs, huge pay cuts, drastic changes in work rules, and the loss of hard-earned pensions. It was a dark time for everyone involved.

The Miami base was closed as a way to aid the company's survival and enhance our chances to better compete elsewhere. The competition in the airline business has and always will remain fierce. I often compare it to a herd of elephants drinking out of a single waterhole. Each elephant looks over its shoulder hoping the other one dies, leaving more water for the ones left standing. The airline business is cutthroat in every sense of the word.

Flying out of Miami for ten years left me with many memories. My frequent travels to Latin America would now end, and many of my fellow employees would be scattered throughout the country. They had truly been the best years of my life; years that would serve to propel me in directions I'd never imagined.

Around that time my close partner Davie was set to retire. I had the honor of flying with him on his final flight. Possessing qualities similar to those of my father, Davie had a heart larger than life. He did countless things for so many, all without expecting anything in return. When he finally retired, his absence left a void that has never been filled.

He loved South America, and I believe his unique connection with the people of the continent was not just an accident. His calm demeanor coupled with his concern for others paralleled what I had experienced during my journeys. Davie seemed to perfectly blend with the Latin culture; no matter what their status, he intuitively knew how to make a connection. Unbeknownst to him, Davie was an American who skillfully bridged the gap between two very different cultures— the American and Latin way of living. I am sure he would never take an ounce of credit for any of what I am suggesting.

Marsha, a soft-spoken and unpretentious lady, had been married to Davie for many years. Like her husband, Marsha was always gracious and giving. With her short blonde hair and normal build, she was always upbeat. She loved every aspect of nature, especially birds, cats and butterflies. During every visit to their home, Marsha would be sure I had everything I needed to be comfortable. Sadly, in her sixties, Marsha passed away from a bout with cancer. She fought like a tiger to the very end but eventually had to let go. I know my close friend misses her immensely; I certainly do.

Without Davie's role, an important ingredient would have been absent in my travels to South America. He had the magical ability to radiate confidence, kindness and tranquility. Davie would always respond "no worries" to any request for a favor; always true to his word, every favor was granted. No matter how dark the clouds might seem, I could always rely on him to find a solution. The ten years I spent flying with him was truly a great ride. I was lucky to have caught such a special wave.

From time to time I think of him climbing those wrong stairs, and his momentary memory lapse with those tricky glasses. In reality Davie was anything but blind and I would have followed him up any steps, no matter how steep; he was a leader, a teacher and a mentor. His character, demeanor, and approach to ordinary people were instrumental in my travels. Without wearing any glasses, Davie could thread the needle of life better than anyone. To this day we remain close friends. As I would only later recognize, our friendship fortified many new and valuable lessons.

With Davie retired and my airline mired in bankruptcy, the company was offering voluntary leaves of absence. I felt it was the right time for me to take off, to step back and do something bold. I gave the offer some thought and decided to accept. I forfeited my salary, yet would be able to maintain my company seniority. When I returned, my pilot status would be relatively unaffected. This opportunity afforded me a chance to reside for several years in South America.

Douglas Andrew Keehn

Eventually I decided to travel to Florianopolis, a city located along the coast of southern Brazil. I had heard many positive things about that part of the country, and thought it was time to finally see it for myself. I boarded one of my company's final flights from Miami to São Paulo and then purchased a ticket on a Brazilian carrier to my final destination. The flight time from São Paulo to Florianopolis was less than an hour. I sat by a window and was taken in by the colorful route. Below were rows of mountains defined by the Atlantic coastline. As we drew closer and lower to the airport, I could see hills and valleys with layers of thick green vegetation.

The initial approach had us gliding over the ocean before the plane turned above a wide bay. I glanced at small boats, flying birds, and a nearby beach community. The pilots made a nice landing in the small Airbus 320, and we taxied slowly to the terminal. Portable air stairs were aligned with two exit doors. It was a beautiful day with a light breeze and pleasant temperatures. Before entering the small two-story terminal, I waved at the flight crew to thank them for a safe voyage. With his window open, the young captain politely waved back.

Although small, the Hercilio Luz Airport is quite capable of serving any medium-size jet. Close to a military installation, the airport actually shares some of its facilities with the Brazilian Air Force. Passing through the baggage claim area, I entered the lower level of the terminal to find the normal rental car agency booths, a small money exchange, and some food for sale. On the opposite side were various airline ticket counters with long lines of waiting passengers. The upstairs portion had a nice café, and across were small jewelry and clothing shops. Large glass windows encased the second level and allowed people to watch arriving and departing flights. For its size, the airport seemed quite crowded. Outside an extended line of taxis was parked to the left. Hailing a cab, I soon found myself weaving through the city.

Also referred to as Floripa, Florianopolis is situated between the coastal cities of Rio de Janeiro and Porto Alegre.

Floripa is the capital city of Brazil's southern state of Santa Catarina. It is mostly composed of one main island, the island of Santa Catarina. Half of the city sits on the island and the other half is on the mainland. Three bridges link the island to the mainland but one is in poor condition. Much of the economy is dependent on tourism, with the main season starting in November and ending in February, the month of carnival. During those months, the population greatly expands and the communities by the ocean come alive. The summer season is the opposite of the United States; the warmer weather prevails during our winter months.

I instantly fell in love with Floripa and its beautiful beaches; Praia Mole, Praia Brava, Praia Campeche and Praia Santinho are just some of the more recognized shores. Approximately forty-two beaches decorate the coastal areas. Also renowned for surfing, Floripa's outskirts contain pristine shorelines draped with sand dunes or mountains; either offered a powerful combination.

My focus was drawn to the small upscale beach community of Jurere International. Located on the northern shore of the island, Jurere has a good mix of older and modern buildings and homes. The town's coast extends for approximately 2.5 miles with a black-and-white stone path running parallel to the shore. The trail is ideal for walking, jogging, or riding a bike. After several trips, I made a choice to purchase a lot in front of the ocean. I always dreamed of waking to the sounds of the ocean and decided to seize the moment. I was excited at the prospect of residing near the ocean and also looked forward to the experience of living outside the United States . . . particularly in a part of the world I had been drawn to for some time.

To purchase a lot and then build a home in Brazil was not an easy task. Just the process of purchasing the lot took over nine months, lots of negotiating, and mounds of paperwork. My first experience with a local realtor was interesting. While waiting on a corner with my American ideologies close at hand, I was expecting a fancy clean car to arrive promptly. I pictured a well-dressed, polished professional offering tours of available properties in Jurere. How truly conceited my narrow thoughts were.

An old beat-up car finally pulled over about forty-five minutes past schedule. I was only about five minutes away from giving up hope that anyone would arrive. The tires were worn, and several hubcaps were missing. I looked inside the passenger's side at torn seats and an interior in desperate need of vacuuming. Surely this wasn't my guide. It just couldn't be! After opening his door, a man slowly walked over to introduce himself. His name was Marcon. Admittedly this didn't come close to the image I'd had in mind.

Marcon was thin, unshaved, and masked by a bush of wildly uncombed hair. Cigarette in hand, his wrinkled shirt was untucked over a pair of drooping jeans. He looked as if he had just walked through a car wash. Beneath his sloppy appearance was a happy glow. He was always relaxed, smiling, and constantly wanted to joke. His calm demeanor and fun personality more than made up for my initial impressions.

I recalled just how many plastic salespeople I had encountered back home, people who were impatient, uncaring and flamboyant. Many were dressed to the tee in name-brand clothing and drove swanky cars. Of course, that wasn't always the case. I did meet many upstanding American realtors but none would dare present themselves in such an unrehearsed manner. Eventually I would purchase a lot from Marcon's boss, and would remain friends with him throughout many years. There was never a time I saw Marcon without a smile . . . never!

After the purchase of the lot and several round trips from Miami, it took approximately eighteen months to finalize construction. For one thing, I had to adjust to the bureaucracy that comes with any foreigner attempting the assembly of a house. Brazil has a system of officiating many legal transactions through offices set up across the country. These offices are referred to as Catorios. The nearest Catorio was located on the other side of a small mountain in the nearby town of Canasvieiras.

Also called Canas, the seaside neighborhood has a long street with offices, cafes, and a variety of stores. Unpretentiously situated along this row of buildings sat the local Catorio. Visiting this establishment became commonplace as so many of my progressions required governmental approval: purchasing land, permits, power of attorney and residency, just to name a few. The Catorio experience for an American is like seeing an attorney, notary, accountant, banker, financial advisor and governmental official all at once.

Each time I traveled to the office, I had to take a number, sit and wait. There were normally four to five ladies who sat at desks behind a counter; computers, printers and filing cabinets surrounded their open cubicles. The boss was an older lady who was very savvy and experienced. Both her and all the clerks were extremely patient. It could take years to skillfully understand all the procedures, rules and regulations involved with this type of business. When my turn came to fill out the necessary forms, each page necessitated either an initial or a signature. Then an official seal or stamp accompanied most of the sheets. To say that stamping is common within the Brazilian Catorio organization would be a huge understatement; it's more like deeply imbedded.

At first glance this system might seem inefficient and outdated. But after time I began to realize that it did offer some solid advantages. There were many procedures and binding contracts accomplished by clerks that in the States would have required several different attorneys. So, although many of the Catorio's fees weren't cheap, they were substantially less compared with similar services back home. Also, although the paper, signing, sealing and stamping system seemed complicated, if you take a step back you realized how many middlemen were eliminated. Of course, it's anything but perfect, but it does have its benefits. It just takes time for a foreigner to get acclimated with all the moving parts connected with the various levels of officialdom.

Another reality that impacted the building process was the weather. In Floripa rain can continue nonstop for weeks. When the rain arrives, the workers do not! In the summer the heat can be brutal, therefore the pace of work is dramatically slowed. There are also weekends and long holidays when not very much gets accomplished. Lunch hour is really two hours, so work ceases between noon and two p.m. Combined, the entire process was more than double what I had expected.

It was always interesting to watch the construction. The setup of the site/foundation didn't resemble what I was accustomed to in the United States. Many of the safety precautions and requirements demanded in the States were absent. Not many hardhats or goggles were around, and workers frequently went without protective shoes. Supports were usually made out of wood branches. The workers were quite remarkable.

By then my command of Portuguese was fair but I could only understand it if it was spoken slowly. They spoke exceptionally fast, making it particularly difficult for me to communicate. My architect Mauricio didn't speak any English but he did have a fair understanding of what I was trying to convey. He was young, energetic, creative and very helpful; throughout all the trials and tribulations, he displayed an enormous degree of tolerance.

Working with Mauricio was Carlos, the chief engineer. Fortunately, Carlos spoke some English. Like most of the workers, his physique was as thin as a pencil. He had a mustache and always had a cigarette dangling out of the side of his mouth. Carlos was a relaxed and composed man. Always very polite, he did a superb job of guiding me through an array of necessary procedures.

To accomplish what I wanted meant that I had to place my American way of thinking out the door. I quickly found out that "quickly" did not exist in this culture; that nothing can, or as I was to learn, should be rushed. The only thing that needed to be developed quickly was my patience.

One of the workers, Spivey, communicated with me via translations from Carlos. Spivey was short, tan- skinned, and never cleanly shaven. A tireless worker, Spivey loved to joke and was also knowledgeable about the island's wildlife. Any questions about the local birds, Spivey was the man with the answers. Although the workers were mostly slender, their physique could be deceiving. They had the strength of steel and were able to work under any conditions. I watched in awe as they operated an entire day with little food or water. Because their clothing was often raggedy, I called them the ragtag team. Not only was the team resourceful, they were exceptionally skilled. When life gives you a lemon, make lemonade . . . the rag tag team, often void of the proper tools, always managed to make things work.

Another gentleman, Marcos, was instrumental in building my house. Marcos was big and tall man in his early forties. He didn't speak any English but he communicated his Portuguese with a deep and confident voice. Owning a GE appliance store on the mainland side of Florianopolis, he was excellent at repairing and installing electronic equipment. He was nothing short of a genius.

Initially my phone lines were wired improperly, and nobody from the phone company could solve the problem. Marcos was able to rectify the situation, and he rewired my entire home in a day. When any of my appliances developed trouble, Marcos found the fix. Even when I had difficulty with any brand of computer, Marcos knew how to deal with the task. He looked at every problem, no matter how difficult, as a challenge. The more arduous the job, the more he would dig in until he found the light at the end of the tunnel.

I watched him stay focused, even if it meant working into the late-night hours on a weekend. At times I was exhausted just observing him meticulously troubleshoot even the remotest of options. But low and behold, the ever-patient Marcos always prevailed. In all my years of residing in the States, I had never met anyone with his mechanical and technical talent. His amazing devotion and specialized brilliance that made him so unique; additionally, Marcos's honesty was humbling. He would never charge a single cent of overtime or pad any fees. His work morality was a level I had never experienced before. I became friends with Marcos, and almost welcomed any excuse to have him return to my home.

Regrettably, soon after I moved back to Florida, I was informed that he had passed away at a very young age. Although I couldn't claim to have been close to him or his family, the news of his death hit me quite hard. I will always keep my memories of his immense kindness and trustworthiness close to my heart. I am grateful that his special qualities will remain embedded in that beautiful home forever.

* * *

Stumbling along, I am sure I did things that were offensive and culturally improper. During the entire time, the crew never displayed any anger, resentment or disrespect. They accepted my American behavior and tolerated my naivety. For this I will always owe them a great deal of gratitude, along with crediting them with my surviving the translation fiasco.

In the end, I took possession of a beautiful home. It was well constructed, and the rooms perfectly captured the panoramic views of the ocean and mountains. I could not have been more elated. The finished product exceeded my wildest expectations. So much thought and effort had managed to blossom into a dream house.

There were some minor details (and I meant "minor" in a facetious way) that didn't go quite as planned. The home turned out to be substantially larger than I had intended. In fact, it was about 30% loftier than proposed. The square footage was just below 800 square meters (over 8000 square feet). This didn't exactly reflect the living area but nevertheless the scope had ballooned into something that had not been anticipated. I was single, and didn't require anywhere near that sort of space.

And it wasn't just the fact that I was single. I saw how so many lived and was keenly aware that this undertaking was overkill. But at that juncture, it wasn't as if I could tear down the entire structure and start all over again. No doubt, I was not as plugged in as I should have been. When all was said and done, the amount that I had budgeted was exceeded by an enormous sum; I spent more than double what I had prepared to invest due to difficulty with communications and the extensive delays. And yes, I readily admit that I was naive concerning the complexities of building a home, especially in a foreign country where the main language was so very different. Anyway, that's all water under the bridge. I took a snapshot of the preceding months to recognize and learn from my mistakes. *C'est la vie.*

Taking a tour of the finished product was soothing. I could finally say that the design was as practical as it was elegant. The front of the home had a steep driveway made of cut black-and-white stones; it led down to a large garage with a solarium. The solarium, planted with cactus and layered with white stones, allowed for a decent amount of sun to light up most of area. One level up was the utility room, kitchen, dining and living room. The kitchen had a black granite island surrounded with a glass counter, and faced the ocean and distant mountains. A sliver oven was mounted along a wall along with white cabinetry.

The open design of the interior was deliberate to allow one room to have an unobstructed flow into the other. The living/dining room was adjacent to the kitchen, and continued around the first floor in an L-shaped pattern. Large sliding glass doors were placed throughout the entire first and second levels on the side that faced the ocean. Beige porcelain flooring dominated. The living/dining rooms had thick glass tables and were guarded by some of those beautiful stone birds I had purchased in Rio.

I placed a large piece of crystal on the first floor to provide the house and any guests with positive energy. My backyard faced the beach and was elevated atop a small hill. Palm trees and walls separated my land from the adjoining properties. Carved into the ground in the shape of a key was a lengthy pool. It was bordered with white cool deck to maintain comfort. When I was away, the local boys would sneak onto the property and help themselves to an afternoon's swim. The backyard was separated from the beach by a walkway and vegetation. A set of long black and tan granite stairs led to the second level.

Upstairs were three bedrooms; two, including the master, had breathtaking views of the ocean, islands and mountains. One dorm faced the street and mountains with only a partial view of the water. Every space was uncluttered, including the hallway that connected all three bedrooms. Facing the ocean was a large balcony, with tiling of white cool deck material. The terrace was wide and extended the entire length of the rear. The elevation allowed anyone to capture the sights and sounds of the oceanfront property.

The front had a neatly cut lawn that carried an Arizona type style; large tall cacti stood watch over the front entrance and offered protection for small blue seabirds. Somehow, through a combination of imagination, determination, ingenuity, luck and patience, the blueprint had been transformed into a peaceful residence.

More than anything else, I was always taken aback by the views. My apartment where I had grown up faced a large enclosed courtyard. Looking across the square I would see rows of brick buildings decorated with ivy vines. Gazing down brought into focus some benches accompanied by large rectangular planters. As a boy, the confined scenery always struck me as suffocating. At times I felt almost claustrophobic. I made a promise to myself that one day I would not only break free of that memory but also, I would elevate myself to a place that offered unrestricted and spectacular scenes. My surroundings would lack red block buildings, and instead would be filled with real life and would capture panoramic sights of the ocean.

Ironically, when my home was completed, I wasn't mesmerized by its interior. Sure, the architectural design was nothing short of phenomenal. But the result of so much time, effort and thought were no match for what had been in place from the very beginning—the intrinsic beauty of the ocean, islands, and the surrounding mountains. My favorite room was the grassy hill in back. Almost every late afternoon I stood there, and with the sun waning I stared quietly into the distance. Across the water I saw the tall mountains of the continent. A point emanating from Gobernador Celso Ramos, a municipality in the State of Santa Catarina, stood proudly out in the sea.

Off to my right and standing alone was the tiny island, the Ilha do Frances Pesca. Directly below my knoll, the marshes and dunes gave harbor to a variety of birds. Echoes of the gentle waves brushing against the shoreline softened the squawking of the Quero-quero's (Brazilian seagulls). The sounds of the different birds took on their own auditory stage and reminded me of the Trinidad sunrises. Florianopolis immersed me in the serenity of its mountains and secluded beaches. The days and nights were engulfed by the sounds of nature that echoed from the distance. On rare occasions, I would be entertained by a school of dolphins covertly passing as their dorsal fins poked through the glassy surface. This time I was in a courtyard that only God and nature could have created.

* * *

The neighborhood of Jurere was made up of *internacional* and *tradicional* sections. The *tradicional* was on the north side of the small area, and was the older of the divisions. Located between the towns of Daniela and Canasvieras, Jurere developed into one of the most sought-after communities in all of Santa Catarina. It stood only about forty-minutes from downtown and fifty minutes to the airport.

The Jurere open shopping area is situated in the heart of town, and contains rows consisting of nice café's, stores, realtors, banks and a variety of other establishments. The open shopping area resembles a large, long courtyard that extends from the town's center to just a few blocks from the beach. Each side of the courtyard contains apartment buildings with businesses situated on the first level. In the morning, the pastry shop's outdoor tables are a good place to catch the locals enjoying their fresh coffee and espresso.

As you walk through the surrounding streets and avenues, you notice quite the spectrum of homes. Their styles range from ultra-modern to antique, and their values can be assorted. Some of the streets are paved while others have scattered stretches of uneven cobblestone. The waves that brush against the sands of neighborhood shorelines remain mostly calm year-round. On a breezy day you might find a windsurfer but there are better beaches for those who like to challenge the ocean's large breakers.

Paralleling the Jurere beach is an assortment of well-manicured homes, restaurants, and a nice hotel. The private homes are separated from the beach by wide mounds covered with trees and a variety of plants. The natural wall acts as a great protector from the daily rising tides. All in all, the planning for Jurere was well thought out. There remains a nice balance between the residences, wildlife, and the adjoining mountains and ocean.

Over time I slowly became acquainted with the island. I never tired of the majestic views of the mountains that draped the shorelines. In the morning and early evening, I tried to take in the sounds of the birds that echoed throughout valleys. Their beautiful bright blue and yellow colors shone. The environmental agency, EBAMA, does a good job of protecting the island's natural surroundings. The beaches, dunes and forests are all vital to preserving the beauty that attracts so many to this special place. The first beach I visited outside of Jurere was called Praia do Mocambique. Also referred to as Praia Grande, Mocambique stretches for 4.6 miles along the eastern shore and is the longest beach on the island. With its light sand, the beach is secluded by rows of thick, tall pine trees. Its pristine coastline captures the essence of the island and serves to explain what lures people to this special part of the world.

Floripa still has many fishermen who can be found netting their catch in small wooden boats. Hardworking and proud, their presence compliments the island's history and natural surroundings.

Now that I was living in the southern part of Brazil, it became apparent that much of the population included people of European descent. My neighborhood didn't have many Americans but there were residents from all corners of Europe. In public, it was not uncommon to hear people using German as the preferred language. Communicating with the locals took quite a bit of adjusting. It was not so much the language barrier but rather the cultural differences that I found to be challenging.

As an American, I wasn't bashful and was used to being direct. The islanders didn't feel comfortable with this approach; normally they spoke only of good news and masked any underlying problems. Unless requested, information was generally not volunteered. I learned it was important to be specific to have a fighting chance of receiving an answer to a question. At times I found myself zigzagging in an attempt to stress my concerns but was often left wondering if I had really received an answer.

Sometimes this made for a good laugh. Americans normally get to the point, at least within the first few minutes of a conversation. This forthright style just didn't blend into the way things were done. Replies and reactions I was used to receiving almost instantly either never occurred or were expressed sometime during the next several weeks. This norm required lots of work for me to conform to it but I improved only on my expectations. I just wasn't good at tap dancing around issues.

Appointments were another topic I found interesting. When I set up a schedule with a utility worker, gardener, electrician, etc., it was not unusual for any of them not to show. In fact, I learned it was acceptable to appear hours or days or even weeks before or after the arranged time. There wasn't any rescheduling phone call or warnings; when they arrived, that was the time for work. After enough practice, I finally figured out that an appointment only inferred a possibility or suggestion, much like the red lights to the cab drivers of Rio.

While at times I felt my patience tested, ultimately, I learned that waiting wasn't such a horrible experience. Many people might consider this lackadaisical attitude utterly ridiculous or just maddening. And even when I thought I had finally adapted, at times I still found this accepted chaos inefficient and downright rude. I will not imply that a noncommittal system should serve as a model; obviously it doesn't. However, another side of this spectrum is also out of balance: the expectation that so many insignificant tasks have to be dealt with immediately, or that if someone doesn't arrive on schedule the universe will cease to exist. There needs to be a happy medium between the desire for instant gratification (or, putting it more softly, a rapid solution) and tolerance. When I resided in Brazil, the scale was greatly tipped toward the latter. Later I was to recognize that even imperfect systems could contain powerfully beneficial effects.

* * *

One afternoon, near the northern part of Jurere beach, I stumbled upon a large cafeteria. Built out of beige brick, the vast, rather uninspiring interior contained several rows of large tables. In the center was an oval buffet, and toward the back was a grill attended by a cook. I was in shorts and grabbed some salad and shrimp. While enjoying my lunch, I noticed a pretty lady with blonde hair, a radiating smile and blue eyes. Two friends accompanied her, so I waited for the right moment to introduce myself.

As she walked toward the front to pay her bill, I finally gathered the courage to ask for her name. To my surprise, she answered in English. Monica was fluent in Portuguese, English and German. As it turned out, she was flight attendant for Varig, a large and established Brazilian airline. Since she was well traveled and frequented the United States, we immediately found a lot in common. We began dating, and the romance lasted several years.

Raised in Porto Alegre, a large city in the very southern coast of Brazil, Monica had been living in Floripa for several years. Her house was located in Jurere Tradicional and was close to where I lived. Constructed of concrete, it was a modern design, tiled on the inside and painted a glowing white. The property was surrounded by tall palm trees and a manicured lawn. The two-story home had winding stairs that led to three open bedrooms. The master bedroom overlooked a mountain densely layered with a rich green forest. At certain times, the top would be draped with a dense fog or low-lying clouds. The upstairs balcony overlooked her backyard, and allowed for views of a nearby farm and hills.

Before sunup, the concert of the various birds ruled the airwaves. Their distinct whistles echoed off the mountains, as only they could understand its true significance. Across the street in the short trees and dense bushes, the camouflaged birds stood motionless to avoid detection. Then, as the sun began to rise, their sounds and singing slowly dissipated into the morning air. A period of silence normally followed only to give way to the nearby cows, goats and chickens.

During the early dampness, a large brown and green iguana might be seen tiptoeing over the lawn. Red tongue testing the surroundings, he often displayed his triangular crown.

Directly in front of the property were tall wooden telephone poles, a favorite perch of the local vultures that roamed the island in search of easy prey. Their curved beaks, huge black wingspans, and wrinkled toes awarded them a threatening appearance. They sat patiently, sometimes for hours, waiting for that perfect moment to take advantage of another's kill.

In the evening, the poles and cement walls across the street were occupied by owls. Very aggressive, their concentration was intense as they scanned the darkness for small animals and reptiles. Turning their heads, their mysterious marble eyes would focus on anything nearby. The stillness of their lens left no hint about what they were thinking. Periodically the echoes of their screeches and hoots could be heard.

Monica loved animals, and she moved to Florianopolis because of the abundance of nature throughout the island. Dolphins and whales swam off shore; plentiful species of colorful birds decorated the forests; horses and cattle roamed the farms. All blended into the background of the beaches and mountains. Monica had a soft heart for animals in need. She owned four dogs: Pitty, Bully, Bibby and Nero, all mutts rescued from the neighborhood streets.

Throughout the islands, many dogs were left to fend for themselves. It's common to see dogs roaming the streets, sidewalks, lots and beaches. Their numbers are so high that they blend into the neighborhoods mostly unnoticed. In poor countries, many people barely have enough residual income to feed themselves, let alone any barking companions. To care for a dog isn't cheap; medical expenses and food bills can add up to a tidy sum. Unfortunately, these economic burdens leave many of man's best friends without personal care.

In Monica's home, Pitty and Bully were the first dogs to be saved from the streets. Without knowing their family history, Pitty and Bully appeared to be mixtures of Whippet and Dalmatian. Pitty was short and slightly stocky while Bully was a bit larger with more of a streamlined body. Both were mostly grey with some black and sprinklings of white. Because of her apparent Whippet similarities and powerful physique, Bully could run as fast as a cheetah.

One sunny afternoon we heard loud barking emanating from the yard of Monica's neighbor. Apparently, a stray dog had wandered into the plot then occupied by two large Rottweilers. The Rottweilers, three times its size, had the intruder cornered. Monica and I ran over and used a garden hose to separate the small female from her captors. I grabbed the stray and of course Monica's eyes did the rest; I was holding new member of the family.

Soon to be named Bibby, she entered Monica's house skinny, smelly, and a shaking mess. Traumatized, Bibby became the third female in the dog family. Another Mutt, Bibby was almost completely black and resembled a beaten-up Beagle. About the same size as Bully, she remained shy and nervous for many months. Bully readily accepted Bibby, and shared her happy and giving personality. Things were a bit more complicated with Pitty. She wasn't that excited about the new resident. The smallest, Pitty was also the smartest. She was the most dominant, and if the situation warranted a growl, a ferocious display of teeth was never far behind. Glad to simply have safe shelter and food, Bibby quickly learned who was boss.

Months later, the winter proved colder than normal. One early morning while entering the garage, I found a German shepherd lying under her car. She was cold and obviously hungry. I thought, *Oh no, better not let Monica see this*. Three dogs was already a lot of work but I admit that my heart had softened. We named the shepherd Julia, and she became a part-time tenant of the garage. Another street dog, Julia normally patrolled the neighborhood during the day and arrived in the evening for some food and to sleep under Monica's car.

She was a medium-sized German shepherd with a perfect combination of golden brown and black fur. Julia was extraordinarily smart and loyal. When we left the home either by car or bicycle, Julia would give chase for miles. When

I went shopping in the nearby supermarket, Mercado 3 *Irmaos*, Julia followed me inside. The small neighborhood store reminded me of Sam's, the grocery store I had known as a boy. It was small and the owner, Mr. Sliva, and his wife were directly involved with the day-to-day business operations. Julia calmly walked beside me as I shopped; nobody seemed to even give her a second look.

"Juju," Monica's nickname for Julia, was much larger than the other three dogs. Because of her size and domination, she didn't mix well with Pitty, Bully or Bibby. Ultimately, we thought it best to let Julia come and go as she pleased and not take her directly under our care. Sadly, over time, she became a nuisance for some of our neighbors. Because she was protective, she appointed herself the guardian of Monica's garage. When cars drove by or anyone walked nearby, Julia displayed her objections. Unlike Pitty, her strength, the display of her teeth, and her size were all taken seriously. Unfortunately, she was frightening many of the residents.

One day I was looking outside Monica's bedroom window as the postman came to deliver the mail. He was carrying a big sack over his shoulders. Out of nowhere Julia appeared. She gave a growl that would frighten any Great White out of the water. The postman abruptly dropped his sack, and his hat flew off as he took off with the speed of a thoroughbred. Packages, postcards and magazines decorated the streets and sidewalks. The entire incident gave me a whole new understanding of the term "express mail."

I ran outside and had to wrestle several tasty envelopes out of Julia's grip; it was already too late for me to rescue the hat. It took the postman over an hour to return, and he wasn't alone. He brought the local police. I had a lump in my throat and knew what was coming. The police were kind yet firm; we were told that if Juju's hostility could not be controlled, she would be taken and put to sleep. I was nervous and loved my great friend. I first had to come to grips with the fact that I had to give her away. Then the more pressing issue was to find her an owner.

As luck would have it, Mr. Silva also maintained a large farm in the nearby municipality of Ratones. He and his wife were always very kind to me, and I thought to ask them if they had an interest in taking care of Julia. Because they saw her as my shopping companion, they were already familiar with her loyal behavior. As much as it hurt, I reluctantly handed over the leash to her new guardians. I was torn because I had let go of a special buddy, yet was relieved that her life would be spared. Juju was now safe, free to roam a farm and enjoy prime food from the supermarket.

With Julia out of the garage, Monica thought the coast was clear. It was but not for long. Another puppy that appeared lost rested in the garage. Having never seen this dog in the neighborhood, we assumed he might have been accidentally separated from his owners. We asked around and with photos in hand, traveled to local animal clinics. The dog was in perfect physical condition and appeared quiet content. After inquiring around for several months, we finally gave up the search. And yes, he became number four, the first male of the team. Monica christened him Nero. I named all the dogs the gang of four.

Full of energy, Nero was accepted by Bully and Bibby. Although he was young, it was obvious he would soon grow to be much larger than the others. And this of course had the leader, Pitty, quite concerned. She would let Nero know that despite her size, she would remain the Queen; there was to be no king, at least not in this house.

Nero was mostly black with a thick white stripe running between his eyes. He seemed to have some mix originating from a Labrador. The stripe on his forehead made him look like he'd taken a direct hit from a vanilla ice-cream cone. Because he was a clown and in constant mischief, I referred to him as banana head. His first mission in life was to dig giant holes, steal socks, and eat new pairs of shoes. Each day something magically disappeared. He was at that age of innocence, and it was always entertaining to sit back and watch.

His strength grew in leaps and bounds, and he packed the energy of a full-blown tornado. To walk him was akin to being pulled by a bull. Like a fireman on alert, Nero was always ready to spring into action. He barked at all the passing bicycles, cars, pedestrians and stray dogs; the garbage men, postal workers, local horses and cows were never exempt from Nero's fury. After all, who were they to dare em' "bark" upon his anointed personal property?

This suburb of Florianopolis had its differences from many communities in the States. At times I thought I was in the Wild West. Dogs ran astray, horses and cows ate grass out of lots, and the nearby goats and roosters weren't exactly the picture of a typical American suburb. As crazy at it might seem, this underdevelopment and disorganization continuously captured my imagination. The lifestyle was a tradeoff of sorts. One had to accept less structure and modernization, and be comfortable with a more simplistic and untamed environment.

In the community, people managed with what they had. If they didn't individually have resources to help the street dogs, they collectively found a way. Although the process of achieving stability wasn't always pretty, its pure simplicity was beautiful. The transformation from disorganization into organization blossomed. Watching people blend so little into so much was always uplifting. In many neighborhoods throughout Latin America, the dogs were obviously not the only ones struggling.

Monica and I would take the gang of four out for lengthy walks. We often wound up along the shores of the nearby community of Daniela. This small and quiet place offered a perfect setting for a late afternoon's walk to enjoy the sunset. Many of the homes were rented solely during the summer vacation. During the off-season, the town and beach were mostly empty; there might be one or two miniature markets open for business.

Similar to Jurere, the beach there is separated from the homes by hedges of vegetation; its waters are mostly calm and clear. During the winter, it was not uncommon for us to walk the entire beach and not see a soul. Every now and then we came across some of the local fisherman preparing their nets for the day's venture. We would stop and exchange some light banter, as they always seemed to have a refreshingly positive mood. Throughout the shores of the island, it wasn't uncommon to run into fisherman. Just beyond the sands you will see them netting their catch in a variety of small wooden boats. Hardworking and proud, their presence compliments the history and natural surroundings of Florianopolis.

Because of Pitty's size, we had to be especially alert as she was viewed as a tasty morsel by vigilant owls. As professional hunters, they were cunning and surprisingly swift. When least expected, it would not have taken much effort to swoop down and pick up a dog her size. Daniela was also home to alligators and packs of wild dogs. During the colder months, the dogs found it more challenging to find food. Their pent-up hunger could make them more aggressive. We learned the hard way that it was frequently not safe to allow our dogs to roam free. On one occasion Pitty and Bully got into a brawl with a group of untamed mutts, and one of them almost got killed. After that episode we always kept them on a leash, even when the community was empty.

While walking Daniela's shores, I looked out in the distance at the mainland with its towering mountains. On a clear day the sun radiated off the tops, and I could feel an energy echoing from some of the peaks. When it was overcast, the clouds and fog wove around the hilltops. I often felt as if I was being walked by the dogs, that I was being taken on some exceptional tour. The mountains, water and forest made a perfect kaleidoscope only nature could have created.

Whenever Monica recognized that I had something on my mind, she would stop our walk and redirect my focus. She reminded me to relax and absorb the positive energy of the dogs, birds, ocean and mountains. When we went into the forest, she pointed out the spectacular sights of the *gralha azu-*

ls (blue jays) hiding high in the branches. Their unique blue colors were camouflaged by the thick pine trees.

One evening I was alone on Monica's balcony. Across the street was a family of stray black and brown colored dogs huddled under a large tree. Several puppies were accompanied by their parents. A local man noticed they were hungry. He stood tall with his black uncombed hair blown by the wind. The man was quite thin, and was shirtless despite the chill. The rest of his attire consisted of an untidy pair of worn, long black pants and black flip-flops. I had already seen this particular man in the neighborhood, and suspected he had little if any money to spare.

Both the parent dogs displayed their teeth as they become agitated with the man's proximity. Unfazed, he walked to a small pet store only two blocks away. Intrigued, I patiently remained on the veranda. After about twenty minutes the man returned with a small bag of food. He opened the bag, grabbed a handful of chow, and gingerly presented it to the dogs. With hunger outweighing fear, it didn't take long for the dogs to accept. Tails wagging full range, their night was made.

Watching in silence, I could feel the connection between the man and the group. In an odd way, they both had a lot in common; they were down to the minimum amount required to survive. Residing in a nearby tiny open shack, the man had little money or any basic resources. The pack was clustered under a tree trying to stay warm, and of course they were famished. They were drawn together by a chemistry that's prevalent in many parts of the world. The chemistry that contains an unwritten yet clearly understood code: do what is necessary to make it through another day. The man knew the dogs needed food to survive the night. And the knowledge of what his sacrifice would accomplish was all he needed to lift his own spirits until sunrise.

I watched him walk back to his shack, realizing that he likely wouldn't eat until morning. I took a mental snapshot and reflected on it later that night. In more ways than one, it symbolized much of what I had experienced during my travels. I would make certain never to lose sight of this special memory.

It's not easy to admit but it's really us who continue to learn each and every day. We learn from each other; we can also learn from man's best friend. We are unknowingly just students of the countless messages nature provides.

* * *

Monica loved to go on drives to explore different places. At times she drove me to the town of Garopaba, a quaint area by the sea to our south. We would sit on some large rocks and watch the determined fishermen, shirts off, wading in the shallows to throw their large nets out over the surface. They were in search of Tainha, a favorite fish of the locals. Often, we remained still, silently admiring the clear blue water as it crashed against the shoreline; we could smell and taste the salt water as it sprayed our faces. On a windy day, surfers waded offshore and patiently waited to catch that textbook wave.

After a day at Garopaba, Monica would drive us along some winding mountains to the tiny ocean town of Gamboa. A very rural and off-the-path place, Gamboa had a dirt road that led toward a hidden beach. The simplicity of the area along with its serenity offered a secret get away. Along the dirt road were some small rickety wooden homes with shanty porches and empty or boarded-up windowpanes. Stray dogs and horses were tied to makeshift posts scattered throughout the green shrubs. Mountains and patches of tall, razor-sharp grass guarded the shore.

I listened to the waves gently rubbing against the unspoiled sand. After enjoying our time at the secluded beach, we drove up the spiraling mountain roads to connect with the highway to Floripa. Rolling down my window, I smelled the purity of the high, thin air. Passing an assortment of homes and farms, I thought what a peaceful life so many must be privately enjoying. My silly imagination considered stopping the car and being welcomed into one of the farmhouses. I had momentary lapses and like a child, fancied what it would be like to trade places with one of the families. Even if just for a day, I wanted to feel the breeze of the hillside and experience the seclusion of the high and sparsely populated topography.

During the holidays, we visited Monica's sister Barbara in the city of Porto Alegre. The trip took all day as we worked our way up and down through the valleys of adjoining mountains. The twisting roads took us past open areas of farming and grasslands. We went by several small fishing and shrimping villages, and some long industrial complexes. The sights were eclectic to say the least.

Porto Alegre is the capital and largest city in Brazil's southernmost state of Rio Grande do Sul. It sits on the eastern bank of Lake Guaiba where five rivers meet to form a large freshwater lagoon called Lagoa dos Patos. The Port has many docks with large ships tied along the piers. In some ways it resembled the Westside waterfront of Manhattan when I was a boy.

Entering the outskirts of the city, we passed several areas that made up an assortment of *favelas*. The sights reminded me of parts of Rio, the fringes of São Paulo, and some of the sections surrounding Lima, Peru. We drove by subdivisions of poorly constructed shacks and fires that smelled of burning rubbish. The scenes were dichotomous to the previous stretches of beautiful hills and ranches. As we drew closer to the city, many buildings came into view. We would stay at Barbara's apartment, which was located on top of a hill overlooking the soccer stadium. I enjoyed my stays in this southern port as it offered a diversity of nice shops, restaurants, and friendly people.

On other excursions, Monica directed us to the north of Florianopolis. We spent some time in the coastal communities of Bombinhas and Camboriu. Bombihnas, the smallest municipality in the state of Santa Catarina, has magnificent blue Caribbean water. The beaches and coves remained mostly unspoiled, and like Daniela, it was largely deserted after the summer months drew to an end. We strolled along the shores and absorbed the peace and privacy. Camboriu is quite different; it's a major beach resort whose population is about six times larger. Rows of tall buildings line the beachfront, and during the rush hours many streets can be jammed with pedestrians. It certainly is a bustling waterfront city.

Monica had a dear friend, Vinny, who remains a flight attendant with a large Brazilian airline company. He was of medium build, thin, somewhat religious, and always cheerful. Vinny was staying in the beachside district of Praia dos Acores in the southern part of the island. On our way to visit him we passed an old monastery constructed by Jesuit Priests. The cloister was built out of solid stone and had a large circular driveway in front of the entrance. Bordered by tall palm trees, it towered atop a hill allowing for a remarkable view of the Morro das Pedras beach.

I always had Monica stop the car so I could walk to the top. I never tired of watching the windswept white caps mixing with the clear green water. The tides crashed the waves into the big rocks along the Morro das Pedras shores. On certain lucky days we could spot schools of dolphins quietly making their own special splashing in front of the Jesuit's castle. I will always carry the magical sights and sounds I experienced from that distinctively elevated knoll.

When we finally arrived at the Praia dos Acores, we found Vinny staying in a compact two-story home. The residence belonged to the parents of one of his friends. The floors were wooden and the small rooms were decorated with older and simple furniture. With the windows open, a nice breeze flowed off the ocean. Monica's friend enjoyed a modest life in a sparsely populated section. The south part of the island was less developed; there wasn't yet the infrastructure to permit much growth. Nevertheless, in some cases its beaches and natural sights outmatched many on the lands northern divide. In my eyes, the lonely Praia dos Acores was a great secret getaway. All of us walked along the sandy shore and eventually enjoyed shrimp dishes offered at a longstanding seaside restaurant. The combination of the salt air, dunes, and the natural bareness of the beach always put me at ease.

Near the center of the city of Florianopolis is the district of Lagoa da Conceicao. And within that area is a beautiful large lagoon that bears the same name. The huge cove offers some of the most spectacular sights on the continent. Mountains encase the lagoon, and pockets of homes are camouflaged within the layers of trees. It's a unique place to discover. I found the serenity of its aura invaluable.

To get to Lagoa we drove through Floripa. The main thru-way, Avenida Beiramar, ran between office buildings, apartments, and the baia Norte (North Bay). The city has a decent shopping center, hospital, and everything else one would expect in a mid-sized Brazilian metropolis. For all the years I resided in Jurere, I didn't spend a large percentage of time within the downtown area. Although the city is indeed the heart of Florianopolis, I always found the true treasures lay in the small towns and villages the decorated the island's shores.

Closer to home, we frequented the beach of Campeche where Monica had a few close acquaintances. Protecting the popular seashore were thick rows of bushes and tall dunes. They masked the beauty of the ocean that sat on the other side. When I squeezed through the shrubs, it was as if a giant curtain had been lifted. A stunning and captivating beach opened up before my eyes. The fresh smell of the salt air was magnetizing and immediately drew me toward the water. Campeche's waves and undertow were powerful, and could pull anyone far from their original spot. Because the wind frequently whipped across the ridges, it was a popular place for flying kites and windsurfing. Different arrays of blue, red, white and green sails decorated the skies and surfaces. Always alive with activity, I loved my days at Campeche.

During my residence I visited numerous communities; Canasvieras, Lagoinha, Cacupe, Ingleses, Ratones, and Praia do Forte, just to name a few. Each had its own distinctive topography and attractions.

CHAPTER 14

Fica Tranquilo

If you want to see a rainbow you have to learn to see the rain. — Paulo Coelho

Oddly enough, through all the places Monica and I visited, I found it difficult at times to simply appreciate the moments spent amid the beautiful surroundings. Instead I was absorbed with personal difficulties. My mind remained a prisoner of my Western way of thinking; I was excessively stressed over minor unaccomplished tasks. Monica would not allow me to remain blind to the island's many natural gifts; she steered me like a large ship, turning me around ever so methodically. She knew I needed to let go, yet my grip on so much junk remained way too tight. How to loosen this and take hold of what really mattered was still a work in progress.

Monica's traveling experience made here polished at bridging the gap between two very different ways of thinking — the American way and the Brazilian way. Her messages were never a demonstration of which process was "better." We both agreed that each culture had some innate aspects that were preferred. However, since I was living in her country, I had quite a steep learning curve. Monica's steady inputs often reinforced some of what I learned from my travels. The difference now was that I would actually have to implement what I had learned.

Living in a particular country is vastly different than simply visiting. It's not solely a question of practicing what you preach—it's also about becoming comfortable with things that you had never experienced, things you don't expect, find correct, or don't fully understand. All are integral parts of the process of adapting. And I will tell you that for an American to reside in Brazil, especially at the outset, can be challenging.

After some time, I began to make a few friends. Living close by was a nice couple, Francisco and Sandra, along with their son Kiko. Francisco, originally from the north of Brazil, was a retired manager. He was thin, clean shaven, and well read. His wife, Sandra, was from Rio and worked in the field of psychology. Their son, Kiko, was enrolled in a school preparing to specialize in business. All three were gracious as I was frequently invited for coffee, lunch or dinner. Francisco spoke English well enough for me to converse with him about several topics. He was an interesting man with extensive knowledge of the Brazilian business community and the history of the nation. At times we would agree to rendezvous at one of the neighborhood restaurants. Sometimes we talked for hours, as I always enjoyed his different views and advice; both helped me to understand how to better integrate into the local society. Francisco, Sandra, and Kiko will always remain in my circle of friends. Their kindness, patience, and consideration were exemplary of what so many in the community offered.

When absent from the States, I always looked forward to having lunch in one of the native cafes. My eagerness wasn't necessarily driven by any expectation of finding some excellent cuisine. The establishments had limited menus and rather ordinary buffets. With all of its tranquility, Jurere wasn't exactly famous for its fine midday dining. Realtors and construction workers made up the bulk of the steady customers; they would take time away from their chores in search of a close place to eat and relax. Around noon, people from the beach mixed with the workers as they strolled in wearing their shorts, bathing suits and flip-flops; the dress was always casual.

At lunch it didn't matter what place I frequented because most of the selections were similar. Rice, beans, sausage, fish, chicken and salad were the norm. Priced by the kilo, the food was reasonably valued. These cafeterias ranged in size from small to large open areas. All offered the option of outdoor seating, especially during summer. During the peak season of tourism, the small community would become quite populated. However, as soon as the period waned, the exodus was apparent. The locals once again dominated the restaurants. For some owners, business became so slow that they often closed down until the start of the following spring.

My enthusiasm about the lunch hour had everything to do with the experience of participating in conversation with neighbors and people from all walks of life. Unlike the midday practice back home, this culture did not promote the theory of grabbing a quick bite or partake in fast food. Lunch hour was really a time to wind down and enjoy the company of others. There was never any underlying understanding that it was imperative to be back at an office exactly on time.

Because the rush back to work mentality was not baked into the cake, it relieved the pressure of having to gobble down a meal. At tables, I rarely saw people using cellphones or any other Internet-related devices. Patrons were easily approachable; they talked to each other and were not bashful about walking over to others. Many readily took time to chat with some of their friends and neighbors. Lunchtime was not about taking a few bites and constantly glancing alone at a phone, computer, or television. Basically, the hour mirrored what I experienced in all of my other Latin travels.

* * *

In terms of my personal safety, I knew that in the States dialing for emergency service entailed a rapid response. If I called for help, several uniformed personnel would speedily arrive at my doorstep. I took this expectation for granted in my new community. As I learned, it was an illusion to believe that help would appear quickly. As with making an appointment, calling for aid had broad implications. Even with an installed warning system, one could not count on a swift reaction if an intrusion was in progress.

It's not as if my neighborhood was plagued with problems; in reality I felt quite safe and rarely needed police assistance. But as I was to learn with Monica, calling the police could trigger a quick arrival, a very slow arrival, or no arrival at all. The level of help was unpredictable. I grew to accept this as another imperfection that would hopefully improve over time. The subject of crime and police protection has long been an issue throughout Latin America. Obviously expecting a random response doesn't exactly add to one's feeling of security.

As was the case in my other travels throughout Latin America, I found the lives of my Brazilian friends were partially shaped by a lack of some important fundamental services. The feeling of insecurity explained many of my neighbor's distrust of those who served to protect. In Brazil and others countries, I try to remain positive that the day will arrive when this mistrust can be repaired and a better system that will gain the population's respect can be implemented. To this day, the populations of many nations need a far greater sense of confidence that valuable help, when called upon, will arrive promptly.

At the beginning of my time in Brazil, I found myself frustrated with a wide range of tasks involving repairs, transportation, shopping and even banking. But over time (and it didn't take long), I surrendered to the reality that things were indeed going to be quite different. Watching Monica's approach, I began to understand it just wasn't healthy or helpful to have exceedingly high American expectations. I would be an arrogant fool to think I could mold how things ought to be accomplished. Undeniably there were times where I was overbearing and found out the hard way; that frustration only led to more frustration, and trying to rush anything only had the opposite effect. I would be left feeling even more exhausted.

Monica came from a culture where the bar of expectation was set to a lower level. She enforced upon me not to let life's little distractions become stressful. Her way of seeing things was that if it didn't get done today then it would be accomplished tomorrow. At first, I looked at this attitude in a negative way, thinking it was just an excuse to surrender. Yet after I accepted this pace, the outlook began to grow on me. It allowed more time to reflect and to take in all that was around. Most anxieties ratcheted down several levels.

Admittedly I never became one hundred percent comfortable with this transformation but I let go and allowed it to lead me with the passing of time. In a sense, I felt as if I was experiencing a withdrawal from a life's worth of demands. The hiring of a worker, Pedro, served to retrain my American pace. Finding Pedro quite by chance, Monica selected him to maintain both our homes. He was an excellent painter and could repair almost any superficial internal or external cosmetic damage.

Well into his forties, Pedro was as thin as a stick. Constantly working outside in the baking sun had hardened his tanned skin. Pedro would arrive whenever he was available; to make an appointment was pointless. But when Pedro came to work, he applied himself in every sense of the word. In flip-flops, he would climb a ladder and, with a cigarette dangling, work tirelessly from sunup to sundown. I used to refer to him as the Camel because for the entire day he never needed a drop of food or water. His energy was boundless, and he never displayed an ounce of fatigue.

Pedro's strength, humility and approach to life served up many valuable lessons. I would peek out from time to time as if in an open classroom watching my teacher write up a lesson. I didn't simply see a devoted laborer; I saw a relaxed, unselfish, and unpretentious man doing all he could for the sake of his family. When I looked at Pedro climbing those long wooden steps, I saw a unique person—someone who would always be high up on life's special ladder.

* * *

After some months, Monica became more comfortable with my company. She decided to introduce me to a middle-age couple named Marlis and Valdemar who were some of her closest friends. Residing just a few blocks away, they lived in a simple two-story house. Their children Luisa, Valter and Victor were all exceptionally well-mannered and were never afraid to display their affection for both parents. Monica and I were often invited for dinner and were treated to some great home cooking. The dining was always accompanied by lots of laughing. Sometimes I would admire their family connection, how they were all so happy and respectful of one another.

From a material standpoint they didn't seem to have much, but from where I sat they appeared to have everything. Never in my experiences back home had I ever seen this level of genuine and unconditional bonding. They were authentic and kind people, and what they offered can never be bought. By bringing me into their world, Monica subtly uncovered what was ultimately important—health, love, family, friendships, laughter, good food, wine, and music.

Other revealing experiences to this very day remain anchored in my mind. One occurred on a sunny Sunday morning when Monica was out of town. I was alone with the dogs and began to feel sick. Because it was a Sunday, all of the medical offices in my neighborhood were closed; I was not exactly sure of how to find a working physician. I got into

Monica's Renault hatchback and headed toward the area downtown. I often accompanied her in this section for some of her routine medical appointments.

Remembering a clinic that was open daily, I decided this would be my best option. Fortunately, the traffic was very light, and I was able to quickly find the correct address. The clinic was attached to a hospital and had a small parking lot located directly outside the entrance. My head pounding, I parked and went directly to reception. In my best Portuguese I conveyed that I needed to see a doctor and was told I would be examined shortly.

A nurse came out, escorted me to a small room, and asked me what was wrong. My Portuguese was not detailed but I did my best to describe my condition. Seeming concerned, she left me alone for a few minutes. My mind drifted back to the procedures I had been expecting. I was accustomed to the normal drill: What is your insurance company? Do you have your insurance card and a photo ID? All the usual questions surrounding payment and the personal information asked before I received attention.

Sitting alone on the high table, it suddenly dawned on me that none of this had so far been requested. What had been asked centered solely on my well-being. Not knowing about the procedures, I was pleasantly relieved; I just wanted to see a doctor. In short time a young medic in his mid-to-late thirties entered the room. He was wearing a white shirt, tie and had a stethoscope draped over his neck. Displaying a five o'clock shadow with his black hair neatly combed, his concern was genuine.

Speaking some English, his mannerisms were calm and confident. After a thorough examination, he wrote a prescription for some antibiotics and assured me I would be fine. Relieved and a bit embarrassed, I mentioned that I didn't have any insurance coverage and I offered to pay with a credit card. The doctor smiled and asked if there was anything else he could do. I answered no and told him I was extremely grateful for his patience and honest concern. Then, a bit puzzled, I repeated my offer to pay.

He told me that I should relax, drive home, and return if I didn't feel better in a few days. The young doctor told me it had been his pleasure to have helped and to forget about paying. I put my shirt on and walked out a bit dazed. Actually, I was shocked; I simply couldn't believe it . . . I had seen a doctor, on a Sunday morning no less, and had been told not to pay? I scratched my head, strolled out to the car, and drove home. The entire process, from the moment I had entered the clinic, was quite unlike anything I had ever experienced before. It was all almost surreal. The concern had not centered on my ability to pay; the interest was exclusively to investigate what was wrong and to find the proper remedy. To this very day, I still have fond memories of that doctor's remarkable kindness.

* * *

Another distinctive experience left me with lasting impressions. One late afternoon I was quickly pedaling my bicycle near my Brazilian home. The sun was setting, allowing the evening's darkness to take hold. I was on an avenue and traveling against the oncoming traffic. Suddenly a car turned into a side street and I slammed into the driver's door. I was thrown off my bike and landed abruptly on the pavement.

Both my arms were cut but I had not been seriously hurt; the front tire, rim, and my bike's gears were destroyed. Slowly getting up, I saw an elderly lady standing by my side. She was startled and quite concerned about my welfare. She was the driver. Fortunately, she spoke some English, and I tried to explain just how sorry I was for hitting her car. Admittedly I was embarrassed; I was quite cognizant that the accident was entirely my fault.

Noticing I was bleeding, the lady parked her car and insisted on taking me up to her apartment. Luckily, she lived on the same block where we had collided, so the walk didn't require much effort. The moment I entered her apartment, I was given some towels and antiseptic to clean my wounds. After I had regained my composure, I was offered a cup of coffee. My host refused to let me leave until she was completely sure I was well enough to travel home. Her only concern was for me.

We talked for a while, and while sitting on her couch I apologized a hundred times. After gaining my strength, I grabbed my mangled bicycle and tightly put my arms around her. Unable to thank her enough, I proceeded on a short walk back to Monica's. My memories of that evening's accident remains with me, and represents a stark contrast to my fender-bender in Fort Lauderdale. The level of concern was literally a world apart in more than just one sense.

* * *

In late 2007, my leave of absence was winding down. Thus, I need to return to my flying career. Based out of Chicago, I was now comminuting to my home in Brazil. The commute was extensive and fatiguing, and often involved traveling all night. The journey normally took more than fifteen hours. In 2009, with mixed emotions, I decided to sell my home and return to the States. I did so with great reluctance because I was very much aware of what I was forfeiting.

As luck would have it, I didn't turn the keys over to a run-of-the-mill buyer. Mr. Joao Carlos, a successful businessman and a complete gentleman, didn't have a shred of arrogance anywhere in his demeanor. He was extraordinarily kind, humble and compassionate. Joao Carlos loved the style of my home and revered its spectacular views. The moment he walked through my house, I felt his positive yet soft energy. I could not have shifted something of such personal meaning to a more deserving individual. Somehow, I think a very special pair of dolphins dropped Joao Carlos by the shores in front of my home; he typified so many of the special qualities that I so admired.

One would think I would have a sense of relief or even joy about my return home. To the contrary, I felt empty. I was a realist and knew my relationship with Monica would suffer; ultimately it did. I was also leaving behind many special friends and a way of life that I had begun to adore. I was waving goodbye to a combination of ocean and mountains that could capture anyone's imagination. To this very day, I owe a great deal of gratitude to the many people of Floripa who touched my life in so many special ways. I am especially indebted to Monica who transformed so much of the way I live. She exemplified the term *fica tranquilo*, "stay calm." Good at inhaling all of nature's gifts, Monica also knew how to filter out many of life's toxins. It was just one of the gifts she passed along that I will forever hold inside.

Feeling the pain of my departure, I promised myself to carry forward all I had absorbed. When I left my home for the last time, I purposely left the door open as a personal reminder that I might one day return. When I got on the plane for the final farewell, Monica waved from the terminal. Unselfishly she had afforded me a special key, one that would not completely fit the typical American lock. Unbeknownst to her, that key would forever unlock the way I saw things. Her gift was priceless.

CHAPTER 15

Compass Reversal

When you're finished changing, you're finished. — Ben Franklin

A s the saying goes, it's never too late to change. Without question, the experience of flying has changed dramatically in recent years. The technology incorporated into modern jet aircraft is truly remarkable. As was my father, I am still amazed by the capabilities of today's commercial jetliners. I remain awed watching the large jets roar down a runway and lift off into the open skies. Improving yearly, manufacturers are producing incredibly efficient flying machines. Due to demand, the airlines have also been pressured to provide the traveling public with modern entertainment. The industry has adapted to meet the challenges of personal communication and the need for the rapid processing of information.

Because I had traveled to and resided in Latin America, I was now accustomed to a different way of life. At times I couldn't help but notice how detached many of my fellow Americans had become. I remember my experience as a passenger on a flight from New York to Los Angeles. It was my lucky day, as I was upgraded in a Boeing 767 from the coach section and placed in the first-class cabin. Life was good—a big comfortable seat with plenty of leg room. Walking down the aisle toward my assigned row, I saw scores of people feverishly typing on phones or computers.

I sat down next to a gentleman who appeared to be in his mid-thirties. Well dressed in brand-name jeans and a green sport shirt, he barely acknowledged my presence. Offering a quick nod, he then redirected his focus back to a large phone. The 767 now pushing back from the gate, and the flight attendants made that dreaded announcement: "All electronic equipment must now be turned off until the aircraft safely lands at the final destination."

The final rush of sending that last message was put into motion. People were typing at the speed of light. To keep out the sun and allow for better movie quality, we were advised to lower our window shades. Seated next to me for the next six hours, my fellow passenger wasn't much interested in talking. I tried to strike up a conversation but my attempt was met with little interest.

It was our turn to takeoff. Away we went into the big blue skies. Reaching our cruise altitude was the opportunity for people to select their movie. At the same time, lots of computers, including my neighbor's, were being used. For a moment, I thought I was seated in an office separated by numerous cubicles. Wanting to look outside, I opened my shade only partially so as not interfere with the movie. Staring out of the window, I daydreamed about my Latin friends. If any of them had been seated next to me, igniting a fun exchange would have been simple.

Time passed ever so slowly, and a change of sounds emanated from the engines. We were beginning the initial decent into the Los Angeles area. Soon came the announcement to close and stow all electronic equipment. Now we were close to my favorite part of the dance. The second our wheels touched the runway, an entire group immediately activated their phones, their devices drawn as quickly as if they were a caravan of bandits whipping guns from their holsters. It was the Wild West of the westerners. Their actions resembled those of a group of addicts denied some technological drug. The ringtone symphony echoed throughout the cabin, and I was a captive of the phone harmonic. I saw this same script repeatedly played out during my frequent commutes.

In my hotel in Los Angeles, I closed my eyes and thought about the flight. Something was bothering me; I felt as if something was missing. At first, I thought of the standard passenger complaints: flights were often delayed; service was substandard; luggage was lost or damaged. It occurred to me just how much was taken for granted. With thousands of daily flights, the miraculous safety record was often overlooked. But this broad aspect wasn't troubling me; I remembered the accident in Fort Lauderdale where the lack of genuine concern had been far more damaging than the actual collision. Much of what is truly important can often go unnoticed. After my travels to Latin America, I had the ability to feel and see things I never could have before.

I wondered why the gentleman seated next to me hadn't been interested in meaningful conversation. Why had a movie superseded any uplifting dialogue? Why was this phenomenon so common when I traveled within the States? This hadn't seemed to be the case when I had been a boy. When I got on a plane, I looked forward to an interesting conversation. An abundance of curiosity and interaction now seems all but lost. I didn't have these empty experiences when I traveled in Latin America. People were genuinely inquisitive and readily open to friendly exchanges. My parents taught me that curiosity was a key element of learning; they said it would keep me thirsty to absorb more information and help in developing ways of accepting new concepts.

A lack of even simple exchanges has permeated our culture. In many cases, we have become an isolated society. Established neighbors often know little of each other's lives. The lack of any real curiosity is even worse than the lack of knowledge. I saw an extension of this coolness in my car accident, and was again reminded of it during my experience as a passenger. Was this comfort with solitude mainly an American experience? Never could I remember a time as a passenger traveling to Latin America when I hadn't taken something positive away. Admittedly I had some success during my travels within the States but my track record of establishing meaningful dialogue had been poor; I found myself politely rebuffed too many times.

People might have felt a sense of accomplishment on the flight to California but from my perspective they walked away with little. Once again, what is not often seen can turn out to be significant. When the shades had closed, the cabin had basically been transformed into a movie theatre. And yet there was no curiosity about what lay underneath. The beauty of the lakes, mountains, cloud formations and lightning far exceeded any panoramic scene from the movie.

How detached we have become from the treasures all around. How this contradicted my lessons and experiences of my traveling and living in Latin America. Entertainment was inherently a distraction, a way of transferring one's focus. What price are we paying for the obsession to be constantly entertained? What has happened to our focus? Have we become so desensitized? The lack of communication, curiosity and concern—call it the three C's—is all too common. How can we even notice this phenomenon if we are growing a society of horses with blinders?

When we landed at Los Angeles International Airport, all the passengers' phones had been withdrawn from their holsters. Had I been surrounded by world leaders and diplomats? In other words, what was the rush? People in the Caribbean and South America didn't have that haste to know syndrome.

Winding back the mental film of my accident in Fort Lauderdale: the gentleman who collided with us had a mindset based on a quick solution. The thought was, "Okay, we hit someone, so let's get out of here as soon as possible." Legally the accident wasn't a hit and run but fundamentally, from a humanitarian standpoint, it represented something far more reaching. The accident in and of itself didn't directly change my life. It did trigger a sequence of significant recollections.

Ultimately life-changing was the moment when I finally began to see what I had been missing within those memories: the many messages that came from others, and also from within, that I had subconsciously set aside. When I pieced them all together, I was finally able to develop a clearer sense of some critical aspects that had been missing from my life. And I knew I wasn't alone, as many in my own culture suffered from these same vacuums. By continuing to listen to and learn from other cultures, I was altering my direction. I was to drawing closer by the day to a simple desire—to be truly happy.

Indeed, something was missing and that something encompassed more than I wanted to admit. I was cognizant of the benefits and conveniences of the Internet, and that today's portable phones can place a powerful computer right at our fingertips. What we are missing, what we don't often see, has caused a somber imbalance in our lives. Compared to our neighbors down south, we have become more removed from so much of what truly matters.

Sitting on my hotel's sofa, I had this uncomfortable feeling. I went into the bathroom and splashed some water on my face. I looked into the mirror and thought of just how out of balance my life had been. A lot remained for me to improve and build upon. I thought of my family, friends, and neighbors, how I had wished they could have traveled with me and seen so many bright candles. The time for me to own up to many difficult realities was becoming long overdue. Within my own culture, a lot of damage needed repair. Our balances needed to be overhauled so that we might rekindle some of the kindness and consideration that used to be evident and openly displayed.

Later in the evening, I felt myself drifting as if I were in a small boat lost in a fog and searching for a rope that could pull me back to shore. The twine was made of the very fibers that had surrounded me as a boy and had made me feel so alive in Latin America. Now immersed in my own culture again, I was searching for that special rope, the cord made of fun, laughter, patience, kindness, concern and simplicity. These ropes exist in our culture but I sense them constantly slipping away. Feeling completely alone, I pictured Nero and the gang of four howling into the night. I saw the genuine smiles of the fishermen of Rio and Floripa. I could hear the laughter of my Latin friends, and the chatter of the beautiful blue jays deep in the forest. So many bright moments I captured in places that supposedly had so much less.

We desperately need to regain our curiosity to allow our hearts to open to what truly matters. The frequency of my travels offered me a chance to continuously reflect on many experiences. I found it often took time to register the importance of the more subtle observations. Sometimes I wouldn't even recognize the significance of what I had seen until several months had passed. Many things I had witnessed were placed in the back of my mind because I had thought them rather trivial. Yet when I added up some of these seemingly insignificant experiences, I felt that real value might be contained in their total. With the passing of time, their relevance come more into focus.

For example, one evening I woke up thinking about my stays in Argentina. I recalled a night when I had wandered into the area of Ricoletta in search of some good coffee. I planted myself at an outdoor table akin to a small cafe and watched as the evening crowds walked by. With each layover I became more accustomed to the moderate pace of the service. I admired their custom of not rushing any client no matter what the order entailed. When I requested a single cup of coffee, and sat for an extended period of time, my inaction was never perceived as rude. Relaxation and respect for one's privacy were firmly implanted in the culture.

Douglas Andrew Keehn

My mind then shifted to the morning of one of my returns to Florida. After landing in Miami, I drove north and then stopped at a large coffee establishment. Even at such an early hour, a long line of anxious coffee addicts extended well outside the premises. Exhausted, I placed myself at the tail end of the line. I had just returned from flying all night from Buenos Aires and had that unstable jet-lagged feeling. Sometimes I felt so fatigued I couldn't sleep.

While in line, I noticed people constantly checking their watches. The customers were not relaxed and seemed anxious about the wait time. The burden of being prompt for work was foremost on their minds. Their expressions were a dead giveaway to how the morning's coffee experience was going: it was stressful. The counter, filled with the normal condiments of cream and sugar, was jammed with people. From where I stood, I could literally hear the sighs and expressions of relief from weary patrons. One would have thought they had just been through a tough battle. Stirring their coffee to perfection, it was then time to find a seat. Laughing to myself, I knew that for most, this journey would not end well; there simply weren't enough seats to handle the bulging capacity.

I was still in my bedroom and couldn't go back to sleep. I remained immersed in this silly coffee comparison. I remembered standing in that American café and wondering just how and where many of those people were going to truly relax and enjoy their coffee. To order the coffee to go, and to sip while on the run . . . was that really satisfying? Could it be that our way of partaking in the coffee experience was analogous to the way we consumed our fast food? At the moment it seemed as if I were watching a burger being quickly devoured only the burger was a cup of Joe.

Enjoying coffee in Latin America was always relaxing. This concept seemed simple enough, yet I rarely found this to be the norm within my own culture. The experience of sitting, chilling, and savoring the taste of the delicate brew was often replaced with a robotic chain of efficiency: order, pick-up, mix, and good luck. This bland script was the complete opposite of what I had looked forward to in Buenos Aires and what I had experienced throughout Latin America.

Even though my mind was fully caffeinated, so to speak, I finally returned to sleep. Then in the morning I wrote down some other scenarios about waiting in line. It dawned on me that some nuisances might tell a story, provide hints about how and why we collectively react as a people. Occasionally while staying in São Paulo, I visited the local post office. In order to mail a package, it was common to wait in line for an extended period of time. The wait on any postal line back home paled by comparison. What I remembered was a remarkable display of patience by the patrons at that Brazilian establishment. Despite the lengthy delay, they were extraordinarily tolerant and seemed accepting of the pace of the clerks.

I had to smirk when I recognized my own experiences at my local post office. How often my time spent in a line was minutes compared to what I had faced in Brazil, yet the people were commonly impatient. At times their frustration boiled over and led to a display of raw anger. Once again, the behavior I viewed outside my own country was dramatically different. The criticisms concerning our postal system are all too familiar. It's supposed snail-paced service and inefficiencies make for easy targets and jokes at any cocktail conversation. But the reality is that, at least from what I have seen in many other countries, our mail system is a gem.

I can almost hear the roars and laughs I just created. The truth is that compared to many systems, our package lines are anything but punitive. When you take a wrapped parcel to be mailed, remember that this isn't the only gift you are holding. You might not be aware of it but you truly are in the midst of a comparatively friendly service. Could our system be improved and become more inefficient? Obviously, it could. Yet to concentrate on the imperfections misses the point. What I found revealing is the positive way in which the Latin people, in this case the Brazilians, dealt with a system

218

that was certainly not as advanced. Their adaptation to any range of efficiencies was commendable.

And continuing on the subject of lines . . . had to conduct transactions in person with phone and utility companies while I resided in South America. There again, I was at a disadvantage because I had come from a background that was not as equipped to handle the required level of tolerance. It was not unusual to wait hours in rooms that consisted of long lines, poor seating, dim lighting, and little if any temperature regulation. Nonetheless, people always remained civil and courteous.

At several international airports outside the US, I encountered harrowing procedures while entering or exiting the country. Some of the maze-like governmental processes could be quite tedious and required more time than I ever imagined. Some intervals felt almost tortuous but I never saw even a shred of complaining. The energy required to survive our customs structure was nothing compared to what I had frequently left behind.

When I piloted a flight of mostly American passengers, any delay might pose problems. If our flight was running behind schedule, I could feel the anxiety of our customers. Some became uptight, angry, and occasionally aggressive. From the sidelines, I cringed just watching the customer service agents handle misguided tempers. The verbal abuse they often suffered was completely unwarranted.

On the other hand, when one of my flights to South America was late, the Latin passengers mostly took it all in stride. It's not as if the airlines gained any advantage for extensive interruptions. The vast majority of disconnects are due to foreboding weather conditions or an unexpected serious mechanical problem. No prudent pilot or passenger would want to risk flying under those circumstances. In the end, there aren't many alternatives to coping with lengthy airline delays. Basically, if you want to get from one point to the next, you can choose to arrive tranquil and relaxed or to land filled with anxiety and anger.

I wondered why our behaviors, tolerances and expectations were so frequently out of balance, even when immersed in only the most minor of inconveniences. Little did I realize just how much of an impact a fast-paced lifestyle would have. We have grown so accustomed to speed we don't even recognize what the enjoyment of a simple cup of coffee should entail. In my own county, I found myself in a constant rush to accomplish even the most innocent of tasks. Too many times I felt as if I were in a pool treading water, and if I didn't work hard enough I would sink to the bottom and ultimately drown.

Over time I began to reinforce some ordinary lessons picked up on during my stays in Latin America. And I made myself a few promises. One was to never have a cup of coffee while on the go. If I was in a hurry then it was a waste of time to order something that should be completely connected with some down time. As was the case with fast food, eating on the run, I also wanted to rid fast coffee from the menu of my personal lifestyle. And I assured myself that I would not allow something as ridiculous as a line to alter my mood. I taught myself to take any wait in stride. When I was a passenger, I would not get wound up over delays. In fact, if the interruption was extensive, I would take advantage of that and relax with a cup of Joe.

For too long I had felt as if I had been running on a treadmill that led nowhere. I was placing too much emphasis on things that didn't warrant a high level of devotion. To help readjust my life, I took a simple page out of the Latin American textbook. The page began and ended with the words step back, or *fica tranquilo*. My time away from the States forced me to open my eyes and uncover the importance of tolerance, tranquility and empathy. Often overlooked, these qualities were key ingredients I needed to incorporate into my life. Their values were indispensable if I were to fundamentally change. I needed to detach from too much rigidity and allow the winds of a different direction to slowly take me to a better place.

Douglas Andrew Keehn

While on my boat off the coast of Fort Lauderdale, I envisioned that my compass was reversed. My mind placed me thousands of miles to the south, allowing the magnetism that emanated from that part of the world to extend to my surrounding waters. I found no reason why I couldn't shut down my engine and just sail with the breezes I found so refreshing.

I questioned whether my life was in a holding pattern. Had I been stuck waiting on some sort of an invisible line? Having been exposed to some very different attitudes, perhaps the time had finally arrived for me get off that line. My life in the States was indeed comfortable but I knew it was anything but complete. As someone in Brazil told me, "Comfortable means just that, comfortable. It does not always imply being happy. Sometimes the path to becoming happy require a process that at times will feel very uncomfortable."

CHAPTER 16
Carefully Packed Parachute?

As we work to create light for others, we naturally light our own way. — Mary Anne Radmacher

When I digress, I think back to certain periods in my life and how so many little experiences offered so much joy. When my mom handed me a few cents, how exciting it was to rush to the corner candy store. I could choose some Mary Jane's and fireball treats along with a pocket full of Bazooka bubblegum. How much delight twenty-five cents used to buy. I recall how fascinated I was taking my first steps onto an escalator, that I was so lucky to have discovered the non-stop action of this giant rolling toy. The sheer euphoria of wheeling out my first bicycle for a spin and showing off its lightning speed.

While on a party boat surrounded by grownups, I felt the exhilaration of catching that first big fish, the elation of the pole bending and battling the mighty beast. I still can hear my dad whispering in my ear promising to take me to my first sporting event; my excitement was such that I could hardly breathe. I would get to see those larger than life superheroes whose faces appeared on all my bubblegum cards. On special occasions, my mom would take me to Woolworths, an old retail chain near our apartment. She would allow me to order a cheeseburger with a refreshing bottle of Coke. How could I have anticipated that she would treat me to such a special gourmet lunch?

As I got older, I remember the combination of ecstasy and terror of my first real kiss. The overwhelming moment of passion felt like it could have become an addiction. And I can still feel my heart pounding the first time I drove a car, the night my uncle allowed me to steer his Chevy on a secluded rural road. The thrill was indescribable, and it seemed like I had just landed on the moon.

How much complete happiness such simple acts brought me at different stages of my life. If I could only capture my special moments in a bottle. Every day I would take a sip and experience how the contents were filled with life's positive energy. Instead, I think just how far out to sea I allowed that bottle to drift. Was it so naïve of me to think that my life should remain as simple and carefree as I grew older? Where had it ever been written that I should so easily let go of the great feelings of joy and simplicity?

If I let that bottle drift too far, I might not ever be able to retrieve the invigorating contents. Finally, I reached a point where I recognized that I, not some imaginary bottle, was drifting. Why should I allow so much exhilaration to continue to slip away? Conversely, why should I, or anyone else for that matter, routinely embrace so much negativity? I had filled up the tank of my existence with what I had thought important. Instead of my life running on full, being whole, I was mostly running on empty. My habits were too structured and at times seemed mundane. It would take a confluence of events to gently coax me in a better direction.

I used to feel guilty or nervous if I left something of importance unfinished. I was overly concerned if I allowed a chore to go uncompleted, even if only for a short period of time. My first step was to recalibrate my thinking about what precisely was important. I had to challenge myself and ask if I was placing too much emphasis on things that were trivial. The lessons I corralled from my experiences outside the States helped me make better sense of my worries. Also, far too often, I had difficulty sleeping; I was restless and found myself constantly tossing and turning while thinking about the next day's tasks. Even on my own terrace on a clear night, I found it difficult at times to just enjoy the view and peace offered by the infinite stars.

I remember one particular evening when I sat on my balcony in Jurere. The tiling was damp, and a light mist fell from low-lying clouds. I just listened to the cicadas vacillating from near silence to a loud whistle. With the dark glow of the distant mountains behind my home, my mind was trying to alert me to something. I was wondering about the tradeoffs for choosing to reside in my Brazilian neighborhood, 4,300 miles south of Fort Lauderdale.

It was easier for me to feel the brunt of what I was forfeiting: the ease of banking and utility payments, the convenience of having premier products at my fingertips, secure police protection, obvious cultural and language understandings, separation from my parents and many of my American friends. What I was gaining was subtle but nonetheless quite important: a large reduction in stress and negativity, a personal sense of peace, connections with unspoiled landscapes, food with less chemical additives, a host of natural juices. My conversations were more relaxed and frequently packed with fun. The simplicity of my surroundings allowed for intervals that were relatively devoid of worry. By experiencing a lifestyle that loaned itself to a softer tone, my ability to see clearly grew exponentially. I didn't need to practice yoga because I was living its teachings virtually every day.

Still alone on my terrace I watched as a half-moon struggled to glow through the cool fog. Looking up, I took to heart the many rewards this part of the world offered. Not much was on my mind, not a shred of care. Yes, I was in a very imperfect country in a very imperfect continent; and yet I had never felt so complete.

Douglas Andrew Keehn

Many Latin cultures are criticized for being a bit slow or lazy. From the American perspective, taking a long time to accomplish something is often frowned upon; we want things done yesterday. From spending time in Latin America, I found that slow should not be confused with lazy, and that practicing at a reduced pace is not necessarily a bad idea. Taking one's time is simply a different approach to life. It's a bizarre yet effective way to build patience, tolerance, and reshuffles the deck of a variety of things that should matter.

With the passing of time, I found myself going through a delicate transformation and carrying pieces of positive energy back from every Latin American trip. My goal was to adjust and find more balance in the way I lived. Consciously stepping back in order to move forward, I found great reward in introspection. I was playing a game of chess with myself, with either side representing the American and Latin cultures. And when I was unsure of my next move, I would take time to think, to relax, and appreciate the benefits of sometimes deciding not to act.

What other aspects of my life changed? I am not going to fool myself or anyone else. I still have that urge to buy things and to relax in luxury. For some time, I owned a high-end car and resided in a large upscale home. Now this is not the case. My next home, wherever it may be, will be quite comfortable; it will not however be on the same magnitude as the one I constructed. I readily admit that I do miss aspects of certain ownerships but my cravings are fewer and far between. I have greatly toned down my frequenting of malls and giant retail outfits. Candidly, I just don't need to surround myself with very much stuff.

So, in terms of materialism, it now takes substantially less to quench my thirst. We are constantly bombarded with both direct and subtle messages that influence our impulses. Television, radio, the Internet, posters and retailers are all integral parts of our daily lives. Like most, I am still very much connected with all they offer. The magnitude of how these powerful entities influence one's way of life is very different in Latin America. Brick and mortar conglomerates didn't clog every corner in the cities and outlying suburbs. Out of sight is truly out of mind.

When I was away, I wasn't as tempted to make frequent purchases because of the reduced range of products available. This narrowing of obtainability was true for a host of reasons. A lower purchasing power for a large segment of the population, and import laws connected with high taxes were just two examples of what contributed to a more condensed selection. And since I didn't find it necessary to watch much TV or to spend an abundance of time on the Internet, I was less influenced by the constant suggestions to shop. My urges to buy were subdued even though I had enough extra income. It wasn't just the physical structures of the stores that were out of sight and out of mind. My compulsion to spend and to accumulate unnecessary stuff was basically absent. I was comfortable with much less and enjoyed the freedom that came with these newly formed habits.

Currently I spend dramatically less time watching television and surfing the Internet. Although I make it a point to stay updated with current affairs, I have cut myself loose from the grips of the twenty-four-hour news cycle. Rarely do I allow myself to reconnect to any high repetition of negativity; it's not healthy and doesn't accomplish anything constructive. After some time, to my surprise, I actually didn't miss the phenomenon of channel flipping. What used to be such an integral part of my time now is basically insignificant.

What interest and entertains us is nothing short of a cultural fingerprint. In the US, we are obviously interested in and captured by television. The bulk of what is presented either via movies, series, or news is a negative story often encapsulated with graphic violence. When I returned to the States, I immediately felt a barrage of negativity hitting me from all directions. When I turned on the television, I literally felt as if I was drowning in a pool of problems. The bad news, violence and sad stories were suffocating. I didn't feel as if I had arrived on the shores of a modern, beautiful and tranquil country. When I traveled and lived in South America, this persistent drumbeat of gloom was rare. Not only was it infrequent, it really wasn't desired.

Unlike my Latin friends and acquaintances, my American colleagues were often gripped with insecurity and unhappiness. There were startling differences in basic contentment. I wondered if that used to be me. Was I going to return to that generally pessimistic mindset? Taking to heart my recent experiences, I didn't want to allow this infection to reenter my life. To combat this cultural tidal wave, I needed to paddle upstream. I wanted to remain calm, happy, and to keep a life simple. I wanted a Rio type of aura to guide me forever.

I often think of my dad, and still regret that I had failed to be by his side during much of his remaining years. His sacrifices, kindness and love are more obvious to me now than they ever were when he was alive. That change admittedly came too late but nonetheless that change allowed me to prosper. I want to emulate his special gift of giving solely from the heart. Through my travels and personal exchanges, I finally realized and cherished his extraordinary qualities. I now try to keep in constant contact with my mom. Quite active and well, my mom is still filled with an abundance of energy and wisdom.

When I travel locally or abroad, I can't help but connect with the plights that so many are forced to endure. I want to better understand their struggles, and continue to learn from their diverse opinions and actions. Having been face-to-face with so many who are less fortunate, I know that everyone has exceptional qualities worth embracing. I consider myself a student for life, and continue to learn from anyone regardless of his or her level of education, background, or nationality. To be judgmental is always a critical mistake.

When I look at people who are struggling, I realize just how fortunate I am, at least for the moment. Circumstances for anyone can quickly change, as we are all unknowingly close to losing our stability. The real test arrives when we reach our weakest point. How we react and the way in which our friends respond are all powerfully revealing.

I have found a better equilibrium in my approach to situations and won't allow myself to be fazed by very much of anything. As I learned, much in life is not time critical; it's only important to strive to enjoy what life offers each and every day. It is essential to laugh, relax, and not take life for granted. As abstract as it might sound, I don't take many things or even myself too seriously.

Through the course of my travels, I ultimately found a redefinition of living. I wanted to augment the American lifestyle with parts from my immersion into Latin culture. Even now, I find it difficult to balance my actions and responses with my culture's daily demands. I frequently catch myself stepping on and off the American treadmill. My personal internal battles continue as I struggle with two very different approaches to life. At times I still see my personal progress as too subtle, too slow, or even erratic. And because my awakenings came from only one corner of the world, I wonder if I have allowed myself to be unequally influenced.

Overall, however, I am at ease with my transformation. Anything but perfect, the process is ongoing and requires lots of maintenance. I will confess that I feel as if I am a cultural drunk, a person who was sobered up by attending experiences outside of my own country. The barrage of luxuries is hard to resist and constantly tests my fragile materialistic willpower. Sure, I fall off the wagon now and then and treat myself to something I honestly don't need. But then my memories check my impulses.

When I think of my interactions in Latin America, I mentally place myself in the middle of a group of teachers. Sitting in a room with chairs placed in a circle, I envision coaches from different walks of life assisting me with my struggles. My desire to adopt a new way of living is similar to what a person goes through during the various steps of rehabilitation. It's slow and has moments consisting of triumphs and failures. The path I have chosen requires lots of give and take. But I feel so much better now than I ever before. Finally, I can prioritize, see and feel what really matters. I don't consider my adjustments to be a cleansing process. I do, however, consider my new approach to life a positive and enlightening change.

On my very first steps into Latin America, I liked the warmth of the water. The temperature was just right, and the air was inviting. Immediately I felt a difference in the direction of the winds; the breeze of the culture offered ways in which I could let go and not feel anxiety. I was swept away. My instincts told me I might be falling into something profoundly different, different in a very good way.

My times with the people of Latin America, as odd as it may seem, reminded me of a beach. The shoreline accepts every wave, bringing in the new and returning the old waters back out to sea. The sand absorbs some of the energy, and the balance returns with the pull of the ocean. Sometimes I felt overwhelmed and surprised by the large waves that crashed overhead. Knocked below the surface, I would have to use all my strength to regain my composure. And there were moments where I felt a strong undertow dragging me far from where I wanted to be. The period between the high and low tides offered a time to reflect, to just listen, breath, and accept the purity of the salt air.

My hope is that I have taken a floating bottle from a different part of our Americas and influenced its unpredictable course. I want this bottle, filled with strong and delicate messages, to work its way northward and wash up on the shores of my country. Allow the winds and currents of change to work their natural magic. I am optimistic that many will catch this drift, break open the bottle, and allow the messages to become truly meaningful in their lives.

We live in a world that today is more connected than ever. The Internet, telecommunications, and modern aircraft have brought us considerably closer. But I often wonder if we are truly taking to heart some of the special waves constantly knocking on our shores? People from all parts, no matter how remote, have a lot to learn and to share.

I am quite cognizant of the many headlines that center on governmental and financial corruption throughout some Latin American nations. The frustration and even rage of the people is apparent. Yet to say that shady dealings have not occurred in the States would be unfair and arrogant. It is true that on balance our system of checks and balances seems to work. However, recently we experienced the biggest financial collapse since the Great Depression. Many Americans lost their jobs, benefits, savings and homes. More than twenty years of wealth evaporated in just a few short months.

The devastating monetary and psychological effects linger to this day. In terms of the ruin, there was a lot of blame to go around. It was estimated that over $19 trillion of household wealth was lost. In the end, you can count on one hand how many high-level people actually went to prison; hardly anyone was held accountable. It's not for me to judge how much fraud was involved. However, I can say with some confidence that the amount of punishment didn't nearly meet the extent of the crimes. Trillions of dollars, not billions, vanished among scores of questionable actions. Yes, too much corruption still permeates areas of Latin America. But in an inconspicuous way, some colossal forms of theft manage to take place right here at home.

America is a nation largely built by immigrants. Even to this day, it's a country sought out by people from all over the world. And the truth is that many of those entering our borders are coming from Latin America. Frequently I am asked if things are so great in Latin America, why are so many trying to plant their roots here? That's a fair question, and I am going to answer candidly within the context of my experiences and our journey.

Douglas Andrew Keehn

First, there isn't just one reason people continue to seek out what America offers. Persons of all socioeconomic statuses come here to enjoy our landscapes or to join relatives who have been established as citizens. But I think the major ingredients most seek center on opportunity and stability: better job prospects, housing, healthcare and education. Many are escaping areas where crime and violence are so rampant that fear dictates almost every aspect of their lives. Others are fleeing governments that are controlling, abusive and corrupt.

Next, the way the question is normally posed seems to contain a tinge of arrogance. It's up to an individual to decide if anything is implied; here again I leave interpretation to your discretion. Nevertheless, I understand why this query is presented in such a way. I come from a culture that often sees issues as either black or white. We too often seek a quick fix or fast answers, and can be overly judgmental and demanding. When I am asked this question, I sense one's quality of life is being directly connected to one's standard of living. Yes, there are indeed instances in which the two correlate. But on our journey, I found an "either-or" answer wasn't sufficient to explain quality of life. By now I hope you might agree that judging real contentment isn't quite that simple.

On the other side of the fence sits the Latin Culture, which I found less structured, vague, slower paced, and not nearly as critical. I learned to view my approach to life through an incorporation of both philosophies; I don't blindly think either culture is automatically superior or inferior. I do look at each individually for the benefits to be utilized depending on a variety of circumstances. Threading a needle between our cultures is complicated. But if you allow yourself to sew each of their fibers into a new design, you will find your new wardrobe life changing.

At times actions require quick thinking, determination, and aggressive responses. And there are periods where acting leisurely, being more open and receptive, and taking a broader view are more prudent. To systematically delete the perspectives of either culture is more than a mistake; it's a lost opportunity that can allow us to see others and ourselves in a very different light. Both the American and Latin cultures stand to learn a lot from each other.

When I first began to write about my journey, I was well aware that to successfully transfer my messages would not be easy. In fact, several friends warned me I was walking a tight-rope and that some of my writing could be misconstrued. Many even advised me to exercise extreme caution in what I said, and noted that numerous readers might take great offense at some of my implications. I took to heart all the pros and cons of bringing my observations to the forefront of my culture. I knew I was on thin ice even to remotely hint that there could be some improvements to the American way of life; especially when the enhancements came from a variety of supposed less successful societies.

It is undeniably risky to even touch on what we value and what our priorities ought to be; how we should look at, critique and define others, including ourselves. Some acquaintances wondered who I was to dare to water down the world's most proven democracy and its widely admired standard of living. Certainly, at times I felt very alone, and wondered if instead of being alongside the dolphins, I would be swimming upstream in a river filled with piranhas. Each chapter took a bite out of my enthusiasm. I had a lot of thinking to do and was particularly conflicted, especially during the early stages. I promised myself that if I were to share the significance of my observations that even the most elusive message would really need to matter.

My life was redirected purely by happenstance. An insignificant car accident forced me to finally see so much that had appeared out of reach, and to listen to what was buried inside my own heart. That accident truly did serve as a spark to the ignition. Placing my cards on the table, cards that I considered a winning hand, was an entirely different dilemma. I needed some type of catalyst to get me through what could be a minefield of misunderstood explanations. I was fearful that I wouldn't be able to convey what I had gained, felt, or even seen. So many hints had been anything but clear and were anything but easy to communicate to a culturally proud audience. If I were to have any chance at impacting people's lives, I would have to look past all of my friend's warnings and personal anxieties, and write with my hands completely untied.

On one late evening I was again thinking of my dad. I was on my porch enjoying the cool west breeze of a Florida winter's night. During a fishing trip, he had described his first night jump during paratrooper training. Laughing, he said he had been so fearful he had needed to be pushed out of the plane. Then he told me more of his experiences as a POW. Whenever possible, the Americans exchanged cigarettes with their fellow Russian prisoners. The two sides from such different parts of the world, sides that had little if any understanding about the other, somehow united. And he talked of how old enemies, when brought together, often wondered just why they had been fighting in the first place.

If fierce enemies can find unity, then why should I fear trying to bring two friendly cultures closer together? Two cultures, each filled with their own individualities, that can clearly benefit from one another. It took an accident to rekindle and realign my many personal outlooks. It took a memory of my dad to finally push me out of the plane (my private comfort zone) and force me to jump out into some very rough terrain. I only hope that I packed my chute carefully.

During my journey, I was not out to convince anyone what is right or wrong, superior or inferior. My purpose was to share a long passage that I found positively transforming. And along the way to point out what I perceived as real human treasures. Whether they were obvious or hidden, large or small, I found them all to be of untold value.

When I now walk through any neighborhood here at home or abroad, I view my surroundings in a vastly different context. It doesn't matter if it's a suburb, a small town or a metropolitan area; I privately take in the beautiful apartments and pristine homes, the towering modern office buildings. I equally note the rundown dwellings, dilapidated houses, and old work structures and factories. Within all of these places are people with unique stories. Many might not see their lives as special but based on my recent experiences, I feel that everyone has something exceptional to offer.

I imagine some will accuse me of being a dreamer or say that I am overly optimistic, that I am a wishful thinker. If that is how some view me, I am at ease with this particular image. I am comfortable with this outlook because of what I have seen, learned and absorbed. In some of the most astonishing homes reside people who can be content or very unhappy. In some of the poorest settings I found a similar spectrum; people's feelings ranging from grateful to depressed hopelessness.

Deep down, with the exception of a very few, most of us want to feel and be thought of as special. We want to know that we have contributed something positive to our family, friends, and acquaintances. We strive to stand out, to be unique in some way. Yet for many, so much valuable potential remains locked up in subjective and guarded vault. The key to finally release so many personal gifts requires one thing above anything else. Truly allow yourself to be open in every sense of the word.

I purposely alluded to this quality at the very outset of our journey. To wash clean the preconceived notions requires a different approach to life. When waves of humility incrementally rinsed away my judgmental toxins, only then did I know I was on track to becoming remade. If you can allow yourself to be a student for life, to patiently and objectively learn and listen to anyone regardless of his or her views, regardless of where he or she is from, that is truly a special achievement. To master this approach will allow you to offer so much more. Follow life's unpredictable scripts and permit people to move you in a variety of uplifting ways. Again, it really does matter that I have opened your mind to a different way of viewing so much that surrounds us.

Through a series of invaluable lessons and experiences, I captured an enormously rewarding lottery. So many were responsible for providing a gift I considered innately rich. Reflect on our journey and never think there are any odds too great to overcome. Nothing prevents you from drawing a winning approach to life. To draw this ticket is much closer than you think. It's not a monetary reward but its potentials are nonetheless priceless.

CHAPTER 17

External Darkness - Internal Light

As the Native Americans say: "Certain things catch your eye, but pursue only those that capture your heart."

On a clear south Florida night, I again visualized those elusive and mysterious dolphins. At the time, I wasn't quite sure what I was honing in on. Strangely enough, I questioned whether I was seeing parallels between the dolphin's auras and something else? A few nights later while washing my boat, I paused thinking of this dolphin quagmire. Upon the bow of my boat, I began to daydream. At that very moment things finally dawned on me—the dolphins might reflect what I had experienced outside the United States.

Their personalities were similar to those of the many people I had come to know. The dolphin's demeanor, grace, adaptability, smile, and enjoyment of life were qualities I had seen in so many people in Latin America. Additionally, their seemingly constant contentment mirrored how I felt when I traveled down south. As if reaching for some personal confirmation, I asked myself if I hadn't seen this sort of behavior and repeatedly feel the sanctity of the dolphin's freedom and happiness.

I shook my head trying to awaken. Leaning against the boat's railing, my energy was waning. I grabbed a hose and splashed water on my face. Then I went back to my townhouse and brewed a cup of coffee. The evening was beautiful, and I wanted to take advantage of the clear night. Mug in hand, I sat on my upper balcony in front of the busy canal. It was a great spot to view the passing boats and yachts. My mind ceased racing but I remained a bit pensive. And then I thought of this crazy analogy tying the personalities and traits of the dolphins with certain people I had met in my journey.

I laughed because on the surface the comparison was a bit silly. But then I decided that perhaps there might be something to this analogy. For some time, I had been searching for a way to frame some very complex issues with something, anything, that most people could comprehend. I needed to draw some comparisons that anyone, myself included, could relate to. The images and realities of the dolphins seemed a rather perfect fit. After all, have you ever thought of a dolphin in a negative way? When we think of dolphins we only have good feelings. Even in captivity, they transfer their excitement and sense of calm. Do they not make you smile and erase your private worries?

In some ways they transcend the core qualities of what life was meant to be: free, fun, and not overly complicated. They simply have a way of inspiring us. When I traveled from the States to places south of the equator, I was repeatedly exposed to these core qualities of life. Things became much less complex. My stays replicated the feeling of being surrounded by schools of dolphins.

Where do dolphins walk? They walk in the many places throughout Latin America, among people who bundle their daily routines with a commendable formula that leaves them extraordinarily resilient, resourceful, and humble. With so many difficulties, they manage to allow rays of happiness to penetrate even the darkest of clouds. The auras projected by the people I encountered were truly reassuring. Often subtle, I was left with positive feelings that were impossible to ignore. Anytime I am dejected or stressed, my mind gravitates back to my times in South America.

Admittedly I am guilty from time to time of displaying a shining grin. I can't help it; I revert to so many special moments. I see the people of Rio, the cheerful kiosk attendant cutting open a fresh coconut, always anxious to share fun stories. I hear the voice of big Tiny Geraldo skillfully dealing his stash of jokes. The images of my special hosts from Lagoa, Paula, Karina and Ramon. I think of the memorizing attributes and echoing messages hidden within the silence of the *capoeira* master.

When I get into a taxi, I immediately wonder if it's the crazy Dario at the wheel. While walking on a pier among patient anglers, I am strolling down the hills of Leblon; I hear the tales of the fishermen who reflect the refreshing fun and softness of many Cariocas. Recalling the times in São Paulo, the faces of the calm bus driver, the playful airport boys, and the ever-curious doorman Chavez remain alive. When I tell my American barber, "Snip, snip," I see photos of Rudolpho's family and an exciting game of soccer. During any busy commute, I know my experience pales compared to what Marcelo and others endure. At breakfast, I want to return to the diner on Alameda Santos and playfully spar with the waiters and patrons. And there is always the shadow of Marta and her gentle energy that forever balances the importance of what money can't buy.

My travels through some poor US areas give me pause, taking me back to my initial impression of Peru. Then I recognized the culture's many treasures exemplified by the wisdom and sweetness of Angelica and Eduardo, the beautiful older couple from Lima. And I am always elevated when I reflect on the giving and inviting personality of Isadora and her tightly knit group. The long lines of buses in Manhattan attach me to the bustling avenue outside our Chilean hotel. I see the portraits of Carolina and Roberto, and will never let go of that incredible evening in Santiago.

Passing an unpretentious outdoor clothing booth, my mind drifts back to Venezuela; I'm still captured by the expression and powers radiating from the salesman on the Caracas beach. A simple walk in my neighborhood is secretly replaced by a jog around the Trinidad park. I have enduring memories of the calmness and contentment of the store clerk, the market salespeople, the Indian servers, and the lady at the spice stall; all were so easygoing and tranquil. The gentleness of the people coupled with the great food always makes me think of my Jamaican nanny, Ines. I can practically taste her unmatched dishes of freshly prepared codfish and feel the warmth of her open love.

Actually, relaxing with a cup of coffee, I think back to the cafés in Buenos Aires where the mild-mannered waiters never rushed me. And as I listen to a radio, I pretend I am watching a pair dancing the tango while elegantly sweeping across a ballroom floor. Accompanied by younger people, I envision returning to Uruguay; the polite manners, curiosity and excitement of the Carrasco teens was nothing short of admirable. I reminisce about the light-heartedness of the Florianopolis fisherman, and my genuine admiration for the patience and honesty of Carlos and Marcos. I picture the larger-than-life smile and contentment of the unrestricted realtor, Marcon. I remember the thoughtfulness of Marlis and Valdemar, and the special bond they had with all of their beautiful children.

I think of the consideration extended by my neighbors Sandra and Francisco, and the extraordinary kindness and care demonstrated by that young Brazilian Doctor. I can't ever forget the compassion extended by the lady with whom I collided while cycling. My eyes can see the unassuming methods of the tireless Pedro, and the modesty and sincerity of Mr. Joao Carlos. And I always feel the warmth of Monica's approach, accompanied by her immeasurable suggestions that had such an influence in my life.

Closer to home, of course I miss the company and selflessness of my dad. Every time I don my uniform and take off into the sky, I know he is still watching in awe. He remains nearby, as my mom continues to hold and share his special quiet messages. Serving as co-captain along with my dad is Davie. To this very day, he carries the rare quality of only wanting to give from the heart.

At times I think all of these people must have been dolphins in their past lives. In their presence, the same special feeling arrives, the sensation of being in my boat encircled by a school of grey and white spirits. How lucky I was to have been part of such an amazing group who demonstrated what really matters in life. Their inherent treasures remain underestimated and frequently go unnoticed.

I wonder if our First World lifestyles have become too artificial and overly structured. Do we inadvertently place ourselves in bad positions and maintain views that are the result of feeling trapped? Have we gotten too far ahead of ourselves and lost sight of too many basic values? Shouldn't we take an objective snapshot of where we are and consider slowing down? Perhaps by even retreating we can strike a healthier balance and ultimately find ourselves in a better frame. Unfortunately, within my own culture, we do not truly understand what we are lacking. There are moments when I feel like I am witness to a giant iceberg slowly melting away. As it thaws, chunks of our core goodness fall into the sea.

As a people, we used to be softer and work more as a national family. I am not for an instant suggesting that we don't have our schools of dolphins, people who are extraordinarily happy, kind and caring. My hope is merely to bring closer to home some other diverse approaches to life. If we are humble and bold enough to hear the echoes of our southern neighbors, we might find ourselves reestablishing many positive and lasting connections, hints that can influence and rekindle the fundamentals of what truly matter. Yes, as Americans we do have our dolphins but here they still swim faster. Maybe it's time for us to rise to the surface and stop for some fresh air. To take a few steps back and walk at a pace that allows the others to catch up.

I can see the day when schools from both parts of our worlds join together and allow the majority to swim through life more gracefully.

Try to visit this special place; a place that is so ordinary it's extraordinary. If her waves are embraced and permitted to sweep you away, you will find yourself a changed person. If you agree to be open and accepting, you will find yourself elevated to a unique and meaningful level, a level you will wish you had arrived at a long time ago. Don't be fooled when you first step off of that boat, bus or airplane. The initial impressions might lead you to think you have landed in a zone outfitted only with external darkness. Rest for a moment, take a deep breath, and be patient. If you can be fearless in the face of change and can look beneath the surfaces, you will find shining from the seemingly external darkness a great and beaming internal light. Look into the eyes and feel the special souls of the people to our south. Regardless of where you live, I hope that you will take a chance as I did and allow yourself to follow in their footsteps.

It's the place Where Dolphins Walk.

Embrace the challenges connected with positive change. The possibilities are infinite.

CHAPTER 18
Final Approach and Landing

The greatest mistake you can make in life is to continually fear you will make one. — Elbert Hubbard

Coming into the final approach, I want to express my gratitude to all of the people of Latin America. Despite all of your difficulties and challenges, many admittedly daunting, you still managed to direct me to an alternate place to land. A place where I could see things in ways I never imagined was possible. My wish is that one day a variety of what you practice will not only be accepted, but will be welcomed into the American way of life.

And to my great American friends, I thank you for flying with me until the end of the journey. I know at times the ride has been slow, and that there have been many changes in altitude. Through all the turbulence, I sincerely hope the experience will have positive and lasting effects on many dimensions of your life. That I might have influenced the way you value many indirect, simple, or even obvious aspects of your surroundings. And if you are so inclined, grab a hold of a rope offered by our Latin neighbors. Allow some of what we have lost to be wrestled back in our direction. If you find yourself seeking change then hold on tight. Stay with your instincts and convictions, and don't let go. You will know when the time is right to finally give way.

Wishing everyone's future has a smooth landing. For now, after we touch down through the clusters of cotton, I will rush to turn on my cell phone and replay the following messages. Please take them to heart.

From my Dad:

Life is like a train. You will always see many people in front of you who appear to be doing so much better but your mind doesn't capture the many people in back of you who are truly suffering and struggling. Be happy and make the best of what you have in the moment. And if you are not able to do this then take a moment, pause, and adjust your rearview mirror.

As painful as it can be, keep in mind that good does not always triumph over evil.

Always give from the heart, and never give with the intention or expectation of receiving anything in return.

Anyone can do well when everything is going well. The real test of character is how quickly someone can pick up and rebuild when so much is going so wrong. This also serves as a litmus test of one's true friends, those who will be by a friend's side when that person is at their lowest points of life.

We have and will continue to fail throughout our lives. Failure is just another process we should take in stride, and use it constantly to learn from and rebuild.

If you are good to people, made them happy and laugh, then the personal reward will be something that no amount of money can ever buy.

From my Mom:

Live your life in a way that makes you happy. It might not seem correct, normal or even wise to many of your friends. But it's your life, and you need to follow the rhythm of your heart and not the beat of others.

From my friends and acquaintances during my travels down South:

Don't ever allow yourself to be a horse with blinders on.

Work to live, don't live to work.

Educated means just that, 'educated.' Educated does not necessarily imply that one is 'smart.' Everyone has something to offer regardless of his or her level of academic achievement. One's selflessness, one's true kindness, are distinguishing and place a person into a category all to itself.

Fica Tranquilo.

When life gives you lemons, make lemonade.

As the song goes: Don't worry, be happy.

If you have never had a particular item of luxury, chances are you won't miss it. However, if you are used to certain comforts, it's quite difficult to let them go. Even for those who are economically privileged, it's prudent to keep all purchases balanced. When things are going right, we often become oblivious to the notion that things can quickly go very wrong.

By doing absolutely nothing, you might actually be doing something extraordinary. At times it can be more beneficial to do nothing at all.

Slow does not always equal lazy, and also should not be confused with bad.

At the end of the day, what really matters is good health, family, friends, passion, food, wine, and music; everything else is just . . . stuff.

If you have an urge to buy something you probably don't need to buy it. And if you think you need something repaired right away you are probably just wrong. Most of the time things can wait, and your life won't change one iota.

To be humble equals strength and is not a sign of weakness.

Winning does not always preclude one from failing.

Laughing should not be a rarity; it should be a frequent part of one's daily routine.

Lunch hour is just exactly what it implies—an hour to relax and enjoy some lunch. Don't allow it to be a work hour.

Douglas Andrew Keehn

You don't have to be religious to allow God to shine on, protect, and guide you.

Americans think too much about making money.

The golden years are not in our distant future. They are the present and right before all of us each and every day. Every moment you have your health and can laugh abundantly is golden.

Comfortable means just that, comfortable. It does not always imply being happy. Sometimes the path to becoming happy might require a process that at times feels very uncomfortable.

From me via the lessons of my journey:

Never fear change.

Taking a few steps back might just propel you forward faster than you could ever imagine.

So much in life involves good old-fashioned luck.

I often found that the best diamonds were people who never owned a piece of jewelry. Although they didn't have any valuable gems, gold or silver decorating their body, their hearts and actions glittered more than any Cartier showcase.

Don't ever lose sight of the expression: "There but for the grace of God go I.

So little can add up to be so priceless, and often so much can prove to be so worthless.

Nothing can ever substitute for the enormous potential of goodness that so many possess; the key is how to unleash that positive energy.

Poor can be so rich, and rich can be so poor.

Ordinary can so often be extraordinary.

We cannot fix—nor should we try to fix—everything we perceive to be out of place. Many things in life we simply don't have control over, and ultimately can't repair or even adjust to our liking. Too much positive energy can be misdirected and wasted attempting to change the unchangeable.

We all have our strengths and weaknesses; our parents are no exception. Love them for who they are. More than likely you are underestimating their positives and overweighing their negatives.

245

Don't squander the time you have left with your parents. If you choose a path of avoidance, it will likely come back to haunt you.

Always be humble. Constantly be open to learning from people of all races and socio-economic backgrounds. We are all teachers and students throughout our entire lives. We might graduate from a particular school but we are all enrolled in passing on and receiving ideas and knowledge until the day we leave the earth. We don't need report cards to tell us how we are doing; we consciously and subconsciously know what our grades truly are.

Always listen, even if you have strong beliefs, opinions, and preconceived notions against what is being expressed. There is no penalty for listening. And even if only 1% of what a person is trying to express resonates in your core, then 1% is still better than zero percent.

No is only the first step to yes.

By the time you get to a certain point in your life, you probably will be able to count the amount of your true friends on one hand.

Are you really walking your dog or is your dog walking you? Who is really the teacher here?

Nothing we can create will equal the beauty nature has already offered.

Absorb the testimony that emanates from one's eyes.

Modern does not always imply better.

Even imperfect systems can contain powerfully beneficial effects.

Progress has many connotations if you are humble enough to look below the surface.

Who is more fragile or vulnerable: the rich or the poor?

How much we subconsciously overestimate the expected, and how greatly we underestimate the significance and powers of the unexpected.

Many dynamic powers are contained within the codes of silence.

Sacrifice can be extraordinarily healing.

So much in life can turn out bittersweet. Concentrate on and absorb the sweet; it will always overpower the bitterness.

CPSIA information can be obtained
at www.ICGtesting.com
Printed in the USA
BVHW081310130819
555687BV00003B/329/P